V. PATTESON LOMBARDI

UNIVERSITY OF OREGON

BEGINNING
WEIGHT
TRAINING

THE SAFE AND EFFECTIVE WAY

D0141199

 WCB Wm. C. Brown Publishers

To Sara, Jean, and Nick
For their never-ending faith, hope, and love

Cover credit: Comstock, Inc./R. Michael Stuckey

Text Illustrator

Diann N. Laing

Consulting Editor

Physical Education
Aileene Lockhart
Texas Women's University

Evaluation Materials Editor

Jane A. Mott
Texas Women's University

Printed in the United States of America by Wm. C. Brown Publishers
2460 Kerper Boulevard, Dubuque, IA 52001

10 9 8 7 6 5 4

Contents

Fundamental Training Principles 87

5

Beginning Weight Training 111

6

Preface

This book is about weight training, the use of resistance to enhance multiple components of fitness. If you are a beginner this text is especially for you because it emphasizes safe and effective exercise techniques. If you are an intermediate to advanced student, teacher, or coach, you will also find that this book is a valuable resource since the key training principles and techniques described are the foundation for all beginning, intermediate, and advanced weight training programs.

My goal in writing this book was to dispel myths about weight training and to teach students how to train in a safe, effective, and enjoyable way for the rest of their lives. If you implement the scientifically-based principles and techniques presented, you will be assured of minimizing your risk of injury and maximizing your improvements.

Since the six chapters of the book are integrated in a narrative style, it's best that you read them in the order that they are presented. Chapter 1 gives a brief introduction to scientifically-based weight training. Fitness components and the energy continuum are used to establish a framework for evaluating weight training. Weight training is contrasted with weight lifting and body building, and myths and misconceptions, advantages and disadvantages are examined from a historical perspective. Chapter 2 reviews guidelines for safe training to reduce soreness and nagging injuries and to promote lifelong participation. Preliminary guidelines including medical clearance, adequate sleep and diet, and proper attire, will help lead you in the right direction. Training guidelines, incorporating warm up and cool-down, equipment orientation, spotting, resistance selection, and general exercise techniques, will ensure that your training is safe, progressive, and worthwhile. Chapter 3 presents the pros and cons of isometric, isotonic, and isokinetic devices to maximize your ability to use equipment available in your facility.

To make it easier to train your muscles, chapter 4 explains what muscles look like, how they work, and how they adapt. Sections on body levers, hand positions, and active movements will help you visualize the connections that allow you to train your muscles with weights. Chapter 5 discusses basic principles you'll need to design and implement a comprehensive fitness plan. The American College of Sports Medicine's guidelines for achieving optimal fitness and body fat are described together with a step-by-step procedure for creating a personal exercise prescription. A special section on periodization is included to help vary your program, reduce boredom, facilitate improvements, and minimize chances of overtraining.

Chapter 6 is the most important chapter of the book. It focuses on the key ingredients for safe and effective training: program design and exercise technique. The heart of the chapter is the Basic Dozen, twelve classes of complementary exercises that have been carefully selected to help you achieve balanced muscular development and tone. Major muscles worked by the Basic Dozen are given in common (lay) and equivalent anatomical terms. Mini-form checks are included as a quick and easy reference to help verify that you are using proper technique. Exercise techniques are then described and illustrated in detail. Important areas to warm up and notes concerning spotting are also given for each exercise. Contraindications are presented as a guide for appropriate exercise selection for those who are conditionally cleared. To help troubleshoot and further refine your form, special sections called Coaches' Corners have been included. These highlight common mistakes made by beginners along with pertinent points used in teaching the particular movement.

A collection of the most frequently requested and useful materials from my files has been pooled to make up the appendices. Included are medical screening and waiver forms, the Basic Dozen warm-up/cool-down routine, charts for predicting maximum lifts, guidelines for safe maximum testing, mini-form checks for the competitive lifts, and sample intermediate and advanced programs. Due to a recent surge of interest, special updated sections on androgenic-anabolic steroids and circuit weight training have also been included. The last appendix is a valuable resource directory of sports medicine associations and equipment companies.

I hope that after using this book, you will be motivated to train in a safe and effective way for the rest of your life.

Acknowledgments

Many have contributed either directly or indirectly to the completion of this text. Without brother Johnny and Sandy Groves I never would have been introduced to weight training. I feel fortunate to have been influenced and encouraged by many outstanding coaches: Ray Hambrick, Jim Costen, Tally Johnson, Steve Spellman, Mel Hulme, Bo Blackerby, Bill Dooley, Al Groh, Sandy Kinney, Mike Mansfield, Moyer Smith, and Dave Stroup. Their thoughts and words are integrated throughout the book. I am most grateful to Paul Hoolahan of the University of North Carolina for teaching me about the importance of exercise technique.

My professor, Dr. Eugene Evonuk, was an infinite source of wisdom and inspiration. He should be credited for much of the information in chapters 4 and 5 on fundamental training principles and muscle physiology. Other exceptional physiologists are recognized for making significant contributions via their outstanding texts: P. O. Astrand, G. A. Brooks, H. A. deVries, T. D. Fahey, S. I. Fox, A. C. Guyton, and J. H. Wilmore. Special thanks to Dr. Edna Wooten-Kolan for her enthusiasm and help with anatomy in chapters 3, 5 and 6.

I have been assisted and supported by the finest group of friends anyone could ask for. Rick Troxel provided unfailing encouragement, expert advice on editing, and a much needed touch of humor. Other past and present members of the faculty and staff at the University of Oregon gave just the right amount of insight and support when I needed it: Vern Allers, Lorrie Brilla, Mary Ann Carmack, Mike Clark, John Downing, Elwin Heiny, Tom Hirtz, Jeff Lander, Janice Lettunich, Pearl Morgan, Bill Mumbach, Vince Nethery, Lou Osternig, Don Pellum, John Postlethwait, Robin Pound, Jim Radcliffe, Mike Reuter, Rick Robertson, Theron Savelich, Doug Seelbach, Dave Symons, and Juanita Webb.

At many times during the writing of this text, it was Diann Laing's superb artwork that kept me going. Gene Lewis and Roger Holm deserve special recognition for last-minute photo processing. Thanks to those who exercised flawlessly during my novice, photo sessions: Troy Davis, Steve Gilchrist, Richard Gustafson, Sara Gustafson, Eric Hohn, Todd Loken-Dahle, Jim Radcliffe, Bobby Simmons, Glenn Villarmia, Carolyn Quinn, Lino Vaccher, Mike Walter, and Rob Willis.

Special thanks to Chris Rogers, Peggy Selle, Kelly Smith, and Sara Fischer of Wm. C. Brown for their patience, enthusiasm, and meticulous editing.

This text has been strengthened by the criticisms, suggestions, and encouragements provided by the expert panel of reviewers: Jay Dee Gunnels (Briar Cliff College), Jeffrey E. Lander (Auburn University), Gene Lee (Metropolitan State College), Maureen Murphy (Pima Community College), Rochel Rittgers (Augustana College), and Jon Sutherland (Gonzaga University).

Most importantly, I thank God for giving me my parents, Nick and Jean and my beloved wife, Sara. Their patience, understanding, and encouragement have transformed my dreams into reality.

Introduction

1

In 1985, 36 million adults in the United States participated in weight training, an estimated 3 million more than those who engaged in running and jogging during the same year (American Sports Data cited in Levine, Wells & Kopf 1986). Together with aerobic dancing, weight training ranks as America's fastest growing physical fitness activity (President's Council on Physical Fitness and Sports 1983; Hurley & Kokkinos 1987). Clearly, for many, weight training has become a life-long activity.

The benefits of weight training can be virtually limitless, provided that scientifically-based principles are used in designing and implementing a program. When properly applied, weight training can be one of the most effective and efficient ways to enhance multiple components of fitness.

This chapter is designed to give you a brief introduction to scientifically-based weight training. In order to establish a framework for evaluating this activity, we'll first look at basic and health-related physical fitness and the energy continuum. After contrasting weight training with competitive weight lifting, we'll explore selected myths, misconceptions, advantages, and disadvantages from a historical perspective. Finally, we'll review some general guidelines to help point you in the right direction as you embark on your beginning weight training program.

Basic Physical Fitness

To achieve basic physical fitness you must develop four major areas: (1) cardiorespiratory endurance, (2) muscular strength, (3) muscular endurance, and (4) flexibility.

Your cardiorespiratory endurance ultimately depends upon your heart being a powerful and efficient pump, while your strength relies upon the maximal force-producing capabilities of your voluntary skeletal muscles. Muscular endurance is the ability of your muscles to contract forcefully for prolonged periods. Flexibility, the capacity of your joints to move freely throughout a range of motion, is limited by your boney structure and by the tautness of your muscles, tendons, and other connective tissues.

Health-related Fitness

Health-related fitness is similar to basic physical fitness, but combines two of its components while adding two others that deal with health. To develop and maintain health-related fitness, improvements are made in (1) cardiorespiratory endurance, (2) muscular strength/endurance, (3) flexibility, (4) percentage body fat, and (5) neuromuscular relaxation.

Despite the bad press about fat, we would have difficulty surviving without it. Fat is our most concentrated energy source, and helps protect our internal organs, cushion our joints, and maintain our body temperatures. However, high levels of body fat are associated with an increased risk of cardiovascular disease (CVD) and cancer (Craddock 1978; National Research Council 1982; Hubert et al. 1983). We may also increase our risk of developing CVD and other diseases if we are constantly tense and driven by a sense of time urgency (Friedman & Rosenman 1974). By doing exercises like jogging and weight training we can reduce our body fat, foster neuromuscular relaxation, and decrease our risk of CVD and perhaps other diseases (Misner et al. 1974; Greist et al. 1978; Hurley et al. 1986; Hurley & Kokkinos 1987; Hurley et al. 1988). By exercising consistently we can enhance our health-related fitness and the quality, if not the quantity, of our lives. Let's take a brief look at the modes of exercise we can use to improve our health-related fitness.

The Energy Continuum

When you cross-country ski, jog, swim, or cycle, you use many large muscles at a slow to moderate pace for a fairly long time. These continuous exercises are often called *aerobic* because they use oxygen or the oxidative energy system (fig. 1.1). All of the energy nutrients (fats, carbohydrates, and small amounts of protein) are burned in the presence of oxygen so that your working muscles are provided with fuel. In contrast, if you sprint, lift heavy weights, or do other short, intense *anaerobic* exercises, you don't use oxygen to burn the energy nutrients. Instead, you use high-energy phosphate compounds and carbohydrates (sugars) already stored in your muscles. During the first few seconds of an anaerobic exercise, adenosine triphosphate (ATP), creatine phosphate (CP), and adenosine diphosphate (ADP) work like tiny, supercharged battery packs to supply your muscles with immediate energy. After the first few seconds, the longer you can continue exercising, the more heavily your muscles will depend upon carbohydrate. Since carbohydrate is the only energy nutrient that can be used when oxygen is not readily available, it is called the nonoxidative or glycolytic (sugar solution) energy source.

As you might guess after looking at figure 1.1, most activities are not purely aerobic or anaerobic, but are distributed across an energy continuum. Since aerobic exercises are continuous and are especially good at burning fat, they are the

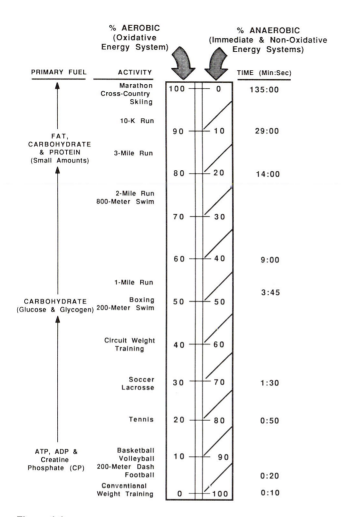

Figure 1.1

The energy continuum and fuels used during different activities. The duration of an exercise determines the fuels used to provide energy. Aerobic exercises use all three energy nutrients while anaerobic exercises use immediate energy sources and carbohydrates already stored in muscles. (*Source:* Adapted from *Sports Physiology* by Edward L. Fox. Copyright 1979 by Saunders College Publishing/Holt, Rinehart and Winston. Adapted by permission of Holt, Rinehart and Winston, CBS College Publishing.)

best for improving cardiovascular fitness and reducing body fat and body weight (Misner et al. 1974; American College of Sports Medicine 1978; Pollock, Wilmore & Fox 1984). However, aerobic exercises do not improve strength appreciably (Hickson 1980) and may even decrease flexibility if done through a limited range of motion. Later in the chapter it will be shown that weight training can be the perfect complement to aerobic exercise for enhancing health-related fitness for a lifetime. But first, what is weight training?

Weight Training versus Weight Lifting

During the early 1900s there were no clear distinctions between weight lifting and weight training. Weights were lifted for the sole purpose of strength or physique exhibitions and competition. In the 1940s Captain Thomas DeLorme established the concept of progressive resistance exercise. He also helped formalize distinctions between muscular endurance and strength training, and weight training and weight lifting (DeLorme 1945).

Weight training is a noncompetitive activity that involves using a resistance to improve muscular strength, muscular endurance, and flexibility. It may also be used to reduce percentage body fat, enhance neuromuscular relaxation, and in some special cases, improve cardiovascular fitness. Thus, the primary goal of a weight trainer is to enhance multiple components of fitness (fig. 1.2). This clearly differs from weight lifting. Weight lifters strive to improve a single component of fitness, muscular strength, which is needed specifically for one-repetition maximum (1-RM) lifts in competition.

It is important that you make this distinction before you start training. Otherwise, your goals as a beginner may be obscured. Remember that lifetime fitness, rather than maximum lifting, is the primary goal of a weight trainer. To get a clearer picture of this distinction, let's take a closer look at weight lifting and the competitive sport of body building.

Subclasses of Weight Lifting

The two subclasses of weight lifting are Olympic lifting and power lifting. Olympic lifts are ballistic, high-speed movements that are used not only by Olympic lifters, but also by athletes in football, track and field, and other power-type sports. The two competitive Olympic lifts are (1) the snatch and (2) the clean and jerk. For the snatch, a wide grip is used to lift the bar in one fluid motion from the floor to a position directly overhead. The clean and jerk is a two-phase movement. For the clean, a shoulder-width grip is used to pull the bar from the floor to a resting place above the shoulders. During the jerk phase, the hips, thighs, shoulders, and triceps are recruited in sequence to thrust the bar powerfully overhead. To master these difficult competitive lifts, athletes must spend many hours practicing specific lifting techniques. The Olympic lifts are detailed in appendix G.

Power lifting includes three major lifts: (1) the squat, (2) the bench press, and (3) the dead lift. The first two are used as the foundation for most weight training programs. The squat is the best exercise for developing lower body strength. It involves carefully positioning a bar on the shoulders, lowering the hips until the thighs are just beyond parallel, and then returning to an upright position. The bench press is "the pillar of strength" exercise for the upper body. It is done by lying on a bench and pressing a barbell from the chest until the elbows are fully extended. In the dead lift, a barbell is lifted from the floor by

Figure 1.2
As a weight trainer, you should seek to develop multiple components of fitness.

using the hips, thighs, and lower back to move from a stooped to an erect position. The squat and the bench press are discussed in chapter 6 with other beginning weight training exercises, while the dead lift is detailed in appendix G.

Body Building

Body building may be viewed as bridging the gap between weight lifting and weight training. It is competitive, but rather than being directed toward the primary acquisition of muscular strength, it aims to achieve muscular balance, hypertrophy, and delineation.

The terms weight lifting, weight training, and body building are often confused. How do the goals for each differ, and what differences in muscular development and general appearance of the body do you associate with each activity?

Fact and Fiction

Weight training is besieged by myths and misconceptions. Most of these have endured since the early days of the nineteenth-century strongmen. In the 1930s weight lifting had such a poor reputation that men who trained were said to have "strong backs and weak minds" and "were forced to use cellars and attics as meeting places and in addition supply their own equipment" (Benninghoff 1938, 96). Even today, this tarnished image is fueled by those who warn that lifting weights inevitably injures joints, stunts growth, creates muscle-boundness, or induces permanent masculinization. Improper training, lack of scientific guidance, and isolated cases being exaggerated or generalized have helped perpetuate these myths and misconceptions. Thanks to recent research, education, and widespread participation, weight training is gradually being accepted as an appropriate activity capable of enhancing fitness for a lifetime. In this section we'll highlight benefits and dispel myths, but also candidly explore the limitations of this popular activity.

Myth 1: Weight Training Injures Joints

It is true that lifting weights may stress and strain joints, but this occurs largely when (1) there is a preexisting injury, (2) warm-up is inadequate, (3) poor exercise technique is used, or (4) logical exercise progressions are ignored.

To help dispel myths and misconceptions about weight training and joint injury, follow these general rules:

1. Obtain medical clearance before you start training to reduce the chance of aggravating previous injuries.
2. Use both general and specific warm-up before moving on to high-intensity exercises (see appendix C).
3. Move in a slow, smooth, and methodical fashion and be "kind to your joints," especially at the beginning and end of a movement. Almost all injuries caused by exercise are the direct result of sudden movements (Allman 1976). Explosive-type weight training is associated with a high (55%) dropout rate and an increased incidence of injury (Reid, Yeater & Ullrich 1987). Be sure to stress the form—and *not* the weight—to minimize joint injury, to improve compliance, and to promote strength gains.
4. If you are injured during a training session, stop exercising. Rest, ice, compress, and elevate (RICE) the afflicted area and consult a sports medicine professional immediately. Ask when it is safe to return to the activity.

We'll focus on these and other important safety considerations in chapter 2 and examine safe exercise techniques and progressions in chapter 6.

Myth 2: Weight Training Depresses Growth and Development

For years my mother said, "You're not 6'7" like your brother Nicky because you use those silly weights so much." Mom may have been right, if at a very early age I had lifted heavily and abused fundamental training principles. Extremely heavy work may stunt growth in children (Kato & Ishiko 1964; Cahill cited in Duda 1986). Dynamic, cartilage-containing growth plates at the end of long bones can be replaced prematurely by bone, which depresses normal skeletal growth and development. These cases are quite rare. It's been estimated that less than 5% of all epiphyseal injuries in children result in disturbances in growth (Pappas 1983).

Regardless of the activity, children can develop chronic debilitating injuries when they are forced to overparticipate or progress according to plans devised for adults. Short-term weight training can be safe and effective for children if they are properly instructed and closely supervised by professionals trained in sports medicine and exercise physiology. However, the long-term effects of weight training on growth and development have not yet been determined (Rians et al. 1987).

Stresses imposed in a logical and consistent fashion upon healthy bones may strengthen bones and prevent bone loss (Dalen & Ollson 1974; Jones et al. 1977; Nilsson & Westlin 1971). This is opposite to effects which occur during long-term bed rest or space travel in an antigravity environment (Issekutz et al. 1966; Donaldson et al. 1970; Krolner & Toft 1983). Although sufficient estrogen and dietary calcium are prerequisites for healthy bones in females, exercises like weight training may be helpful in preventing age-related bone loss (Korcok 1982; Stillman et al. 1986).

Misconceptions about growth and development have also been fueled partly by those who have observed short-statured body builders and have somehow concluded that lifting weights stunts growth. Small persons, like others, may be attracted to weight training to increase muscle mass and bolster self-confidence.

Help perpetuate the truth about weight training's effect on growth and development by adhering to these general guidelines:

1. Consult a sports medicine physician for medical clearance before you or your children begin training with weights.
2. Make sure that your children receive proper instruction and are closely supervised by professionals trained in the fields of sports medicine and exercise physiology. Children should use light weights and high-repetition schedules (≥ 10–12) and avoid maximum lifting.
3. Encourage your children to engage in a variety of activities to improve their overall fitness. Many low-impact, body-resistive games and exercises can be used to build strength, including climbing, push-ups, chin-ups, and tandem stretching-strengthening movements (Kozar & Lord 1983) (fig. 1.3).
4. Train by using slow, smooth, methodical movements to reduce shear, tensile, and compression forces and to decrease the risk of epiphyseal and other injuries.

A   B

Figure 1.3

Children can use a variety of indoor (A) and outdoor (B) body-resistive games and activities to increase their strength. Some modified types of weight training for short periods can be safe and effective for children when they're closely supervised by trained sports medicine professionals. However, the long-term effects of weight training on growth and development have not yet been established.

Myth 3: Loss of Flexibility, Speed, and Coordination

In the 1930s Dr. Peter Karpovitch, a leading authority in exercise physiology, said, "Observe some good lifters in running. Some of them lack decidedly in form . . . and speed. Some of them cannot run" (Karpovitch cited in Gillesby 1938, 16). I am certain these men that Karpovitch observed were not poor runners because they lifted heavy weights, but rather because they trained improperly and avoided running. Misconceptions like these have prompted even seasoned coaches to profess that lifting weights "slows you down." Nothing could be further from the truth about a properly applied weight training program.

As with other myths, this third myth has been preserved by those who have generalized from isolated cases or have abused fundamental training principles. Certainly, if you don't stretch, exercise through a limited range, or work only muscles you can see, you may create imbalances and lose flexibility. However, there is no question that if you train properly with weights, you can improve your flexibility (American Academy of Pediatrics 1983; Sewall & Micheli 1986; Rians et al. 1987). Even if you do heavy resistance training, you won't decrease your flexibility provided that you select exercises that balance opposing muscle groups and work through the full range of motion (Massey & Chaudet 1956). To ensure that you will maintain or improve your flexibility, include specific stretching exercises in your fitness program (Micheli cited in Duda 1986).

In chapter 4 we'll see that training with heavy weights recruits "fast" rather than "slow" muscle fibers. Fast fibers are used for short, high-force activities, whereas slow fibers are used for prolonged, low-force activities. Consistent heavy resistance training enhances intrinsic muscle strength (DeLorme 1945; Thorstensson 1976; Costill et al. 1979; MacDougall et al. 1980). Overwhelming evidence indicates that this increased strength is accompanied by an increased speed of muscular contraction (Stone & Kroll 1978; American Academy of Pediatrics 1983). Contrary to what you've read or heard, slow, controlled strength training will not decrease your speed, but more than likely will enhance it. You may even improve your reflexes by strength training. Compared to endurance-trained runners, power lifters have a shorter reflex time for contracting their quadriceps (frontal thigh muscle) following a tap of the patellar tendon (tendon below the kneecap) (Kamen, Kroll & Zigon 1981).

Like Dr. Karpovitch, you may have seen athletes who appear to be uncoordinated after they have trained with weights for extended periods. This is because they have failed to continue practicing their specialized sports' skills while weight training. Old skills become new skills that must be performed with a "new" body. Apparent lack of coordination is not due to training with weights. Rather, lack of practice time devoted toward specific skill acquisition causes the particular skills to degenerate. In chapter 5 we'll take a close look at the specificity principle, which states that to improve a specific skill we must practice it.

To help clear up misconceptions about the effects of weight training on flexibility, speed, and coordination, follow these simple guidelines.

1. Always use both general and specific warm-up before training. Do cool-down stretches to improve flexibility and minimize soreness (see appendix C).
2. Select complementary exercises in your program to balance the development of your muscles. This will maintain or improve flexibility as well as reduce the risk of injury.
3. Do all weight training exercises in a controlled fashion through the full range of motion (FROM).
4. When using weight training to improve strength for a particular sport's skill, be sure to set aside time for practicing that specific skill.

Myth 4: Women Hypertrophy as much as Men

Healthy women who do not take steroids or other muscle-building drugs experience only small changes in the size of their muscles when they train with weights (fig. 1.4) (Capen, Bright & Line 1961; Wells, Jokl & Bohanen 1963; Wilmore

Figure 1.4
In response to weight training, healthy women who do not use anabolic steroids can expect substantial gains in strength with little increase in size.

1974; Brown & Wilmore 1974; American Academy of Pediatrics 1983). While the relative increases experienced by men and women may be similar, the absolute changes tend to be greater for men (Cureton et al. 1988). If you're a woman and you handle near maximal resistance for six months, you may see minor increases in the size of upper body measurements (≤ 1/4″), but you won't change or may even slightly decrease the measurements of your lower body and abdominal region (Wilmore 1974; Brown & Wilmore 1974). Although some researchers disagree (Cureton et al. 1988), most attribute the greater hypertrophy in men to their twenty- to thirtyfold higher circulating levels of testosterone (Hettinger 1961; Brown & Wilmore 1974; Mayhew & Gross 1974; Wilmore et al. 1978b). A few women produce excessive amounts of male hormones because of hyperactive adrenals (suprarenals), two small endocrine glands named for their position directly above the kidneys. Even though these women may be more susceptible to muscular hypertrophy, this condition rarely occurs. Intense weight training can elevate testosterone (Fahey et al. 1976), and growth hormone (Vanhelder, Radomski & Goode 1984), which may act to facilitate muscle growth.

More studies are needed to determine the long-term effects of weight training on anabolic hormones in women and men.

Help clear up misconceptions about weight training's effects on women by adhering to these rules:

1. Avoid using steroids to promote muscle growth. The side effects are largely irreversible in women and children and are especially damaging to the heart, liver, and reproductive system (see appendix J).
2. Do relatively high repetitions (12–20 per exercise set) if you are primarily interested in increasing your muscle tone.
3. Along with weight training, engage in consistent aerobic exercise at a low to moderate intensity, three to five times per week for 15 to 60 minutes (American College of Sports Medicine 1978, 1986; Pollock, Wilmore & Fox 1984). This combination is guaranteed to reduce your body fat, increase your strength, and do wonders for your physique.

Myth 5: Muscle Turns to Fat

Many self-proclaimed fitness experts say that muscles turn into fat as a natural consequence of inactivity. Muscle can't turn into fat and fat can't turn into muscle. In chapter 4 we'll see that a muscle is made of bundles of fibers or muscle cells. These specialized cells contain protein filaments made of amino acids folded in a unique pattern. In contrast, a fat, also called a triglyceride, is composed of one alcohol piece and three fatty acids. Thus, muscle and fat are quite different chemically and can't be magically interconverted.

Muscles may appear to turn to fat in formerly well-built athletes who stop working out. However, what has actually happened is a distinct, two-phase process. Muscles have atrophied or decreased in size due to the absence of a training stimulus. Also, like most of us, athletes base their diets on their habits rather than their needs. If we consistently eat huge volumes of food and reduce our activity levels, we're doomed to depositing excess calories as fat.

Fat deposition is further accelerated by a reduction in metabolic rate that occurs naturally as a consequence of aging (fig. 1.5). This "creeping obesity" is more pronounced in women because the metabolic rate in females declines more rapidly. Metabolic differences between the sexes are largely due to the male hormone, testosterone, which can increase metabolic rate by about 10%–15% (Guyton 1986).

Don't lose hope—you can elevate your metabolic rate dramatically by exercising. During exercise, well-trained athletes can increase and sustain their metabolic rates about 2000% above normal (Guyton 1986). Even at rest, an aerobically trained person can burn more fat than one who is untrained. This is because enzymes specific for fat metabolism have increased in response to an aerobic training stimulus.

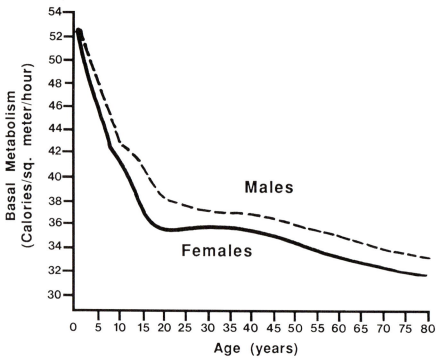

Figure 1.5

Normal basal metabolic rates at different ages for each sex. Since metabolic rate decreases with age, caloric intake should be reduced and activity level increased in order to maintain an optimal level of body fat. (*Source:* From *Textbook of Medical Physiology,* 7th ed., by Arthur C. Guyton, M.D. Copyright 1986 by W. B. Saunders Company. Computer illustration by Diann Laing, redrawn with permission of the publisher.)

Emphasize the following, not only to dispel this myth, but also to improve the quality and perhaps the quantity of your life:

1. Decrease your total caloric intake when your activity level declines, but never consume less than 1200 Calories (kcal) per day or eliminate important nutrients. It is difficult if not impossible to satisfy your nutrient requirements (especially for carbohydrates, vitamins, and minerals) if you dip below this level. By using the modified Four Food Group Plan described in Whitney and Hamilton (1987), you can be virtually assured of satisfying your daily needs.

2. Remember that if you eat 3500 kcal above what you need, your body will store it as a pound of fat. By consuming 500 excess kcal (equivalent to about two beers or a piece of chocolate cake with ice cream) each day for one week or 117 excess kcal (roughly a glass of table wine) each day for one month, you'll be sure to gain a pound of fat (Hamilton & Whitney 1982). Your nutritional plan, like your exercise program, should be based on consistency.

Figure 1.6
Neither massage specific to an area nor rubber suits can be used to spot reduce. The safest
way to reduce percentage body fat is through consistent exercise and sound dietary planning.

3. Seek an enjoyable aerobic activity that you can perform safely for the rest
of your life. Without a doubt, this is the key to maintaining an optimal level
of body fat (American College of Sports Medicine 1978, 1984, 1986; Pollock, Wilmore & Fox 1984).

Myth 6: Spot Reduction

We can't achieve those rippling, washboard abdominals promised on television
ads by rumbling our waist lines with vibrating belts, by suffocating in rubber
scuba-like gear, or even by doing hundreds of sit-ups (fig. 1.6). Although "body
shaping" sessions with electrical stimulation are said to be specially designed to
melt away those ugly pounds of fat, none of the techniques or devices you've
heard about work to spot reduce.

It has been demonstrated conclusively that the thickness of fat beneath the
skin does not depend on the activity of underlying muscles (Gwinup, Chelvam
& Steinberg 1971; Wilmore 1974). Fat is mobilized from various deposits

throughout the body, not in or around the specific site used (Wilmore 1974). Recently, a variety of electrical stimulation devices have been tested and proven to be entirely ineffective for fat reduction (Keller et al. 1988; Lake & Gillespie 1988). The only sure way to spot reduce is to surgically remove the fat via a costly intervention called liposuction (also called suction lipectomy).

A rubber waist belt may cause you to lose weight due to loss of water, but hopefully you'll replace it in your next stop at the water fountain or in your next meal. When worn in saunas, steam baths, or other hot places, rubber suits and belts may severely disrupt water and electrolyte balance. These delicate balances are essential for controlling body temperature, transmitting nerve impulses, and contracting muscles.

Unless you choose the surgical route, the most effective way to lose subcutaneous fat is by consistently exercising and modifying your diet. To help you maintain a healthy level of body fat, we'll examine guidelines for safe exercise in chapter 5. You can develop a comprehensive nutritional plan by consulting texts by Hamilton and Whitney (1982), Williams (1983), and Whitney and Hamilton (1987), listed in the reference section at the end of this book.

Other Myths and Misconceptions

There are other less-publicized myths and misconceptions about weight training and intelligence, ego, narcissism, homosexuality, and the use of steroids. Most have been perpetuated by those who have made generalizations about single cases. We won't elaborate upon these since they've been dispelled by recent widespread education and the enormous public interest in weight training. By adhering to scientific training principles and implementing safe and effective exercise techniques, we can help promote the truth about this enjoyable, lifetime activity.

Advantages and Disadvantages of Weight Training

Enhances Strength, Local Endurance, Flexibility, and Relaxation

Weight training is the most effective and efficient way to increase strength and muscle tone. The improvements you make will depend upon your initial condition as well as the intensity, duration, and frequency of your training. High-resistance, low-repetition (≤ 6) programs are ideal for developing strength, while low-resistance, high-repetition (≥ 12) routines are best for improving local muscular endurance. Even if you are sixty to seventy years of age, you can expect increases in muscle size and strength that are qualitatively similar to those experienced by younger persons (Brown et al. 1988).

By examining myths and misconceptions, we've seen that proper weight training can maintain or improve flexibility. It can also be used as a time to relax and melt away tensions from work or simply as a time to socialize, be with friends, or meet new people. In this way, weight training can help improve neuromuscular relaxation.

Although no form of exercise is complete, a special type of weight training called circuit weight training (CWT) is the best way to improve multiple components of health-related fitness. CWT is exercising through a sequence of weight training stations while limiting the rest between sets. Appendix I illustrates sample CWT programs. Let's take a brief moment to examine some of the claims made about this special form of weight training.

Increases Aerobic Capacity?

You might be able to use CWT to maintain or slightly increase your aerobic capacity (Peterson 1976; Wilmore et al. 1978b; Kimura, Itow & Yamazaki 1981; Gettman et al. 1979; Gettman, Ward & Hagan 1982; Messier & Dill 1985). You have the best chance to accomplish this if you are untrained, have a high percentage body fat, and limit your rest intervals to 15 seconds or less between sets (Wilmore et al. 1978b; Gettman et al. 1979; Gettman, Culter & Strathman 1980; Kimura, Itow & Yamazaki 1981; Gettman, Ward & Hagan 1982; Messier & Dill 1985). Unlike the changes you'll experience with a typical aerobic program, most of the improvements you'll make will be due to increases in lean body mass (Gettman, Culter & Strathman 1980; Gettman & Pollock 1981). Your ability to improve your endurance won't depend on the type of equipment you use (Gettman & Pollock 1981).

Despite claims by equipment companies and fitness clubs, there are no guarantees that you'll increase your endurance by circuit weight training. Recently, two well-designed studies demonstrated that untrained, middle-aged males substantially improved their strength but did not improve their aerobic capacity following sixteen weeks of intense CWT (Hurley et al. 1984a; Hurley et al. 1988).

By training aerobically for four to six months, you can improve your endurance by as much as 15%–25% (Pollock 1973; Pollock, Wilmore & Fox 1978; Gettman & Pollock 1981), but you won't improve your strength appreciably (Hickson 1980). An effective way to increase your endurance and strength is by doing both types of training (Girandola & Katch 1973; Dudley & Fleck 1987). To enhance your strength development, it may be best to perform strength and endurance training on alternate days (Sale et al. 1988).

Decreases Body Fat?

When you exercise aerobically, after about 5 minutes your heart rate is elevated and maintained in a target range at about 70%–85% of its maximum (fig. 1.7a). Your breathing is continuous and rhythmical, and your heart rate and oxygen uptake are almost linearly related. Thus, during aerobic activities, your heart and lungs are beautifully synchronized. If you do conventional strength training with its pauses between exercise sets, it's doubtful that your heart will achieve this target range (fig. 1.7b). In circuit weight training, the rest between sets is reduced or eliminated in an attempt to maintain an elevated heart rate.

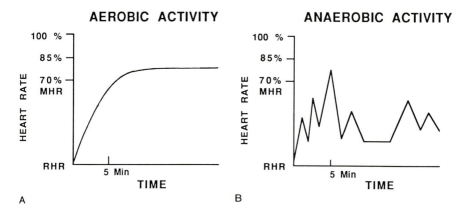

Figure 1.7

Heart rate versus time for aerobic and anaerobic activities. *A,* typical response during aerobic activity; *B,* response during conventional weight training.

Your heart rate may be high when you circuit weight train ($\geq$70% max), but the amount of oxygen you use will be low to moderate ($\leq$40%–50% of VO$_2$max)(Wilmore et al. 1978a; Hempel & Wells 1985; Hurley et al. 1988) (fig. 1.8). Irregular breathing patterns used in resistance training are most likely responsible for this lack of synchrony between the heart and lungs. In chapter 2 we'll take a closer look at why it is important to breathe continuously when you are training.

Since CWT doesn't use much oxygen, it's not as effective as jogging or other aerobic exercises for decreasing body fat. When you circuit train with weights, you burn up about as many calories as in jogging at 4–5 mph (12–15 min/mi), cycling at 11.5 mph, or playing a vigorous game of volleyball or tennis (Wilmore et al. 1978a; Hempel & Wells 1985) (fig. 1.9). It's been estimated that you'd have to complete between 20 and 31 Nautilus Express Circuits (roughly twice the number of slow- to medium-paced jogging sessions) to lose just one pound of fat (Hempel & Wells 1985).

If you circuit weight train for an 8- to 20-week period, your body weight won't change significantly (Peterson 1975; Allen, Byrd & Smith 1976; Wilmore et al. 1978b; Gettman et al. 1978; Gettman et al. 1979; Gettman, Culter & Strathman 1980; Gettman, Ward & Hagan 1982; Hurley et al. 1984a; Messier & Dill 1985; Hurley et al. 1988). Your percentage body fat may stay the same (Wilmore et al. 1978b; Kimura, Itow & Yamazaki 1981; Hurley et al. 1984a; Hurley et al. 1988) or slightly decrease by about 1%–3% (Wilmore et al. 1978b; Gettman et al. 1978; Gettman et al. 1979; Gettman, Culter & Strathman 1980; Gettman, Ward & Hagan 1982). You have the best chance of reducing your percentage body fat if you are overfat (δ 16%–20%, $\circ$ 26%–30%) or obese (δ >20%, $\circ$ >30%) (Wilmore et al. 1978b; Gettman et al. 1978; Gettman et al.

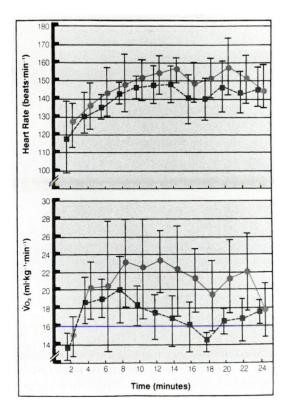

Figure 1.8

Heart rate and oxygen uptake responses to the Nautilus Express Circuit. Average values are plotted for men (circles) and women (squares). Mean heart rates ranged between 140 and 148 beats/min, while peak heart rates varied between 156 and 166 beats/min. Oxygen consumption is considered satisfactory at about 45, when values are expressed in milliliters of oxygen per kilogram of body weight per minute (ml/kg/min). The highest oxygen consumptions elicited by circuit weight training averaged 21 ml/kg/min for the women and 26 ml/kg/min for the men. Thus, while heart rates may reach values >75% of maximum during NEC training, oxygen consumptions are generally <40% of maximum. This means that circuit weight training does not satisfy requirements needed to make it aerobic. (*Source:* From L. S. Hempel and C. L. Wells, Cardiorespiratory Cost of the Nautilus Express Circuit, *The Physician and Sports Medicine,* 1985, 13, p. 91. Reprinted with permission of the publisher.)

1979; Gettman, Culter & Strathman 1980). The most significant change in your body composition will be an increase in lean body mass rather than a loss of body fat (Wilmore et al. 1978b; Kimura, Itow & Yamazaki 1981; Hurley et al. 1984a). Heavy resistance training increases lean body mass and body weight (Misner et al. 1974). Combining endurance and strength training reduces body fat, reduces or maintains body weight, and increases muscle mass (Misner et al. 1974; Hickson 1980; Gettman, Ward & Hagan 1982).

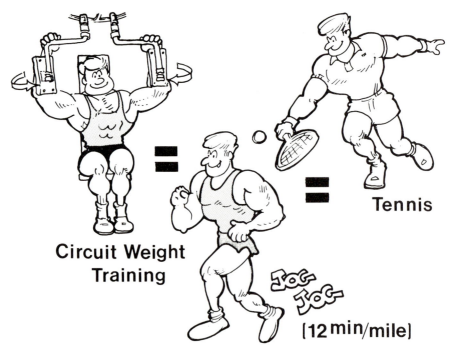

Figure 1.9
The energy one expends while circuit weight training is equivalent to jogging (walking) at 4–5 mph or playing a game of tennis. (*Source:* Based on data from Wilmore et al., 1978a and Hempel and Wells, 1985.)

Reduces Cardiovascular Disease Risk?

Long-term CWT can decrease diastolic blood pressure and low-density lipoprotein cholesterol (LDL-C, the "bad" form of cholesterol), and increase high-density lipoprotein cholesterol (HDL-C, the "good" form of cholesterol) (Hurley et al. 1986; Hurley et al. 1988). These changes can occur independent of changes in aerobic capacity. Even though you may not be able to increase your endurance much by engaging in CWT (especially if you're well-trained), you can reduce your risk of cardiovascular disease (CVD). As you might guess, a highly effective program for reducing CVD risk would include aerobics, CWT, and a balanced diet which minimizes cholesterol, fat, and sodium intake.

Emphasis for the Beginning Weight Trainer

Dr. Karpovitch may have been wrong about the relationship between lifting weights and speed, but he hit the nail on the head when he stressed, "In using weight lifting, one should remember that it is not a complete system of body development" (Karpovitch cited in Gillesby 1938, p. 16). At the same time, Dr.

Figure 1.10
Professor Arthur Steinhaus of George Williams College felt that lifting weights developed skeletal musculature out of proportion to the heart. Steinhaus, together with Dr. Peter Karpovitch of Springfield College, emphasized that weight lifting was an incomplete exercise that must be supplemented by endurance activities.

Arthur Steinhaus, another leading authority in exercise physiology, wrote ". . . weight lifting develops the skeletal musculature out of proportion to the heart" (Steinhaus cited in Gillesby 1938, p. 16). Both Steinhaus and Karpovitch emphasized that those who trained with weights should not ignore a balancing program for the heart (fig. 1.10). Since the days of these exercise pioneers, it's been confirmed that the aerobic fitness of weight lifters and other strength-trained athletes is well below that of endurance athletes and similar to or only slightly greater than that of inactive persons (Saltin & Astrand 1967; De Pauw & Vrijens 1972; Fahey & Brown 1973; Fahey, Akka & Rolph 1975; Lombardi & Evonuk 1985).

While circuit weight training may help you improve many areas of health-related fitness, don't forget a balancing program for your heart. Envision your weight training program as a single part of a comprehensive program that in-cludes (1) flexibility exercises, (2) an aerobic base of either walking, jogging, swimming, cycling, and/or cross-country skiing, (3) weight training, and (4) a scientifically–based nutritional plan.

The differences between weight training and weight lifting bear important implications for your program and lifetime fitness goals. Regardless of whether you're a beginner, an intermediate, or an advanced weight trainer, you should place major emphasis on perfecting exercise technique and less emphasis on how much weight you handle. This doesn't mean that you ignore the work load, but that scientific exercise technique takes full priority over maximum lifting. Simply stated, *stress the form, not the weight.*

By reducing the time you devote to maximum lifting, you'll avoid severe muscle soreness and nagging injuries, and be less intimidated and more easily encouraged. You'll also be more likely to improve multiple components of your health-related fitness and enjoy the benefits of weight training for the rest of your life.

A comprehensive health-related fitness program requires several elements in addition to weight training. What are these elements? Which specific supplementary activities will be best for you in terms of your interests, availability, and time schedule?

Summary

Basic physical fitness is a combination of (1) cardiorespiratory endurance, (2) muscular strength, (3) muscular endurance, and (4) flexibility. Health-related fitness adds two other components: (1) neuromuscular relaxation and (2) percentage body fat. Weight training, the noncompetitive use of resistance devices, can be used to improve many components of basic and health-related fitness. It is distinct from weight lifting, which is competitive and solely directed toward increasing strength for 1-RM lifts. Aerobic activities like jogging, swim-ming, cycling, and cross-country skiing require large amounts of oxygen and burn all three energy nutrients. Short-duration, high-intensity activities like sprinting and weight lifting are anaerobic and use immediate energy sources and sugars already stored in muscles. Aerobic exercises are best for improving cardio-vascular endurance and reducing body fat.

There are many fallacies associated with weight training. Through the years, these have been perpetuated by poor training techniques, lack of scientific guid-ance, and isolated cases being exaggerated or generalized. Weight training only damages joints when there are preexisting injuries, warm-up is inadequate, or improper exercise techniques or progressions are used. Proper weight training does not retard growth and can actually enhance the development and strength of bones. Contrary to popular belief, weight training may be used to increase speed, flexibility, and coordination. In order to improve specific sports' skills, one must not allow time devoted toward weight training to supersede practice time. Most healthy women experience minimal gains in muscle size when they train with weights. Muscle and fat cannot be interconverted and exercise cannot be used to spot reduce. The best way to ensure a healthy percentage body fat is by consistently exercising and eating a well-balanced diet.

Individual programs should be designed to improve all components of health-related fitness. Cardiovascular endurance is best achieved through consistent aerobic exercise, while muscular strength, endurance, and flexibility may be improved through proper weight training. Programs should also include flexibility routines and scientifically–based nutritional plans. When training with weights, the form and not the weight should be stressed to minimize nagging injuries and muscle soreness and to encourage lifelong participation.

Guidelines for Safe Training

2

Weight training is an activity with inherent risks. In this chapter we'll identify important guidelines for safe training to reduce your chances of soreness and injury. As a beginner, it's easy to be discouraged by severe soreness and nagging injuries, especially when you first start exercising. By following the guidelines in this chapter, you'll enjoy your initial workouts and be encouraged to pursue weight training as a lifelong activity. You'll also help dispel myths and misconceptions about weight training by implementing safe and effective training principles.

Preliminary Guidelines

Medical Clearance

Regardless of your age or past experience with sports, you should be examined by a licensed sports medicine physician before you begin an exercise program. In addition to a standard physical, you may be asked to complete a medical questionnaire (appendix A), musculoskeletal exam, blood chemistry test, and graded exercise stress test (GXT) before you are cleared for training. Comprehensive medical screening provides vital information about your current health and fitness, which is needed to design a safe and effective personalized fitness plan.

After you have been tested, you should be provided with an explanation of your results as well as written clearance for weight training and other specific activities. To maximize your safety, the fitness staff at your facility may request that you submit a copy of your medical records. Additionally, for liability purposes, you may be asked to sign a waiver form (appendix B) before you begin training.

Neither coaches nor personal trainers have the authority to clear you for participation. Your personal sports medicine physician is solely responsible for your medical clearance. He or she will place you into one of three categories: (1) not cleared, (2) conditionally cleared, or (3) unconditionally cleared for weight training. Let's take a brief look at each of these classifications.

Not Cleared for Weight Training

A physician may not clear you for weight training if you have heart disease, high blood pressure, or another form of cardiovascular disease (CVD). During moderate to heavy lifting, a type of breath holding called Valsalva's maneuver increases pressures within the chest and abdomen. These pressures limit or even abolish blood flow to and from the heart and add considerably to its work load (Compton, Hill & Sinclair 1973). This is much like pinching off the gas line in a car while forcing it to climb up a hill. It's easy to see that Valsalva's maneuver is not a suitable stress for an already weakened heart. In some cases, patients with CVD may be conditionally cleared provided they handle light weights and breathe continuously. Mild to moderate aerobic exercise and light dumbbell work are often prescribed for CVD patients to improve their cardiovascular fitness and strength.

Adults with orthopedic abnormalities like degenerative arthritis or children with growth plate problems like Osgood-Schlatter disease may not be cleared for weight training. Physicians often direct clients with these and other bone disorders to seek activities which minimize skeletal stresses. Due to the supportive, cushioning effects of water, swimming often provides a pleasing alternative.

Conditionally Cleared for Weight Training

Some persons are conditionally cleared for weight training provided they modify or avoid exercises that aggravate their specific condition. For example, those with low back syndrome (LBS) can substitute leg presses for squats to increase back support and minimize discomfort. It's important to note that in most cases, LBS is caused by inactivity that weakens abdominal and low back muscles and tightens hamstrings and hip flexors. Proper stretching, weight training, and aerobics may be the ideal prescription for eliminating LBS entirely.

Those with kneecap grinding (chondromalacia patellae) can strengthen their thighs without knee pain by doing eccentric-only ("negative") exercises on standard machines or concentric ("positive") exercises on special machines designed to control speed. To minimize problems with balance, the orthopedically handicapped, partially sighted, or blind can train safely by using stationary devices instead of free weights (fig. 2.1).

Children and Conditional Clearance

In 1979 there were an estimated 35,512 weight lifting injuries that required visits to emergency rooms. Most injuries occurred in the home, while over half involved 10–19 year olds (U.S. Consumer Product Safety Commission 1980; Legwold 1982; American Academy of Pediatrics 1983). Children and adolescents are most likely to sustain growth center injuries between 12 and 13 years of age (Wilkins 1980; Peterson & Peterson 1972; Pappas 1983; Shankman 1985). Overhead lifts appear

Figure 2.1

Exercises may be modified so that those who are conditionally cleared may benefit substantially from weight training. In some cases, using stationary machines instead of free weights may be the only change that's needed.

to be the most dangerous (Ryan & Salciccioli 1976). Many injuries can be prevented if youngsters use proper exercise technique and low resistance (Rowe 1979).

Healthy children may be conditionally cleared for weight training by a sports medicine physician. Conditional clearance means that a child avoids maximum lifting and competition and is always closely supervised by professionals trained in sports medicine. Supervision is the key to a child's safety. When closely supervised by sports medicine professionals, children may improve their strength, jumping ability, and flexibility by training with weights (Micheli 1983; Servedio et al. 1985; Pfeiffer & Francis 1986; Rians et al. 1987).

Children should be encouraged to participate in a variety of different activities to improve all areas of their health-related fitness. If they express an interest in training with weights, be sure that they are closely supervised by a sports medicine specialist.

Cleared for Weight Training

Hopefully, you'll be fully cleared for weight training, which means that you can participate without restrictions. If this is the case, you should emphasize (1) upper-body–lower body or superior-inferior balance and (2) front-of-body/back-of-body or anterior-posterior balance. In chapter 5 we'll examine these balances and other fundamental training principles more closely.

Why is medical clearance essential prior to weight training?

Adequate Sleep and Diet

In many ways, the benefits you derive from weight training will be limited by your sleeping and eating habits. If you don't get adequate sleep your body will be doubly taxed during an intense workout. Lack of sleep can impair concentration and increase the risk of injury. Not only will a sound night's sleep help your weight training, but a solid workout may even improve your ability to sleep. Recent research indicates that as fitness increases, sleep quality improves (Shapiro et al. 1984).

The foods you eat are the source of energy for your daily activities. By balancing your diet, you'll not only feel better, but you'll also prime your muscles, bones, and other organs to respond to the stimulus of training. To develop a comprehensive nutritional plan for optimizing health-related fitness, consult texts by Hamilton and Whitney (1982), Williams (1983), and Whitney and Hamilton (1987).

Dress for Safety

Wear hard-toe athletic shoes with nonslick soles when weight training. Nonslick soles reduce the risk of slipping, while hard-toe shoes minimize foot and other injuries if free weights or dumbbells are mishandled. Lifting shoes are ideal but are a relatively expensive investment for beginners. New cross-training shoes manufactured by some companies provide an alternative.

It's preferable to wear cotton or other light, absorptive material to maximize sweat absorption and heat dissipation. Clean cotton gear also helps decrease the transfer of bacteria and minimizes wear and tear on various pads and equipment. (The equipment at your facility should be cleaned and disinfected regularly.) It's often handy to carry a towel so that you can wipe hands, pads, or other slick areas to improve your grip and stability.

Belts, Wraps, and Other Supportive Devices

Wrapping or taping vulnerable knees, ankles, wrists, or elbows may provide additional support. If you use wraps make sure they're not so tight that they cut off your circulation or increase joint forces (the kneecaps may be more vulnerable to injury when tight knee wraps are used). Athletic supporters for males and sports bras for females also help with comfort during weight training and other forms of exercise.

Figure 2.2
Remember that safe and effective programs are based on an awareness of individual differences. Realize that starting weights will vary dramatically depending on your initial fitness, experience, age, gender, previous injuries, goals, and exercise selection.

Although some question the effectiveness of weight belts, experienced lifters maintain that a quality belt gives extra support and tightness to the lower back and abdominal regions. It seems logical that belts may work by decreasing the volume of the intra-abdominal area, enabling the lifter to generate greater intra-abdominal pressures which help resist external forces placed upon the vulnerable spine. Heavy weight belts are associated with higher intra-abdominal pressures and may support the lumbar spine better than light weight belts (Lander 1987).

Increased pressures may also act to impede blood flow to and from the heart. If you use a belt for heavy lifting, remember to breathe continuously.

Be Aware of Individual Differences

Safe and effective programs are based on an awareness of individual differences (fig. 2.2). To minimize your risk of being injured and discouraged, avoid competing with others. Realize that starting weights will vary dramatically depending on your initial health and fitness, experience, age, gender, goals, and exercise selection. Before you start training, give your instructor pertinent data about yourself to make it easier to design a personal program to meet your specific needs.

Be Aware of Body Position

Whether you're performing an exercise, observing, or relaxing between sets, be aware of your body position in relation to others. Be especially aware of others when you're training in a crowded weight room. Keep your hands, feet, and hair away from machine cams, rotors, cables, and chains. Fortunately, many newer machines have protective coverings for chains and other movable parts.

Avoid Horseplay

Injuries may occur when two or more persons are involved in horseplay while others are lifting seriously. This is especially dangerous during free-weight sessions and should not be tolerated. Facility regulations should be enforced to maximize safety for all participants.

On the first day of class, what information should you give to your instructor to maximize your safety and make it easier to select starting weights?

Training Guidelines

Warm Up and Cool Down

Following medical clearance and optional signing of a waiver you're ready to participate. Before you start training, take the time to warm up thoroughly. Warm-up increases temperature and blood flow to a particular area, decreases muscle viscosity, and may benefit performance (Shellock 1983).

The first phase of your warm-up should be general in nature and should include light aerobics (e.g., walking or easy jogging) followed by a standard stretching routine (see appendix C, Basic Dozen warm-up/cool-down routine). Do twelve or more stretches to loosen major muscles in your lower body, abdomen, lower back, upper body, and neck. To reduce your risk of being injured, do static (controlled) rather than ballistic (bouncing) stretches. For each stretch, use a slow 5-count to proceed from a fully relaxed to a fully stretched (yet comfortable) position. Since your muscles reflexively shorten when they are suddenly stretched, you must move slowly and maintain the stretch for at least 20–30 seconds. Following this pause, use a slow 5-count to return to your original starting point. Never bounce or "pop out" of a stretch (fig. 2.3). By stretching consistently, you'll elongate your muscles, loosen surrounding connective tissue, and improve your flexibility.

After you warm up generally, warm up specifically by focusing on the muscle or group of muscles you plan to use for a particular exercise. For example, use one to two light weight, high-repetition sets of squats as a specific warm-up before moving on to more heavily weighted squat sets. Of the three types of warm-up

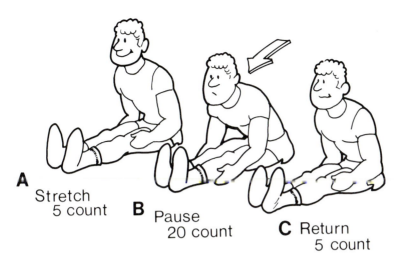

A Stretch
5 count **B** Pause
20 count **C** Return
5 count

Figure 2.3
When you warm up generally, be sure to move in a slow, controlled fashion. Use a 5-count to move to a fully stretched yet comfortable position. Stay there for at least 20 to 30 seconds and then slowly return to the starting position. Detailed stretches are illustrated in appendix C.

(generalized, specific, and passive), specific is the most beneficial because it increases local muscle temperature and gives you a chance to rehearse the movement you're about to do (Shellock 1983). Lower and upper body exercises that engage large muscle groups (e.g., the squat and bench press) require more extensive specific warm-up.

When you have finished training, don't just stop. Your muscles have been working hard to actively massage the blood back to your heart. If you stop suddenly, severe pooling of blood in your lower body can induce dizziness or blackout. Cool-down will not only prevent massive shifting of blood to your lower body, but may even help reduce your chances of getting sore.

Set aside at least 10 minutes for a cool-down. Cool down by first doing specific and then general stretches (appendix C). A cool-down is an excellent time to do abdominal and lower back work along with light aerobics and stretching.

Why is it important to move slowly into and out of a full stretch?

Check Equipment

Wherever you train, safety should be a top priority. Before workouts are permitted, a supervisor or instructor should ensure that the facility is in order and free of hazardous, nonfunctional equipment. Nonworking or dangerous items should be removed or replaced with new devices designed with safety in mind. When machine repair is pending, the surrounding area should be effectively cordoned off to reduce the risk of injury.

Always verify that the device you're planning to use is safe to train on. Look for signs indicating that the device is not in working order. Check for unstable support boards, frayed cables, cracked plates, stripped bolts, and missing collars and weight keys. Report dangerous or nonworking equipment to the management.

Equipment Orientation

Even the same equipment is often slightly different from weight room to weight room. If you aren't sure what to do or what to look for, ask the supervisor or instructor. It may be quite helpful to attend a facility orientation session before you start training.

Secure Movable Equipment Parts

Adjust and secure seats, uprights, and other movable equipment parts prior to training. Before using a circuit machine, be sure that the weight key is locked in place. A standard key can be secured by inserting and twisting it clockwise or by pressing and releasing a button on its end. To protect your lower back, contract your abdominals and fasten belts if they are present. When you use free weights, secure collars before you start exercising. Be especially careful when adjusting spring-loaded bench presses, inclined bench presses, or power racks. Many of these newer devices require resistance placed on the uprights to make adjustments safe and easy.

Before using a piece of equipment, it is essential to understand exactly how it is adjusted and operated in order to avoid injury. Give examples of spring-loaded, cable, and cam-type equipment, and describe how each device is safely adjusted and operated.

Use Spotters

When you use free weights, have spotters nearby in case you have difficulty. It's especially important to have a spotter for heavy attempts since you're virtually helpless if you don't complete the lift. If you don't have a training partner, ask an instructor or supervisor for help. To reduce your risk even further when using free weights, use power/squat racks with adjustable safety supports.

Regardless of your experience, use a spotter for all high-risk movements. You'll be the most vulnerable during the squat, bench press (standard or supine, inclined and declined), military press, behind-the-neck press, and triceps extension (supine). If you are just starting out or happen to be carrying a few extra pounds, you may also need some help with body resistive movements like the parallel dip and pull-up. Adjust bars and racks to the lowest position so that you can support yourself quickly and easily by placing your feet on the floor. Work on alternative exercises to develop the strength needed to do body resistive movements safely.

You may even improve the quality of your training by having a spotter. When you know a spotter is there, you'll feel more at ease completing a difficult exercise set. A spotter may also help you verify your technique, complete the range of motion, or do negative resistance (eccentric) work.

For maximum lifting, two to three spotters are best, but they must be skilled and act in a coordinated fashion during the actual attempt. Having one skilled spotter may be safer than having two unskilled ones who haven't practiced together.

As a general rule, spot someone only when they are using less than or equal to the weight you can handle easily for the same lift. For example, if your 1-RM for the squat is 250 lb, don't volunteer to spot someone attempting a 275 lb squat unless other experienced spotters can assist you.

Although spotting techniques for the Basic Dozen beginning weight training exercises are detailed in chapter 6, these general guidelines may help you spot a variety of movements:

1. Master the technique of an exercise before attempting to spot it.
2. Observe experienced spotters in action prior to spotting.
3. Practice by spotting instructors or experienced lifters who are handling reduced weights during light training sessions.
4. It is essential that you communicate while you're spotting, but minimize idle chatter to avoid distracting the lifter.
5. Check to see that weights are evenly distributed and collars secured.
6. When spotting, assume a ready position with a solid base of support (fig. 2.4c).
7. Be close enough to provide help but far enough away to avoid distracting the lifter.
8. To give a lift-off, use an alternate or pronated grip and guide the bar smoothly off the support rack or floor to the starting position (fig. 2.4b). Don't let go of the bar until the lifter gives a signal that the bar is steady and under control.
9. Focus your attention on the lifter during both the hard (concentric) and easy (eccentric) parts of the movement (compare a and c in figure 2.4).
10. If the lifter fails the attempt, guide the bar smoothly until it's safely secured in a rack or other stable position.

Choose a Low Resistance and Use Logical Progressions

Select a logical starting weight based on your initial strength for the specific exercise. If you're not sure, choose on the light side. You can always go up, but you may not be able to go down safely. Chapter 6 gives the trial starting weights for the Basic Dozen beginning weight training exercises (see table 6.2, p. 116).

Don't attempt heavy (1- to 2-RM) lifts during your first several weeks of training. Near maximal and maximal lifts require considerable skill and increase the likelihood of injury. Make sure that you satisfy the requirements for safe

A

B

C

Figure 2.4

A. Improper spotting technique. Be sure to focus your eyes and attention on the person performing the lift. B. Guide the bar off the rack using an alternate or pronated (palms-down) handgrip. Don't let go of the bar until the lifter gives a signal that the weight is under control. C. Watch carefully during the performance of each repetition.

maximum testing before you attempt a 1-RM lift (see appendix D). When starting out, it's best to estimate your maximum so you can determine the appropriate training intensity for each exercise (see appendix E).

Be logical and gradual when you increase resistance. This allows your body to adapt to the new stresses of training. Despite what others may say, don't try to increase the weight you handle every workout. In chapter 5 we'll see why this can be disastrous. To reduce your risk of soreness and injury, gently overload rather than forcefully over-overload your muscles.

Use Lower Body Muscles in Lifting

Many beginners are injured when they rely on their lower backs rather than their hips, thighs, and legs to lift weights from the floor. Most of these injuries can be prevented by using proper lifting technique.

To lift an object, assume a squat position with your knees bent, abdominals contracted, and eyes focused on a point above (fig. 2.5a). By contracting your abdominals strongly, you can decrease the forces acting on the cushioning pads (discs) between the vertebrae in your lower back by as much as 30% (Morris, Lucas & Bressler 1961; Morris 1973). Drive your head and shoulders "to the sky" as you move to an upright position (fig. 2.5b). To reduce your risk of muscle pulls, stretch inner thigh (adductor), posterior thigh (hamstring), anterior thigh (quadriceps), and lower back (erector spinae) muscles before lifting.

Bend Knees and Contract Abdominals when Standing

Any time you do an exercise from an upright position, be sure to stand with your feet slightly wider than your shoulders, your knees bent at a constant angle, and your abdominals contracted (fig. 2.6). By doing this, you'll reduce the stresses on your lower back considerably. You can protect your lower back even further by strengthening your abdominals and lower back, stretching your hamstrings and hip flexors, and reducing your percentage body fat.

Stress the Form, Not the Weight

Proper exercise technique is the single most important factor in making improvements. It is also the most neglected. Many weight trainers and competitive lifters would make dramatic gains if they stressed exercise technique more than the weight they handled (fig. 2.7).

Weight training exercises are designed to stress specific muscle groups. When you recruit extraneous muscles to maneuver a heavy weight, you increase your risk of being injured. You also diffuse stress away from the muscles you intend to isolate and detract from the benefits of the exercise. Although we'll discuss specific techniques in chapter 6, let's take a brief look at some general exercise guidelines.

A

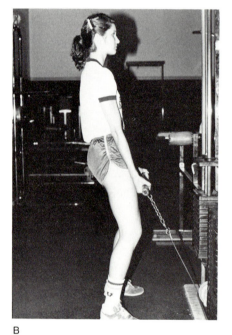

B

C

Figure 2.5

A. Protect your lower back by contracting your abdominals and using your hips, thighs, and legs when lifting. B. Move to an upright position by driving your head "to the sky." Note in the figure that the hips are not elevated during this movement. B. and C. Isolate muscles by stabilizing the axis of rotation. In this case, the front arm muscles (biceps and brachialis) are more fully isolated by pinning the elbows just to the outside of the abdominal area. This decreases recruitment of front shoulder muscles (anterior deltoids) during a curl.

A   B

Figure 2.6

A. If you stand with your knees straight and your hips extended, your iliopsoas muscles tug on the vertebral column and make you more susceptible to lower back injury. B. When standing, it's best to contract the abdominals, flatten your back, and keep your knees flexed at a constant angle. By doing this, you'll collapse your iliopsoas muscles and take the stress off your lower back

Stabilize Rotational Axes

Concentrate on stabilizing the axis of rotation of the particular joint you're using in an exercise (fig. 2.5b and c). This will maximize isolation of the specific muscle(s) the movement is designed to work.

Use Slow, Smooth Methodical Movements

Explosive-type weight training is associated with a high dropout rate (55%) and a high incidence (30%) of head and neck pain (Reid, Yeater & Ullrich 1987). By using slow, smooth, and methodical movements, you'll increase the tension in your muscles, dramatically improve your strength, minimize undesirable joint forces, and decrease your risk of being injured (Hill 1922; Fenn, Brody & Petrilli 1931; Allman 1976; Caiozzo, Perrine & Edgerton 1981; Kanehisa & Miyashita 1983b; Reid, Yeater & Ullrich 1987).

Figure 2.7
Be sure to stress the form and not the weight. This will reduce your risk of injury and enhance your strength gains.

Special Techniques for Circuit or Stationary Machines

When you use circuit weight training machines, free the plates from the weight stack before you begin exercising. Don't allow the plates to touch the weight stack until you are finished with the repetitions for a given set. Between repetitions, keep a paper-thin distance between the plates so that the brunt of the weight is on your muscles rather than on the weight stack. This will maximize the tension you develop in your muscles. Be sure to move in a controlled fashion and be kind to your joints, especially at the beginning and end of each movement.

Breathe Continuously

When you lift objects, it's tempting to use Valsalva's maneuver, which means that you bear down, hold your breath, or force against a closed glottis (the glottis is the space between your vocal cords). You'll find that it's hard not to hold your breath when you handle a weight that's more than half of your maximum.

By using Valsalva's maneuver during lifting, you increase pressures within your chest and abdomen. This makes your heart work harder to pump blood to the rest of your body. Muscles that contract powerfully during lifting also act to

BREATHE CONTINUOUSLY

EXHALE   INHALE
CONCENTRIC PHASE ECCENTRIC PHASE

Figure 2.8

Breathe continuously to reduce pressures inside your chest and abdomen and aid blood flow back to your heart. As a general rule, inhale before you start, exhale during the hard (concentric) part, and inhale during the easy (eccentric) part of an exercise.

impede the return of blood to the heart. In contrast, when you exercise aerobically, your heart does not have to work against added pressures because you breathe continuously and contract your muscles less forcefully.

Blood pressures as high as 480/350 mm Hg in body builders doing a series of double leg presses and 232/154 mm Hg in subjects using only 50% of 1-RM have been recorded (MacDougall cited in Carswell 1984; Freedson et al. 1984; MacDougall et al. 1985). Given that a normal value for resting blood pressure is 120/80, these pressures are extremely high. Notice that both the top (systolic) and bottom (diastolic) pressures are elevated during lifting. This means that the heart never has a chance to relax. High pressures during heavy lifting can severely limit or even abolish the output of the heart, decrease blood supply to the brain, and induce blackout (Compton, Hill & Sinclair 1973). By breathing continuously, you'll mimic breathing patterns used in aerobic exercise, decrease pressures inside your chest and abdomen, and reduce stresses on your heart and vessels (fig. 2.8).

Figure 2.9

The heart and its vessels, the brain, spinal cord, lungs, and other organs can be adversely affected by breath holding (Compton, Hill & Sinclair 1973). Intra–arterial measurements indicate that extremely high blood pressures can occur during heavy lifting (Freedson et al. 1984; MacDougall cited in Carswell 1984; MacDougall et al. 1985). Emphasize continuous breathing, especially during 1-RM and heavy resistance exercises, to reduce stresses on the cardiovascular and other body systems. If you have high blood pressure, avoid heavy lifting. Be sure to consult your physician before starting an exercise program.

Valsalva's maneuver may be advantageous for supporting the spine during heavy lifting (Lander cited in National Strength and Conditioning Association 1987a). However, the mechanical advantages of using Valsalva's maneuver to support the spine are offset by the undesirable effects on other organs and systems (Davis and Troup cited in Compton, Hill & Sinclair 1973). The heart and its vessels, the brain, spinal cord coverings and cerebrospinal fluid, lungs, and other organs can all be adversely affected by breath holding (fig. 2.9) (Compton, Hill & Sinclair 1973). To reduce pressures and to protect vital organs, always breathe continuously when training with weights.

You are cautioned throughout this chapter to breathe continuously. What are the adverse effects of holding the breath while lifting?

Summary

Weight training is a high-risk activity. By following simple guidelines, beginners can minimize soreness and injuries and have enjoyable initial training experiences. Medical clearance is a must before starting a fitness program. A sports medicine physician is the final authority for medical clearance. He or she may clear, conditionally clear, or not clear a client for weight training. Cardiovascular or orthopedic abnormalities may limit clients in their training.

Adequate sleep and a proper diet are needed to reap the full benefits of exercise. Hard-toe, nonslip shoes may prevent loss of footing and injury. Belts, wraps, and other supportive devices may be helpful. A thorough facility and equipment check should be completed prior to training. Hazardous or nonfunctional devices should be replaced or secured. Both general and specific warm-up should precede weight training to increase temperature and blood flow and reduce the risk of injury. Stretches should be done in a slow, methodical fashion. Specific warm-up is the most useful because it provides for rehearsal of a movement that is about to take place. A cool-down following exercise prevents pooling of blood in the lower body and may minimize delayed muscle soreness. Successful programs progress logically and are based on an awareness of individual differences.

Use spotters when free-weight training. Spotters should be close enough to provide help but far enough away so as not to be distracting. High-risk movements which require the most spotting are the free-weight squat, bench press, military press, and supine triceps extension. Secure seats, bolts, pins, clips, collars, and screws prior to lifting. Use lower body muscles rather than back muscles to lift weights from the floor. During upright exercises, bend the knees and contract the abdominals to protect the lower back. To maximize intramuscular tension and reduce the risk of injury, do exercises in a slow, controlled manner. Above all, stress the form and not the weight. Breathe continuously to decrease the intrathoracic and intra-abdominal pressures.

Exercise and System Classifications

3

Muscle contractions are classified as (1) isometric, (2) isotonic, or (3) isokinetic. In this chapter we'll briefly examine these general types of contractions to help classify weight training exercises and equipment.

Although it is convenient to place machines and movements into one of three categories based on the types of contractions they require, it may not be entirely realistic. Even when we perform everyday chores, we contract some of our muscles isometrically to stabilize body parts, and others isotonically or isokinetically to ensure smooth, coordinated limb movements. One contraction type may evolve from another, as when working muscles first contract isotonically but later contract isometrically when they are fatigued.

The following classification system may be idealistic, but it will build a framework for understanding the many machines and exercises encountered in the weight room. Hopefully, this understanding will help you maximize the benefits you derive from training on the unique equipment available in your facility.

Isometric Exercise

The word **isometric** comes from the Greek words *isos* and *metron,* which together mean equal measure or equal length. A muscle is said to contract isometrically when there is no visible change in its length or in the angle of the joint that it crosses. In the next chapter we'll discover that during an isometric contraction small filaments within muscle fibers must contract and shorten slightly. This may not be detectable with the naked eye, but does occur on the microscopic level.

If you push against a relatively immovable object like a wall, the triceps muscles in the back of your arms fail to overcome the resistance. Your elbow joint angles do not change appreciably and the velocity of your forearms equals zero. Your triceps are said to contract isometrically because you have used them to apply a force but no movement has occurred. All of us have experienced this type of contraction when we've tried to lift heavy boxes or other seemingly immovable objects.

Hettinger and Mueller (1953) found that midrange isometric training at 75% of maximum for 6-second intervals increased strength. During the 1950s and early 1960s isometrics were popular with athletes. After it was determined that

Figure 3.1
Sample isometric squat exercise using a power rack. Even though isometrics may be inexpensive, they provide limited benefits; they strengthen muscles only at specific joint angles at which training takes place.

muscles were strengthened only at the specific angles where training occurred, the use of isometrics became limited (Bender & Kaplan 1963; Gardner 1963; Kanehisa & Miyashita 1983a; Brooks & Fahey 1984). Today, some athletes use isometrics to improve strength at "sticking points" in a range of motion. Isometrics are mainly used by patients to rehabilitate joints or by body builders to practice posing for competition.

Isometrics are not as effective as dynamic exercises for increasing heart rate and they induce unfavorable increases in blood pressure (Sharkey 1966; McArdle & Foglia 1969). When you do isometrics or other static exercises, be sure to breathe continuously to decrease the stress on your heart and vessels. If you have high blood pressure or other cardiovascular problems, it's probably best to avoid isometrics.

Isometric exercise equipment can be inexpensive. All that is needed is an immovable object or some resistance which is too great to overcome (fig. 3.1). Occasionally, you may like to use isometrics when traveling on the road or when you need a change of pace. Remember that by using isometrics, you can strengthen your muscles, but mainly at the specific angles at which you train them. Whether you're involved in common daily activities or competitive athletic events, make more dynamic forms of exercise your primary focus.

Isotonic Exercise

The word **isotonic** is derived from the Greek words *isos* and *tonus,* meaning equal tone. It's actually a misnomer, since muscles that contract isotonically don't maintain the same tension or tone throughout the range of motion. The words **dynamic, anisometric,** or **nonisometric** might be more descriptive of this type of contraction.

A muscle contracts isotonically when it overcomes a resistance and its length and corresponding joint angle visibly change. This dynamic type of contraction is in complete opposition to a static, isometric contraction.

During isotonic movements, limbs proceed with a velocity through a range of motion. However, this velocity is not necessarily controlled. When the velocity is controlled or set equal to a constant, the movement satisfies one condition of isokinetics, which we'll discuss later in this chapter.

Isotonic equipment and exercises are the most popular for weight training (fig. 3.2). Isotonic training can be further subdivided into four categories: (1) constant resistance, (2) dynamic accommodating or variable resistance, (3) plyometric training, and (4) speed resistance training (Brooks & Fahey 1984). Before we take a look at each of these groupings, let's compare the different phases of an isotonic contraction.

Concentric versus Eccentric Movements

When you do an isotonic exercise you complete two separate movements: (1) the concentric, positive, or shortening phase and (2) the eccentric, negative, or lengthening phase. You concentrically load your muscles when you go up stairs, while you eccentrically load them when you go down stairs.

When movements occur at a constant velocity, there is greater electrical activity during concentric compared to eccentric phases (Bigland & Lippold 1954). The oxygen used during positive, concentric work is about four to six times greater than that used during negative, eccentric work (Asmussen 1953; Knuttgen, Petersen & Klausen 1971). The concentric phase of a weight training exercise is more effective in stimulating strength gain and hypertrophy, especially when muscles contract to at least 75% of their maximum tension (Guyton 1986).

Eccentric movements are associated with severe muscle soreness (Friden, Sjostrom & Ekblom 1981; Francis 1983). To reduce muscle soreness during the early phases of your program, minimize eccentric loading.

How can you avoid muscle soreness in the early stages of weight training?
What phase of an isotonic exercise is more effective for increasing strength?

Constant Load Isotonic Exercise

When you use a work load that appears to be constant for an isotonic movement, you're said to be doing a **constant load exercise.** Constant load devices like free weights, dumbbells, and most circuit machines are the most common forms of isotonic equipment (fig. 3.2). "Standard" or "typical" may be a better adjective for describing this type of isotonic exercise.

A

B

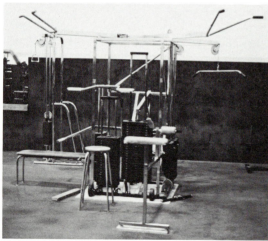

C

Figure 3.2

Isotonic exercise equipment. *A,* fixed, free-weight barbells, *B,* dumbbells, and *C,* a circuit training machine by Universal.

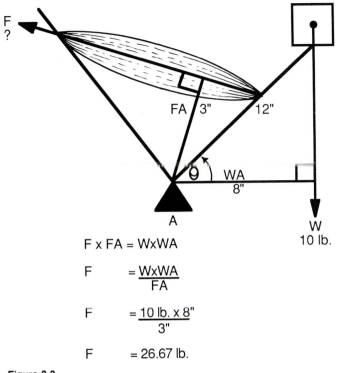

$$F \times FA = W \times WA$$

$$F \quad = \frac{W \times WA}{FA}$$

$$F \quad = \frac{10 \text{ lb.} \times 8"}{3"}$$

$$F \quad = 26.67 \text{ lb.}$$

Figure 3.3
The principle of levers states that any lever will balance when the product of the force (F) and the force arm (FA) equals the product of the weight (W) and the weight arm (WA). In order to calculate the force needed to balance a particular resistance, isolate and solve for F in the equation. The lever pictured is a class III lever, the most common in the human body.

You may notice that even though you use the same weight during an isotonic exercise, the difficulty in overcoming the weight varies greatly according to the particular angle of your joints. The true resistance or effective weight that your muscles experience is equal to the weight you handle times the length of the weight arm of your acting lever. The weight arm is the perpendicular distance between the line of resistance and the axis of rotation (fig. 3.3). Thus, even though the weight you handle may appear to be "constant," the force you need to balance that weight changes according to the angle of your joints. Exact values can be calculated by using the principle of levers:

$$F \times FA = W \times WA$$

where F = force or effort required to balance the opposing weight,
FA = the length of the force arm (effort arm) which is the perpendicular distance from the line of force to the axis of rotation (fulcrum),
W = the weight or resistance used, and
WA = the length of the weight arm which is the perpendicular distance from the line of resistance to the axis of rotation.

The above equation represents the equilibrium state. If you want to overcome a resistance, you must apply a force greater than that which balances the system (fig. 3.3). As your joint angles change during a typical isotonic exercise, so does the force you must exert to overcome the resistance. To calculate the force needed to balance a particular resistance, isolate and solve for F in the equation. The only variable that will change will be the weight arm (WA). You are required to exert maximum force when the line of resistance is perpendicular to the limb that is used as a lever (Wells & Luttgens 1976). This occurs when WA is at its maximum. In chapter 4 we'll see how muscles attach to form different types of levers.

When you do constant load isotonic exercises, you are limited by the weakest angle in the range of motion. This is commonly called a *sticking point*. As you approach a sticking point, your muscles slowly begin to contract isometrically instead of isotonically. Even though you can overcome the weight at most joint angles, you can't increase the weight until you improve your strength at this "weak" joint angle. In other words, constant load devices don't maximize muscular tension throughout an entire range of motion. Dynamic accommodating resistance and isokinetic devices were designed to achieve this goal. Although some advances have been made, weight training equipment is far from perfected. Each particular device has specific strengths and weaknesses (table 3.1). More objective, scientific research is needed to substantiate claims made about specially designed equipment.

Table 3.1 Characteristics of Weight Training Exercises and Systems

	Exercise or System		
Characteristic	Isometric	Isotonic	Isokinetic
Type of Contraction/ Synonym	Static	Dynamic	Dynamic[a]
Relative Expense	None or low	Low[b] to high[c]	High
Maintenance	None or low	Low[b] to moderate[c]	Moderate to high
Portability	Not required	Easy[b] to difficult[c]	Moderate to difficult
Concentric loading	Yes	Yes	Yes
Eccentric loading	No	Yes	No[d]
Accommodation	No	No[b]/Yes[c]	Yes
Intramuscular tension	Low to high?	Moderate[b] to high[c]	Moderate to high
Potential for delayed muscle soreness	Low	High	Low
Potential for rehabilitation	Limited	Moderate to high	High

[a]Since the velocity on isokinetic devices may be set to zero, static contractions are also possible.
[b]For free-weight barbells, dumbbells, and most other constant load devices.
[c]For isotonic dynamic accommodating resistance (DAR) devices.
[d]New isokinetic devices by Chattecx (Kincom) and Loredan (Lido) have built-in options for constant velocity eccentric loading. These are exceptions to typical isokinetic machines.

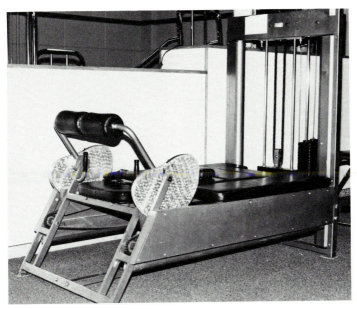

Figure 3.4
A. Nautilus dynamic accommodating resistance, duo-symmetric hip and back machine. B. Most DAR devices are characterized by an odd-shaped cam, which is designed to maximize intramuscular tension throughout a range of motion by varying the weight arm (see WA in figure 3.5).

Dynamic Accommodating Resistance

Dynamic accommodating resistance (DAR), also known as variable resistance, is a form of isotonic exercise that provides a compensating resistance by varying the length of the machine weight arm (also called a moment arm). Nautilus, Cam II, and similar machines are typical DAR devices (fig. 3.4a). In most cases, accommodating resistance is achieved by using an odd-shaped (cardiodlike) cam (fig. 3.4b).

Simplified Cam System

A. Start

B. Finish

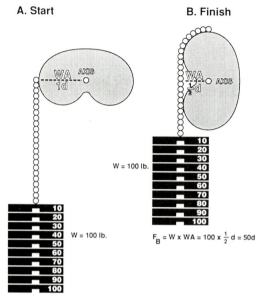

W = 100 lb.

W = 100 lb.

$$F_B = W \times WA = 100 \times \frac{1}{2}d = 50d$$

$$F_A = W \times WA = 100 \times 1d = 100d$$

Figure 3.5

Simplified cam system. The force needed to overcome the 100 pound weight stack in position *B* (finish) is one-half that needed to overcome the weight stack in position *A* (start). This is due to the change in length of the weight arm, WA, from d to ½d. Cam position *A* is matched with the strongest joint angle whereas cam position *B* is matched with the weakest joint angle. Despite this intriguing matching, accommodation on cam-type machines is by no means perfect.

When you move through a range of motion while exercising on a DAR machine, the weight arm (WA) varies according to the shape of the cam. Changes in weight acting on the machine's axis of rotation are directly proportional to changes in WA. Thus, the force you would need to overcome the resistance in figure 3.5a is far greater than that needed in figure 3.5b.

Some DAR machines (e.g., those made by Universal) do not rely on odd-shaped cams, but rather use sleevelike devices which directly adjust the length of the weight arm. Whether a cam or sleevelike compensation device is used, the goal is to maximize the muscular tension throughout the range of motion. This is achieved by matching long weight arms (WA) with "strong" joint angles and short weight arms with "weak" joint angles. Unlike typical equipment, there's not just one sticking point, but supposedly sticking points at every angle throughout the range of motion (Berger 1984). You may sense this as an evenness or smoothness when you train on DAR machines.

The theory of dynamic accommodating resistance is quite intriguing. Nevertheless, it has not been scientifically established that DAR devices are superior to standard equipment for developing muscular strength and endurance (Brooks & Fahey 1984). In fact, since various odd-shaped cams do not fully accommodate and different muscles may respond quite uniquely, it's idealistic to propose that muscle tension may be maximized throughout a range of motion.

In most cases, DAR devices are quite expensive and difficult to move. This makes them less attractive compared to free weights and other simple equipment. Free weights also provide more freedom in exercise selection and multi- rather than single-planar movements which are more akin to everyday life. A new machine designed by Lapko has attempted to combine the advantages of DAR and free-weight systems (see appendix K). Although it's hard to compare different systems because of problems in equating work loads, more research is needed to determine the effectiveness of DAR and other special isotonic devices.

Why is it that even though you use a constant weight such as a dumbbell in an exercise, the force required to move the weight varies throughout the range of motion?

Plyometric Training

Plyometric training, also called implosion training or training for explosive power, originated in the 1960s in the Soviet Union and Eastern European countries (Radcliffe & Farentinos 1985). This type of training is said to bridge the gap between pure strength training and the application of skills used by athletes in competition (Rogers cited in National Strength and Conditioning Association 1986).

Ply comes from the Middle English word **plien,** meaning to apply, while **metric** is from the Greek word **metron,** meaning measure. A person who trains plyometrically rapidly applies a strong, sometimes violent (loading) force to their muscles to elicit a muscle-spindle reflex (also called a stretch or myotatic reflex). Muscle spindles, located deep within the belly of muscles, are receptors that are especially sensitive to changes in muscle length. When stretched during a plyometric drill, these receptors send messages to the spinal cord which increase the outflow of motor nerve impulses to the elongated muscle. Thus, when a muscle is stretched, so are its muscle spindles, causing a reflex contraction of the muscle to return it to its optimal length. We'll see in chapter 4 that other special receptors called Golgi tendon organs help protect the muscle by relaxing it when extreme tension develops.

Plyometric drills include bounds, hops, jumps, leaps, skips, ricochets, swings, twists, and other movements (Radcliffe & Farentinos 1985). A typical plyometric exercise starts with a sudden stretch of muscles initialized by a deep descent jump. The depth jump is followed by involuntary and consciously timed contractions that are intensified by the stretch reflex during a return ascent phase.

During a depth jump or descent phase, other muscles besides those being stretched react to the suddenly applied force. While some muscles are being stretched, others may be suddenly shortened, stretched, or unchanged. In fact, during a depth jump, one end of a muscle like the hamstring (posterior thigh) may shorten, while the other end may lengthen. This opposition may effectively negate any stretching and result in an isometric-type contraction of the posterior thigh. Some researchers believe that these limited range, isometric-type contractions may be one of the reasons that many people have tight hamstrings. While rapid stretching of one muscle may evoke a stretch reflex in that particular muscle, it may also evoke reflex inhibition or a negative stretch reflex in an antagonistic muscle. It's hard to pinpoint exactly what happens in this complex situation, especially when many two-joint muscles are involved.

The nerve fibers responsible for rapid sensing of dynamic changes in the muscle-spindle complex send impulses to the spinal cord between 80 to 120 meters per second. It's difficult to imagine that by practicing, we can improve or intensify something that occurs so rapidly. However, recent research has suggested that the muscle-spindle reflex is fatigable and perhaps trainable (Gollhofer et al. 1987). There's a need for more information about how plyometrics and other types of training influence our ability to regulate the stretch reflex.

With plyometrics, the major emphasis is placed upon integrated development of the body's musculature. Plyometric exercises are often included in training programs for athletes since rapid jumping, leaping, and change-of-direction skills are used in all sports. Athletes who use plyometrics may benefit because they are practicing skills required for their specific sport or activity. This is merely an application of the specificity principle, which states that if you want to improve jumping, leaping, and change-of-direction skills, you should practice these skills specifically.

The major problem with plyometrics is that tremendous compression, shear, and tensile forces are generated during the often violent training sessions. Additionally, irrational American athletes, attempting to improve upon Soviet techniques poineered by Verkhoshanski (1969), have used the concept that "more is better" and now may be seen leaping with heavily weighted vests and leg weights from tall buildings rather than from moderate-height benches and platforms.

Plyometrics may benefit those involved in athletic events, but should not be used by those who are pregnant, elderly or just starting a program. If plyometric training is used, it must be preceded by extensive general and specific warm-up (see appendix C). Logical, stepwise progressions are critical in planning an extended plyometric program. Plyometrics should not be used during initial phases of rehabilitation. It's preferable to increase strength by using controlled isokinetic or isotonic movements to reduce the risk of injury.

If you'd like a more detailed look at plyometrics and logical program designs, consult the text by Radcliffe and Farentinos (1985) listed in the reference section at the end of the book.

Speed Resistance Training

In speed resistance training, one attempts to move the weight as rapidly and forcefully as possible. Speed resistance training, like plyometrics, is practiced predominantly by athletes involved in power sports. While Olympic lifts and other speed resistance movements may be appropriate for competitive athletes, they may not be appropriate for pregnant women, children, the elderly, or other members of the general public.

The Olympic lifts—the clean and jerk and the snatch—are isotonic speed resistance movements. These competitive lifts are described in appendix G. Olympic lifts require considerable skill, strength, coordination, timing, and balance that are unique to the particular movements (Jesse 1977; Allman 1982).

Athletes who participate in gymnastics, weight lifting, and football have the greatest risk of lower back injury (Alexander 1985). During Olympic lifting, the lower back is particularly vulnerable to injury because it's subjected to powerful extension (Jesse 1977; Alexander 1985). Most back strains and sprains occur when an underdeveloped, unprepared, or overloaded spine is subjected to a sudden violent extension contraction, especially when rotation is also involved (Cantu 1980).

Almost all injuries caused by exercise are the direct result of sudden movements (Allman 1976). As a beginner, it's best to perform isotonic exercises in a slow, controlled fashion. By doing this you'll generate greater intramuscular tensions and reduce joint forces as well as your risk of being injured (Hill 1922; Fenn, Brody & Petrilli 1931; Allman 1976; Reid, Yeater & Ullrich 1987).

If you'd like to pursue speed resistance training, seek the guidance of a qualified coach. Be sure that you've developed your back extensively by doing forward flexion, rotation, and lateral flexion exercises. Jesse (1977) recommends that until they've worked their spinal muscles for a full year, no athlete should be allowed to lift or jerk over 40% of their body weight overhead.

Speed resistance training and plyometrics generate strong joint forces and thus invite injury. What precautions should be taken when using these forms of training? For what groups of persons are these ballistic activities contraindicated? What groups might benefit from both types of training?

Isokinetic Exercise

The word **isokinetic** comes from the Greek words *isos* and *kinetikos,* and literally means "equal for putting into motion" or more simply, same speed. An exercise is said to be isokinetic when (1) limbs move at a constant velocity, (2) muscles contract at or near maximal tension through the entire range of motion, and (3) only concentric contractions are involved (Hislop & Perrine 1967). No movement is purely isokinetic according to these idealistic conditions. An isokinetic device by Hydra-Fitness is illustrated in figure 3.6.

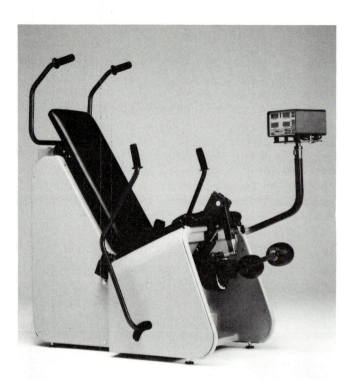

Figure 3.6
An isokinetic device. The Omni-tron (total-power) machine manufactured by Hydra-Fitness.
Although there are some exceptions, most isokinetic exercises satisfy three conditions: (1) limbs
move at a constant velocity, (2) muscles contract at or near maximal tension throughout the
range, and (3) only concentric contractions are involved. (*Source:* Courtesy of Hydra-Fitness, A
Division of Hydra-Gym, P.O. Box 599, Belton, Texas 76513.)

Some newer-model isokinetic machines by Loredan (Lido) and Chattecx
(Kincom) have included an option for constant velocity eccentric movements (see
appendix K). These machines are technically classified as isokinetic, yet they
have both concentric and eccentric options. Perhaps a new definition of isokinetics may involve satisfying only the first two of the three conditions listed previously.

It may help to view isometric exercises as a subset of isokinetics. Since muscles are not able to overcome the resistance in isometrics, the limb velocity is
equal to a constant, namely zero. Assuming one exerts maximal effort, maximal
tension is developed even though it's only at a specific joint angle. Isometrics
include only the concentric phase of an exercise.

Antagonists are muscles that act in opposition to agonists, which are the prime
movers during an exercise. Most isokinetic exercises do not include an eccentric
phase, but involve a concentric agonistic movement followed by a concentric antagonistic movement. For example, if you worked your thighs on an isokinetic
machine, during the first concentric or hard part of the exercise you'd work the

front of your thigh, while during the second hard part you'd work the back. For most isokinetic machines (except for a few newer models mentioned above), there is no easy or eccentric component. This makes them especially good for rehabilitation, since it's the eccentric or negative part of an exercise that is associated with delayed muscle soreness. Another plus of isokinetic machines is that when patients move through the range of motion, the resistance imposed by the isokinetic dynamometer is nearly proportional to the force needed to overcome it. In essence, there's a built-in safety mechanism in isokinetic devices that can be viewed as dynamic and accommodating (Hislop & Perrine 1967).

Like the concept of DAR isotonic exercise, the concept of isokinetics is theoretically appealing. However, there are practical problems associated with isokinetic devices. The viscosity of the fluid within isokinetic cylinders or fluid compartments may change due to weather conditions or heat produced by friction during exercise. Changes in viscosity may dramatically affect a machine's ability to accommodate.

There are no movements that occur at a constant velocity since movements must at some point in time start and stop. This becomes obvious the first time you exercise on an isokinetic machine. Initially, you'll sense a no-load phase in which your muscles barely develop any tension. During this time, you must accelerate the device arm to reach the machine's preset velocity. When your limb achieves this preset velocity, it will collide with the device arm, signifying the beginning of a distinct collision phase. You are now unable to move your limb at a velocity greater than the setting on the machine. As you approach the end of the movement, you decelerate your limb so that you can begin the next phase that involves contracting antagonistic muscles.

Sawhill (1981) found when subjects performed isokinetic leg extension/flexion movements, the device arm moved at a constant angular velocity only 18% of the total time at a rotational setting of 400 degrees per second. Both Sawhill (1981) and Lander (1982) further emphasized that the percentage of purely isokinetic activity decreases as the speed of rotation increases. While studying six highly trained males performing an isokinetic bench press, Lander (1982) observed the following:

At 27 degrees per second the bar moved isokinetically during only 70% of the activity . . . only 50% of the activity was isokinetic at 100 degrees per second. In other words (at 100 deg/sec), half of the time was spent accelerating and decelerating the device instead of accommodating to the subject's strength potential as it appeared to do during the constant velocity phase (pp. 69,83).

The concept of a purely isokinetic or dynamic accommodating resistance machine is idealistic. Contrary to what many fitness companies say, it seems clear that there are no perfect forms of resistance exercise. Remember that you, not the equipment, make the difference. As a famous coach once said, "You can make the best of rocks and stones." Regardless of the systems that are available in your facility, you'll benefit the most by being consistent and practicing strict exercise techniques.

How do isometric, isotonic, and isokinetic exercises differ, and what are the advantages and disadvantages of each?

Summary

Muscle contractions may be grouped into one of three general categories: isometric, isotonic, or isokinetic. Weight training exercises and devices may also be classified in this way. These classifications are idealistic as daily chores may involve combinations of all three contraction types. An exercise is isometric when a force is exerted but there is no movement. In contrast, during isotonic exercises, the resistance is overcome and movement takes place. Isometric exercises are limited to strengthening muscles at the particular angle at which contractions occur. Isotonic exercises consist of two phases: (1) a concentric or hard part and (2) an eccentric or easy part. The eccentric phase is associated with delayed muscle soreness and requires less oxygen than the concentric phase. Subcategories of isotonic exercise include constant load, dynamic accommodating (variable) resistance (DAR), plyometric, and speed resistance training. Constant load devices are the most common and include free weights and dumbbells. DAR machines attempt to increase muscular tension by matching long weight arms with "strong" joint angles and short weight arms with "weak" joint angles. However, accommodation is by no means perfect. Plyometrics and speed resistance training emphasize the development of explosive power for athletic competition. To reduce the potential for injury during these types of training, athletes should use extensive warm-up and systematic progressions. Beginners should avoid explosive-type exercises and use controlled movements to reduce joint forces and the risk of injury. Isokinetics involve moving a limb at a constant velocity. However, as the velocity is increased, less and less of the activity is purely isokinetic. Thus, despite manufacturers' claims, there is no perfect form of exercise. Benefits of weight training are achieved by consistently implementing sound exercise techniques.

How Muscles Work and Adapt

4

A weight trainer without knowledge of muscle structure and function is much like a potter who knows nothing about clay, shapes, or art forms. By enhancing their perception and creativity, potters and other artists learn to translate freely their innermost feelings into tangible works of art. Likewise, you'll find it's much easier to train and shape your muscles when you develop an appreciation for how they work and adapt.

This chapter will explain what muscles look like, how they work, and how they adapt. First we'll examine different kinds of muscles and their smaller components. We'll see how the brain and spinal cord trigger muscles to contract and synchronize them to ensure smooth movements. We'll look briefly at the changes that occur in muscles when specific stresses are imposed upon them. In the final section, we'll examine body levers, hand positions, and active movements to help you understand the connections that allow you to train your muscles with weights. Hopefully, after learning how your muscles work and respond to different exercises, you'll be realistic about setting goals and sensitive to changes which take place in your body.

Cardiac, Smooth, and Skeletal Muscle

Like other animals, we have three basic kinds of muscles. Although they are similar, cardiac, smooth, and skeletal muscles look and work a bit differently (fig. 4.1). Each muscle is organized in an extraordinary way to help meet the challenge of sustaining life.

Cardiac (heart) muscles easily conduct electricity because their cells are leaky to sodium and are fused together in a tightly merged lattice. Even though we rarely think about it, our hearts, empowered by their own pacemakers and special conductive systems, beat steadily over 110,000 times per day. Without this stable, rhythmic pumping, life-giving nutrients are left undelivered, suffocating wastes linger on, and working cells rapidly approach death.

Smooth muscle lines the digestive tract, vascular system, and walls of many organs. Like cardiac muscle, smooth muscle may be easily excited because it's leaky to sodium. Peristalsis, a wavelike action which occurs when we digest food or eliminate waste products, is triggered by smooth muscle contraction. By flexing or relaxing, smooth muscles lining our vessels help regulate blood pressure and

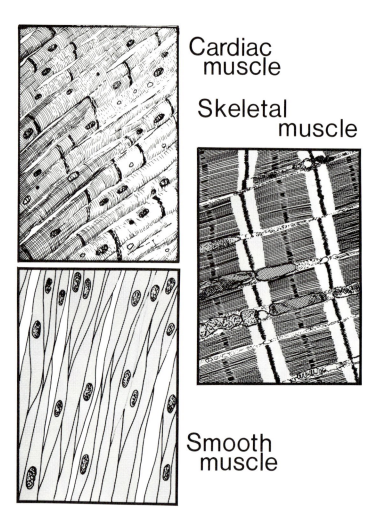

Cardiac muscle

Skeletal muscle

Smooth muscle

Figure 4.1

Cardiac, smooth, and skeletal muscle tissue slices as they appear under a microscope. The skeletal muscle view from a high-powered electron microscope illustrates the detailed arrangement of filaments within a single muscle fiber. Both skeletal and cardiac drawings appear striated or striped. The larger, oblong structures are mitochondria, cell "powerhouses." The dark bands in the cardiac fibers are intercalated discs, which fuse fibers together to form a lattice. These minimize resistance to current flow and allow the heart to contract as a single unit, even when only part of it is stimulated. Smooth muscle fibers are also tightly "glued" so they contract together. The smooth muscle fibers, like those shown from the wall of the gut, are arranged in sheets. As with cardiac fibers, each smooth fiber has a single circular or oblong nucleus that acts as the brain of the cell. In contrast, skeletal fibers have many nuclei.

nutrient distribution. Smooth muscles also play a prominent role in the development of cardiovascular disease (CVD). When the inner walls of arteries are injured, smooth muscle cells migrate to help with healing. However, this normal healing can be impaired by cigarette smoking, high blood pressure, and high blood cholesterol, leading to plaque formation and CVD.

Skeletal muscles make up about 40% of total body weight, whereas cardiac and smooth muscles together account for only 5%–10% (Guyton 1986). Our ability to control our skeletal muscles is what makes them so unique. By practicing with them, we can learn to perform incredible feats involving balance, flexibility, endurance, and strength. Let's take a closer look at what these voluntary muscles are made of.

Skeletal Muscle Makeup

Skeletal muscles, like other muscles, are made of special cells called fibers. Each skeletal fiber usually extends the entire length of a muscle. Muscle cells range from a few inches, like the tiny fibers of the vocal cords, to over one meter in length, like the sweeping fibers of the sartorius of the thigh. An entire skeletal muscle is surrounded by a glistening sheath or epimysium which is continuous with the muscle's tendons (fig. 4.2). Silvery, rainbow-tinted tendons usually attach muscles to bones, but sometimes attach them to other muscles or connective tissue.

Muscle fibers are organized in bundles called fascicles or fasciculi (fig. 4.2). Like the muscle itself, each fasciculus is enmeshed in its own glistening coat or perimysium. Resembling small, multicolored wires within a gigantic telephone line, muscle fibers also have their own delicate sheaths called endomysia.

A single skeletal muscle fiber has many nuclei, the control centers containing genetic blueprints that regulate heredity and daily cell activities (fig. 4.3). The fluid within the muscle fiber (sarcoplasm) bathes typical cell components including contractile microfilaments (actin and myosin), meshlike communication networks (endoplasmic or sarcoplasmic reticula), destroyers of foreign invaders (lysosomes), protein manufacturing plants (ribosomes), and final package-processing and releasing stations (Golgi complexes). Muscle fibers, especially those that are endurance trained, also contain many regularly spaced mitochondria, "powerhouses" which provide us with most of the energy we need (figs. 4.1, 4.3).

It would be easy to spend many years examining all of the "little organs" within a muscle fiber. In the next section we'll focus on the essential components that are directly involved in muscle contraction.

Actin and Myosin

Muscle fibers contain several hundred to several thousand threadlike structures called myofibrils (fig. 4.2). In turn, each myofibril is composed of thousands of tiny actin and myosin myofilaments. **Actin** is named for the Greek word meaning ray, since it looks like a spiraling ray of light. The word **myosin** means muscle

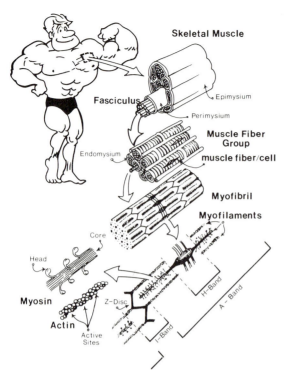

Figure 4.2
Skeletal muscle organization from the macroscopic (gross) to microscopic level.

sinew or muscle cord. You've probably noticed that the prefix *myo* often is used to indicate that some structure or process is closely related to muscle (e.g., myofibril = muscle fibril, myofilament = muscle filament, myotatic reflex = muscle stretch reflex). Even though there are twice as many actins as there are myosins, the larger myosin molecules account for the greatest amount of protein (68%) in skeletal muscles (Guyton 1986).

The thin actin filaments lie side by side with the thick myosin filaments (fig. 4.2). The parallel stacking and overlapping of actin and myosin create distinct bands which make skeletal fibers look striped or striated when viewed with a microscope (cardiac fibers also look striped, but they are less organized) (figs. 4.1, 4.2). Bands are either dark or light, based on their ability to scatter or organize light. The dark A bands alternate regularly with the light I bands (figs. 4.1, 4.2). The A stands for anisotropic, meaning that the band prevents light from shining through by scattering it. In contrast, the isotropic or I band lets light seep through and appears lighter in color (Guyton 1986).

You'll notice in figure 4.2 that the A band contains both actin and myosin while the I band contains only pure actin. The H band (zone) is pure myosin. In

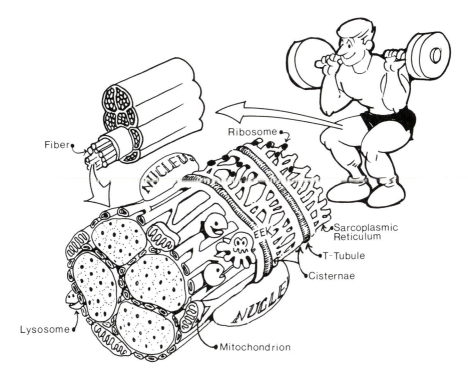

Figure 4.3
Schematic of skeletal muscle fiber.

the center of the I bands are zigzagging Z discs (lines) which link together adjacent sarcomeres. Like bricks used to build the foundation of a house, sarcomeres, which extend from Z disc to Z disc, are the basic building blocks of skeletal muscle fibers. Sarcomeres can become quite inflexible when they aren't used.

Special Parts of Actin and Myosin

Before we explore the sequence of events in contraction, we must take a closer look at the important parts of actin and myosin.

Actin is like two strings of beads that are twisted together (fig. 4.2). For every complete turn of these strings, there are a dozen or so active spots, sites on actin that are strongly attracted to a part of myosin. These spots are covered when a muscle is relaxed so that actin and myosin cannot unite.

Myosin is made of a central core and cross-bridges. The central core looks like the heavy stalk of a broccoli plant or the axis of an elongated bicycle wheel. The cross-bridges extend out from the core much like flower buds pop out of a broccoli stalk or spokes radiate out from the center of a wheel (fig. 4.2). Cross-bridges contain globular heads that are attracted to the active spots on actin.

Just like the thickened ends of spokes fit tightly into small holes on a bike rim, the myosin globular heads fit neatly into the active spots on actin when muscles contract.

How Muscles Work

Filaments Slide during Contraction

By using x-rays and high-powered microscopes, Hugh Huxley and Andrew Huxley found that A band lengths were the same, while I band and H zone lengths were smaller in contracted versus resting muscles (H. E. Huxley 1965; A. F. Huxley 1975; Stryer 1981). Although these researchers worked in different laboratories, they both proposed that muscles contract by sliding thick and thin filaments past each other (fig. 4.4). This is known as the sliding filament model.

The Sequence of Events in Muscle Contraction

Once a muscle fiber is stimulated by a motor nerve its membrane becomes leaky to sodium. Positively charged sodium ions rush in, reversing the charge the fiber had in its original resting state. This change in charge (also called depolarization or an impulse) moves in a wavelike fashion across the membrane of the muscle. Transverse (T-) tubules rapidly carry the impulse deep into the fiber toward small sacs, which store calcium (fig. 4.3). Once triggered by the impulse, these sacs dump their calcium into the fluid of the muscle fiber. When the calcium reaches a high enough level, it sticks to a part of the actin, changes its shape, and exposes the active spots. Only then can the myosin globular heads attach to the active spots and pull the actin filaments closer together. The level of calcium inside a muscle fiber determines whether contraction or relaxation takes place.

When the active spots are exposed, the myosin heads attach to them and then tilt in a power stroke toward the central myosin stalk. Energy is needed both to tilt and dislodge the myosin head from the actin. By performing this sequence over and over, the actin moves along the myosin like a caterpillar crawling along a thick branch. Thick and thin filaments are pulled closer together causing the myofibrils to shorten and the muscle to contract (fig. 4.4). Before the muscle can relax, energy molecules called ATP must be remade and special pumps must pump calcium back into its storage bags. This entire complex process can occur as many as one hundred times per second.

Muscle Control, Integration, and Communication

In this section we'll see how the central nervous system, made up of the brain and spinal cord, controls and synchronizes muscle actions so that our movements are smooth and rhythmical. We'll also take a brief look at how muscles communicate with one another by using special receptors and unique spinal cord circuitry.

Relaxation Phase

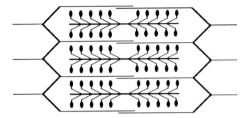

1. Excitation by nerve fiber
2. Conduction by T-tubules
3. Ca^{2+} release by SR

Contractile Phase

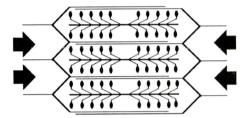

Figure 4.4

When muscles contract, actin and myosin filaments slide past each other. A nerve impulse causes the muscle cell membrane to depolarize or reverse its charge. The impulse is carried deep into the fiber by T-tubules to storage bags containing calcium. Calcium is dumped into the fluid within the fiber (sarcoplasm), sticks to a part of actin, and changes its shape so the active sites are no longer covered. The globular heads of myosin bind to the active sites and the filaments are pulled together. High-energy molecules (adenosine triphosphate, ATP) are needed to fuel muscle contraction. Before relaxation can take place, ATP must be remade and calcium must be pumped back into its storage sacs. The above complex process can occur as many as 100 times per second!

Connections that Provide for Voluntary Control

When you choose to contract specific skeletal muscles, you excite a particular area of your motor cortex, the front, outer barklike crust of your brain (fig. 4.5). From the motor cortex, electrical messages travel down higher motor nerves to the front part of your spinal cord. These signals are transmitted by a chemical called a neurotransmitter to lower motor nerves. When stimulated, lower motor nerves carry messages over tiny nerve branches directly to muscle fibers. Myelin, the fatty, creamy substance which encases motor nerves, enables impulses to travel the length of a football field in less than a second. This extremely rapid conduction velocity is needed for survival.

Brain

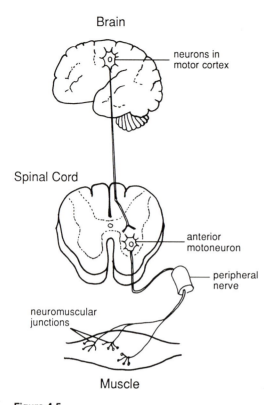

neurons in
motor cortex

Spinal Cord

anterior
motoneuron

peripheral
nerve

neuromuscular
junctions

Muscle

Figure 4.5
To move your muscles, you first excite higher motor nerves located in the motor cortex, the front, outer, crustlike part of your brain. Nerve signals travel to the front of your spinal cord, where they are relayed to lower motor nerves by a special chemical neurotransmitter. When a lower motor nerve is stimulated, its boutons dump their stored neurotransmitter (acetylcholine, Ach) into the space between the nerve and the muscle fiber. This transmits the signal from your nerves to your muscles, telling them to contract.

Each tiny nerve branch from a motor nerve ends in a single bouton (French for button), which fuses near the middle of a skeletal muscle fiber. Boutons contain sticky bags of a special neurotransmitter which are dumped into the space between the nerve and the muscle fiber when the motor nerve is stimulated. Without the neurotransmitter, the nerve signal would not be transmitted across the nerve-muscle gap and the muscle would fail to contract.

The Cerebellum Conductor

The cerebellum ("little brain") at the lower back of the head acts as a processing center for muscle actions. Your eyes, ears, muscles, joints, skin, and other body parts continually send feedback about themselves and the environment to your central nervous system. This up-to-date sensory information is used by the cerebellum to refine movements already in progress.

Figure 4.6
The cerebellum or "little brain" is the conductor of an elaborate muscle orchestra. Based on feedback from a variety of sources, it coordinates muscle contractions to allow for smooth, continuous movements.

Like the conductor of an elaborate orchestra working feverishly to refine music from several musicians, the cerebellum labors hectically to integrate and streamline input from a variety of sources (fig. 4.6). To produce a masterpiece, conductors must estimate when and where the music from many instruments will unite in time and space. To allow for beautiful, coordinated movements, the cerebellum must predict the position of each body part at any given instant. Conductors soften and slow the music of some players, but harden and speed up that of others. During complex skills, the cerebellum dampens limb movements that are too powerful or quick but allows acceptable movements to continue. Like a conductor who receives critical input from the nearby first violinist, the cerebellum acquires important sensory feedback from the vestibular apparatus in the inner ear. This information is used to instantaneously refine signals from the motor cortex to maintain body position and equilibrium.

With many long hours of practice, both an orchestra piece and a complex athletic skill can be perfected and performed with little thought. These unconscious or subliminal skills are probably stored in the sensory cortex, the back shell part of the brain. Later, like computer programs, skills are triggered into action when appropriate cues are given.

The importance of the cerebellum is made more vivid by observing a patient with cerebellar damage or disease. Like an orchestra without a conductor, these persons exhibit ataxia (Greek for lack of order), a condition marked by jerky and uncoordinated movements.

Receptors for Regulating Length and Tension

As mentioned briefly in chapter 3, muscles contain two types of receptors which help maintain their set-point length and tension. Muscle spindles located deep within the bellies of muscles are sensitive to changes in muscle length. By providing constant feedback to the brain and spinal cord, muscle spindles help dampen or smooth out typical body movements (Guyton 1986).

Golgi tendon organs are sensory receptors embedded within the silvery tendons that attach muscles to bones or sometimes to other muscles. Unlike muscle spindles, the Golgi tendon organs are most receptive to changes in tension. Without continuous sensory feedback from our muscle spindles and Golgi tendon organs, we'd have tremendous difficulty controlling our muscles. Let's take a brief look at how these receptors work.

The muscle spindle contains special intrafusal fibers which are different from extrafusal fibers found elsewhere in the muscle (fig. 4.7). In fact, the central part of intrafusal fibers cannot contract because it contains very little actin or myosin (Guyton 1986). It is this central baglike portion of the muscle spindle that is highly receptive to dynamic changes in length.

The Myotatic or Stretch Reflex

You may have had the tendon below your kneecap tapped at a visit to the doctor's office. This is done to check your spinal cord stretch reflex (also called the myotatic or muscle-spindle reflex). This reflex is triggered in plyometrics or other quick-loading, change-of-direction drills.

When a doctor taps your tendon, muscle spindles in your frontal thigh send out signals over sensory nerve fibers (fig. 4.7). These nerve fibers, which enter the back part of your spinal cord, can send impulses at a velocity of 70 to 120 meters per second (Guyton 1986). As with motor signals, important sensory signals are sent extremely quickly because they are critical for survival. Sensory messages travel along an uninterrupted path until they reach large (alpha, α) motor neurons, located in the front gray part of your spinal cord. At the synapse or communication point between sensory and motor nerves, a special transmitter is used to transmit the important message. Large motor nerves respond instantaneously by sending out impulses to excite the stretched muscles in your frontal thigh. Your muscles contract to return to their normal length. Your doctor would see your foot kick up slightly and say that your reflexes are normal.

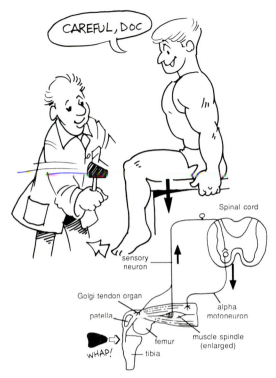

Figure 4.7

The myotatic or stretch reflex. When the tendon beneath your kneecap (patella) is tapped, muscle spindles deep in the fibers of your quadriceps detect a change in length. Sensory nerves that enter the back part of your spinal cord rapidly transmit this information to motor nerves in the front of your spinal cord. The excited motor nerves fire instantaneously, causing your quadriceps to contract so that it returns to its normal length. When severe tension develops in tendons, Golgi tendon organs respond by making muscles relax to protect them from being damaged.

At the same time that the large α motor nerves in the front gray part of your spinal cord are stimulated, so are nearby smaller (gamma, γ) motor nerves. These motor nerve cells send excitatory signals to the outer portion of your muscle-spindle intrafusal fibers, causing them to contract. This adjusts the sensitivity of your muscle spindles so that your brain and spinal cord always receive correct information concerning the length of your muscles.

Golgi Tendon Reflex

Golgi tendon organs differ from muscle spindles in that they are receptive to changes in tension rather than length. When triggered by a sudden increase in tension, Golgi tendon organs send sensory signals to the spinal cord so that muscle tension is adjusted reflexively. However, unlike those sent by muscle spindles, messages sent by Golgi organs act to inhibit motor nerves. This prevents further muscle contraction and promotes relaxation. Thus, Golgi tendon organs protect your muscles from being damaged should you develop extreme tension in your tendons (Guyton 1986).

If you jerk weights excessively when training, you increase the risk of injury as well as your chances of firing your Golgi tendon organs. You may be wasting a lot of time since your muscles will receive signals to decrease rather than increase their tension. The best way to increase muscle tension and enhance muscle strength and tone is to practice strict exercise technique.

Why are the stretch and Golgi tendon reflexes important?

Reciprocal Innervation

Muscles are located in strategic positions around the body to balance each other when they function. For each prime mover or agonist that causes a desired movement, there is an antagonist which opposes that movement. In an orchestra, the cellos balance the violas, but must be integrated with other instruments to make the music virtuous. Similarly, agonists are balanced by antagonists, but must be supported by other muscles to elicit smooth, coordinated movements. Even the simplest movement, like curling a barbell, requires the cooperative action of many muscles.

To curl a barbell, you flex your elbows by contracting the brachialis and biceps muscles in the front of your arms (fig. 4.8). Together, these muscles serve as agonists, while the triceps in the back of your arms act as the antagonists. If your triceps contracted powerfully, curling the barbell would be a difficult task. Fortunately, like other anterior and posterior muscles, muscles in the front and back of the arm are reciprocally innervated. This means that when agonists contract, nerve signals fired back to the spinal cord act to inhibit motor impulses to the antagonists, causing them to relax. In an opposing movement like the triceps extension, the agonistic triceps contract, while the antagonistic biceps and brachialis are inhibited.

When your schedule is tight, you may use agonistic-antagonistic training to help reduce your total workout time. This type of training, commonly called supersetting, takes advantage of reciprocal inhibition. By alternating agonistic and corresponding antagonistic exercises, you'll hardly stop training, yet you'll force your muscles to relax before and after you work them. Supersetting is ideal for circuit training since it minimizes rest time between sets and elevates heart rate to provide for more overall conditioning.

To maximize the advantages of supersetting, you must be precise in your exercise selection. Muscle groups (and corresponding exercises) which may be paired for supersetting include the anterior and posterior thigh (leg extension and leg curl), the chest and upper back (bench press and pull-up, lat pull, or bent-over row), the lower back and abdomen (back extension and curl-up or sit-up), and anterior and posterior neck (neck flexions and extensions). You may choose

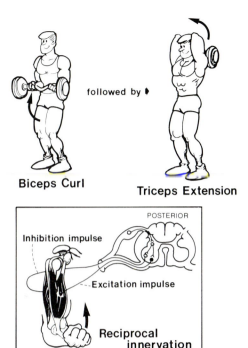

Biceps Curl

followed by ◗

Triceps Extension

POSTERIOR

Inhibition impulse

Excitation impulse

Reciprocal innervation

Figure 4.8
Our anterior and posterior muscles are reciprocally innervated; when one contracts, the other relaxes. You can take advantage of this when you train and reduce your total workout time by supersetting. For example, intersperse biceps curls with triceps extensions.

to alternate upper and lower body exercises like the bench press and the squat. Although in this special case there is no direct reciprocal inhibition, this type of supersetting can be used to reduce total workout time, to increase blood flow, and to create an invigorating and challenging workout.

Reciprocal relationships not only exist between the front and back of your body, but also between your right and left halves, which are nearly mirror images (fig. 4.9). When you contract your right biceps (and brachialis), nerve messages are sent across your spinal cord to inhibit your left biceps and to excite your left triceps. Your spinal cord circuitry also provides for simultaneous coordination of analogous lower body muscles (fig. 4.9).

Dumbbells are smaller hand-held weights that are used to isolate muscles by exercising limbs independently. Generally, dumbbell movements require more technique and balance and allow for more freedom of movement compared to barbells or stationary devices. You can demonstrate reciprocal relationships between opposite sides of your body by performing a simple task with dumbbells.

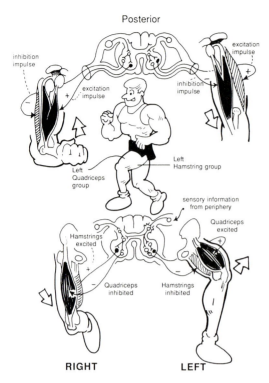

Figure 4.9

Similar muscles on opposite sides of your spinal cord also receive important information from each other. When you contract the right biceps of your arm, signals are sent across your spinal cord causing your left biceps to relax and your left triceps to contract. At the same time, signals are sent to analogous lower body muscles so that the right thigh "biceps" (hamstrings) is activated, while the right thigh quadriceps (frontal thigh) is inhibited. This special spinal cord circuitry pre-programs our bodies to move in a smooth, coordinated fashion. Although we can willfully override this circuitry to move in a different way, pre-programming takes over in life-threatening situations.

Place two dumbbells, one relatively light and the other heavier, in front of you on the floor. Stand with your feet shoulder-width apart, knees bent, abdominals contracted, and eyes straight ahead. Position both of your forearms parallel to the ground with elbows halfway flexed and palms facing up. Have a friend place the light dumbbell in your left hand. After your hand drops slightly, your left biceps (and brachialis) will respond to the weight of the dumbbell by contracting and lifting the hand up. (When your biceps does this, what does it tell your left triceps to do?) Continue to hold the light dumbbell with your left elbow flexed halfway. Now have your friend place the heavier dumbbell in your right hand. Your left hand will drop reflexively. To support the heavy dumbbell, your right biceps contracted powerfully and sent messages to your spinal cord that inhibited your left biceps.

By training with dumbbells, you can take advantage of reciprocal relationships between the right and left sides of your body. When you train with a barbell (or train unisymmetrically), similar muscles contracting on opposite sides of your body send messages to relax each other. This may act to decrease the total weight that you can handle (Ohtsuki 1983). You can reduce the effects of this reciprocal inhibition by performing alternate (or duo-symmetric) dumbbell exercises. This means that you relax one limb while you work the other. Start and end an exercise set by using your weak rather than your strong side so that you minimize instead of promote strength differences. By performing an alternate dumbbell versus a comparable barbell exercise, you'll be able to handle more total weight and more fully isolate and tax your muscles. However, the main disadvantage is that it will take you twice as long to finish a standard set. When time is not a factor, complement standard barbell movements with dumbbell exercises to add a refreshing variation to your training routine.

Right- and left-side reciprocal inhibition is important in common activities such as walking, running, bicycling, and swimming. When one joint flexes, the same joint on the opposite side of the body extends. This provides for smooth, synchronous, and efficient movements. Think about how your limbs move as you walk or run or observe your pet dog or cat in action. It's incredible how our special spinal cord circuitry gives us so much freedom, yet guides us when we move in complex, rhythmical ways.

What is the common name for agonistic-antagonistic training? Select four pairs of exercises that illustrate this type of training.

How Muscles Adapt

Hypertrophy versus Atrophy

The word **hypertrophy** comes from Greek words meaning "above nutrition" or, more simply, "over growth." Muscles that increase in size and strength are said to hypertrophy when they're trained consistently with moderate to heavy weights (fig. 4.10). Individual muscle fibers increase in size while their corresponding myofibrils, containing actin and myosin, increase in size and number. As mentioned in chapter 1, compared to females, males have higher testosterone levels and experience more absolute hypertrophy when they train with weights.

When muscles are overloaded in a logical and progressive way, they respond by increasing their functional capacity. Bones which serve as attachments for muscles also become thicker and stronger in response to the stress of exercise. In fact, the entire body, including its nervous, hormonal, cardiovascular, and other systems, adapts to reasonably applied stresses. Gradual adaptations take place so that in the future, the same stresses are less disruptive to the body's internal balance. When further adaptations are desired, stresses must be increased and varied periodically. In the next chapter, we'll take a closer look at principles about overload, variation, and other fundamental rules of training.

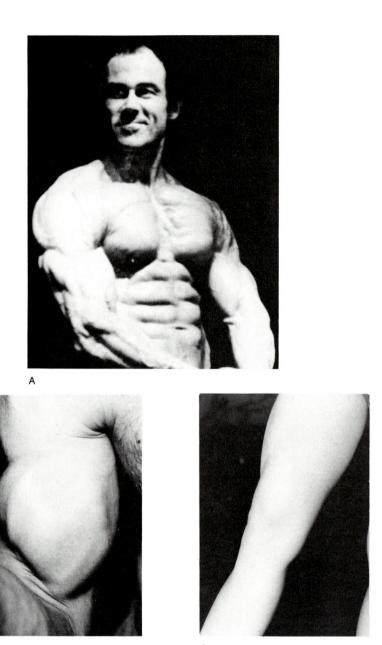

A

B   C

Figure 4.10
Hypertrophy results from constant overloading of skeletal muscle. *A.* Upper body hypertrophy and delineation in a male bodybuilder who has trained for 28 years. *B.* Biceps hypertrophy in a recreational weight trainer (male). *C.* Lower extremity hypertrophy in a female athlete. Unless they take steroids or have excessively active adrenals, women experience only minor degrees of hypertrophy when they train with weights.

A decrease in the functional capacity of the musculoskeletal system occurs when stresses are reduced or eliminated. The old saying "if you don't use it, you'll lose it" is true. Without the stress of exercise, muscle fibers atrophy or decrease in size and strength (atrophy means without nutrition or without growth). As mentioned in chapter 1, bones also decrease in size and strength during prolonged casting, bed rest, or space travel. Likewise, many other body systems "detrain" when exercise stresses are avoided. The fastest proven way to enhance hypertrophy and limit atrophy in our muscles and bones is by training with weights.

Hyperplasia?

When cells hypertrophy, they increase only in size. In contrast, in hyperplasia, cells multiply and increase in number. Hyperplasia is a common feature of normal body cells during their early development and is also characteristic of abnormal cancer cells.

Some researchers have suggested that muscle fiber hyperplasia may be triggered by heavy resistance strength training (Gonyea, Ericson & Bonde-Peterson 1977; Edgerton 1978; Gonyea 1980; Ho et al. 1980; MacDougall et al. 1982). However, it's hard to verify these claims because there are many problems associated with muscle sample preparation and fiber counting. Even when repeated samples are taken from the same muscle in one person, there's a tremendous variation in fiber number (Halkjaer-Kristensen & Ingemann-Hansen 1981; Elder, Bradbury & Roberts 1982; Lexell, Hendriksson-Larsen & Sjostrom 1983). Pieces of fibers may be mistaken as split fibers or as satellite cells, thought to be forerunners of new, hyperplastic cells.

Growth hormone (GH) increases both the size and number of muscle fibers in children and adolescents (Serono Laboratories 1984). GH levels also rise naturally as much as 260% above normal during and after intense weight training (Vanhelder, Radomski & Goode 1984). Perhaps sensitized muscle fibers increase their number in response to natural surges of growth hormone promoted by heavy training. It's also quite possible that younger athletes induce hyperplasia by taking large amounts of synthetic GH. Nevertheless, until techniques are further refined, it will be difficult to verify that hyperplasia occurs in response to intense weight training.

Skeletal Muscle Fiber Types

Slow, Intermediate, and Fast Fibers

Although there are many ways to classify skeletal muscle fibers, they are usually typed or grouped according to what they look like and how they work. You can see from table 4.1 that the use of many synonyms and abbreviations makes things a bit complex. We will simplify this by classifying fibers as one of three major types: (1) slow, (2) intermediate, or (3) fast.

Slow fibers are smaller and contract more slowly and less powerfully than fast fibers. They're usually deep red in color because they have large amounts of

Table 4.1 Comparison of Major Skeletal Muscle Fiber Types

Characteristics	Muscle Fiber Types		
	Slow	Intermediate	Fast
Common names & abbreviations	Type I	Type IIa	Type IIb
	Slow-oxidative (SO)	Fast-oxidative glycolytic (FOG)	Fast-glycolytic (FG)
	Slow-twitch (ST)	Fast-twitch (FT)	Fast-twitch (FT)
	Slow-fatigable (S)	Fast, fatigue-resistant (FR)	Fast-fatigable (FF)
	Tonic	Phasic	Phasic
Size	Small	Intermediate	Large
Color	Deep red	Red	White
Speed of contraction	Slow	Fast	Fast
Fatigue resistance	High	Intermediate	Low
Oxidative capacity	High	Intermediate	Low
Glycolytic capacity	Low	Intermediate	High
Mitochondrial content	High	Intermediate	Low
Myoglobin content	High	Intermediate	Low
Capillary density	High	Intermediate	Low
Myosin ATPase stain (high pH)	Light	Dark	Dark
Succinate dehydrogenase stain (high pH)	Dark	Dark	Light
Myosin ATPase stain (low pH)	Dark	Light	Light

Note: Table compiled from a variety of sources including deVries, 1986; Brooks and Fahey, 1984; Fox and Mathews, 1981; Edington and Edgerton, 1976; Dubowitz and Brooke, 1973; and Peter et al., 1972.

myoglobin, red pigment molecules in muscles that bind and store oxygen. Their rich blood supply also helps give them a vibrant, reddish tinge. Slow fibers have a high-oxidative capacity, which means they can burn oxygen efficiently to produce large amounts of energy for prolonged work. Slow fibers are laced with many regularly spaced mitochondria, powerhouses which use oxygen to burn fats, carbohydrates (sugars), and sometimes proteins. Since slow fibers can contract for extended periods, they are often called fatigue-resistant fibers.

The slow, postural (antigravity) muscles that enmesh your spine work constantly to keep you straight while you're standing or sitting. You've probably never noticed these muscles unless you've gotten a kink in your neck from sleeping in a cramped position or from lifting a heavy object improperly. Right now, the slow contractions of your masseter muscles on either side of your jaws are keeping your mouth from being wide open while you read this sentence.

Fast fibers can develop tremendous tension but only for short periods of time. (Because of this, they are also called fast-fatigable fibers.) Since their blood supply and myoglobin are limited, fast fibers are white or pale in color. They're largely anaerobic (poor users of oxygen) because they have few mitochondria. Even though fast fibers are not well-suited for using fats and proteins for making energy, they have high-glycolytic capabilities, which means they are good at using carbohydrates (glycolytic is Latin for sugar dissolving).

You've probably been delighted by the sight of a frog springing across lily pads or rocks in a pond or creek. The frog is empowered by the explosive contractions of its fast sartorius (thigh) muscles. Or perhaps you've been impressed by the high-speed, rhythmical beating of a hummingbird's wings, fueled by powerful contractions of resilient, fast pectoral (chest) muscles. Your own fast ocular fibers that control eye movements can contract in less than 1/100 of a second. Without a doubt, fast fibers can be critical in survival situations.

Intermediate fibers have characteristics midway between slow and fast fibers. They're also known as fast-twitch oxidative, glycolytic fibers. They can contract with reasonable tension for fairly long periods by using all three energy nutrients. Intermediate fibers are light red (pink) in color and contain a moderate number of mitochondria. Since these fibers have characteristics of both extremes, they're thought to change most easily with intense training.

The large, stomach-shaped muscles in your calves (gastrocnemii) contain a good number of intermediate fibers. These are needed to contract relatively forcefully and quickly when you participate in extended activities like jogging and cycling (Guyton 1986).

Determination of Fiber Types

A small plug of muscle or **biopsy** is obtained with a special needle after an incision is made in the skin of a subject. Tissue samples are sliced into tiny, thin pieces which are treated with different enzymes to make them colored (fig. 4.11, table 4.1). After they've been stained properly, fibers can be typed and counted by viewing them under a high-powered microscope.

Whether or not you know it, you've had intimate experience with fiber typing. As a young child, you probably developed a preference for certain parts of chicken like the breast (mostly pale, fast fibers) or the thigh (mainly slow, dark fibers). While eating, you might have noticed that the breast of a migratory bird like a duck is far redder than that of a domestic chicken. The redder tinge of the fibers is due to the extensive blood supply and myoglobin needed to sustain muscular contractions during migrations of several hundred to thousands of miles.

Distribution of Fiber Types

Most animals have a combination of fast, slow, and intermediate fibers with the distribution based on requirements for survival. The muscle mass of a shark is uniquely divided with over 80% of it composed of fast fibers. These are heavily recruited during the high-speed, whiplike swimming that the shark uses to stalk and attack its prey. The remainder of the shark's energy-efficient, slow fibers are called into action during cruising or migration periods.

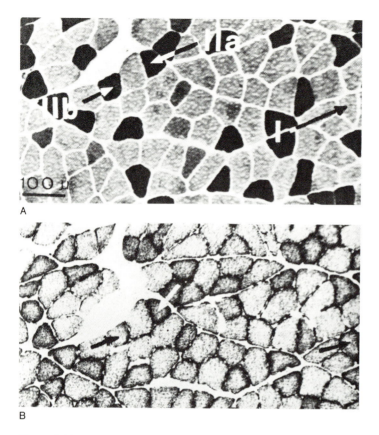

A

B

Figure 4.11

Transverse slices of skeletal muscle fibers viewed with a microscope. Fiber slices are incubated with different enzymes to make them colored. A. The slow fibers (I) are light, while both fast (IIb) and intermediate fibers (IIa) are dark in this tissue section. B. Tissue section treated with a different enzyme to distinguish fast and intermediate fibers. The same slow fibers from the previous photo appear dark, while the same fast fibers appear light. The intermediate fibers (IIa, white arrow in this photo) also have aerobic capabilities like slow fibers and are darker colored. (Source: Micrographs courtesy of Timothy P. White, University of Michigan. Originally appeared in **Exercise Physiology** by George A. Brooks and Thomas D. Fahey. Copyright 1984 by John Wiley and Sons. Reprinted by permission of Dr. White and MacMillan Publishing Company, current publisher.)

The muscles of weight lifters, sprinters, and other power-event athletes often contain a high percentage of fast fibers. In contrast, muscles of cross-country skiers, long-distance runners, cyclists, and other endurance athletes have more slow fibers.

Can Fiber Types Be Changed?

Since most endurance athletes have more slow fibers and most strength athletes have more fast fibers, does this mean that by training intensely you can change your fiber types and instantly become a professional dancer or football player?

Probably not. Basically, the old adage is true: "Sprinters are born, not made." The fiber types that you have are determined by the genes you've inherited from your parents.

All fibers innervated by the same motor nerve are of the same type. Fibers can be "changed" by separating nerves from slow fibers and skillfully reattaching them to fast fibers. The changes are a bit less dramatic when the switch is made in the opposite direction (from fast to slow fibers).

Don't be discouraged. Although your genes act as the limiting factor, your training can make a world of difference. Recent studies on animals have demonstrated dramatic transitions in the characteristics of fiber types with high-intensity exercise (Green et al. 1984). Fast and intermediate fibers become more like slow fibers with extensive endurance training, while slow and intermediate fibers become more like fast fibers with chronic strength training.

Training Specific Fiber Types

It's easy to misinterpret the words *slow, intermediate,* and *fast* as they apply to different fiber types. Contrary to what you've heard, a fast fiber is not always used during a fast movement. Fibers are recruited largely according to the force rather than speed requirements for a particular action (Brooks & Fahey 1984). In other words, if you move your hand quickly overhead, you won't recruit many fast fibers because the resistance to that action is low.

Of the three fiber types, slow fibers are the smallest and easiest to recruit; the small cell bodies of the nerves that nourish them can be triggered easily. As a movement becomes progressively more difficult, more intermediate and fast fibers are recruited. The cell bodies of motor nerves that control these fibers are larger. Large fast fibers are used extensively during one-repetition maximum (1-RM) lifts when muscles are taxed maximally.

Many have said, "I'm using light weights and high-speed repetitions so I won't slow myself down." As we saw in chapter 1, loss of speed is one of the most popular misconceptions about weight training. By doing many quick repetitions with a light weight, you'll recruit mainly slow fibers because you won't tax your muscles enough to recruit fast fibers. You can recruit more fast fibers by training with heavier weights and by using slow, smooth, and methodical movements. However, you still may not improve your ability to use these fibers in a high-speed activity. Chapter 5 explains why the best way to train your muscles for a particular activity is by practicing that activity exactly.

Which type of muscle fiber is advantageous for a sprinter? a marathon runner? a basketball player? a pole vaulter? Can the characteristics of fiber types be modified? If so, how? If not, why not?

Adaptations to Training

Muscles adapt specifically to particular stresses imposed upon them. These changes can be so specific that they occur entirely independent of other changes in the muscle. For example, with strength training you can increase the size and strength of your muscles without improving their ability to use oxygen or burn fat. In contrast, by endurance training your muscles you can enhance their capacity to use oxygen and burn fat without significantly increasing their size and strength (Holloszy & Booth 1976). Since endurance and strength training are essentially at opposite ends of a continuum, it's difficult to develop superior strength and endurance in the same muscle (see chapter 1, fig. 1.1).

Specific Changes Due to Endurance Training

If you consistently endurance train your muscles, you'll enhance enzymes and structures associated with aerobic metabolism. The most prominent among these changes include the following:

1. Increased size and number of mitochondria, the energy-producing power-houses in cells.
2. Increased levels of mitochondrial (aerobic) enzymes, including those specific for burning fats (triglycerides).
3. Increased vascularization of muscles, which improves circulation.
4. Increased stores of fat in muscles accompanied by decreased fat in the bloodstream. This occurs along with an increase in enzymes involved in the activation, transport, and breakdown (beta-oxidation) of pieces of fat (fatty acids).
5. Lowered production of lactate (a metabolic waste product), which enhances a muscle's ability to perform for extended periods.
6. Increased myoglobin (muscle hemoglobin), which helps transport oxygen through the muscle fluid to the mitochondria.
7. Higher resting-energy levels, which inhibit sugar breakdown.
8. Increased aerobic capacity of all three fiber types.

Endurance-trained athletes have aerobic enzyme values up to 150% higher than sedentary persons (Gollnick et al. 1972). However, changes occur specifically in the muscles that are trained. Cyclists have the highest levels of aerobic enzymes in their thigh muscles, while canoeists have the highest levels in their shoulder muscles.

Specific Changes Due to Strength Training

When muscles contract powerfully during strength training they rely on previously stored sources rather than oxygen for needed energy. These sources include high-energy compounds—ATP and CP—and stored sugar called glycogen (see chapter 1, p. 2). Strength training enhances anaerobic capacity by increasing enzymes associated with glycolysis and the immediate energy system. Some of the specific changes that occur in muscles due to long-term strength training include the following:

1. Preferential increase in the size of larger fast versus smaller slow fibers. This hypertrophy is accompanied by an increase in the number of myofibrils with their actin and myosin.

2. Increased CP as well as creatine phosphokinase (CPK), an important enzyme that enhances a muscle's ability to get energy during short-term, high-powered activities.
3. Increased enzymes that help store and dissolve sugar. These include glycogen phosphorylase (GP) (an enzyme which helps cleave sugar [glucose] pieces from glycogen) and phosphofructokinase (PFK) (a key regulatory enzyme in glycolysis).
4. Decrease in the number of mitochondria relative to muscle tissue.
5. Decrease in vascularization relative to muscle tissue.
6. Reported splitting of fast fibers that may result in hyperplasia. This may not be established until biopsy and counting procedures are refined and athletes who don't use steroids or growth hormone are examined.

If you'd like to study more about how muscles change specifically with training, consult the reviews by Holloszy and Booth (1976) and Gonyea and Sale (1982) listed in the reference section at the end of the text.

Muscle Soreness

Sometimes we don't seem to adapt well to the stress of exercise. We get extremely sore because we've been inconsistent or have abused our bodies during a weekend game of basketball, an extended bike ride, or a wilderness hike. When first training with weights, even though you may proceed carefully, you'll probably experience some muscle soreness. Muscle soreness is an inevitable consequence of adaptation to the stress of exercise. This section is designed to give you some insight concerning the different types of soreness you may encounter in your training, as well as some helpful hints about reducing soreness when it occurs.

Acute and Delayed Muscle Soreness

There are two distinct kinds of muscle soreness. You've probably had acute soreness while you exercised intensely or just after you finished. Acute muscle soreness is quite painful and is easy to experience during weight training. All you have to do is perform an exercise until you can't do it anymore!

Acute soreness is triggered by powerful muscle contractions compressing vessels and reducing the blood supply to the working area. When the blood supply is scanty (ischemia), nutrients are not delivered and a muscle's supplies fall short of its demands. This induces low levels (hypoxia) or a complete lack of oxygen (anoxia). The intense pain gradually subsides during the rest period when the blood flow and nutrient supply return to normal. Since the powerful contractions have stopped, the vessels in the muscle can reflexively widen (vasodilate) so that nutrient supplies can help balance the previous demands. In fact, after finishing an intense set, you'll notice that blood vessels overcompensate. Muscles you've worked become swollen and tight because they are engorged with blood. In physiology, this is called hyperemia. In the weight room, it's called the "pump."

Unlike acute soreness, delayed or residual muscle soreness is usually experienced 24–48 hours after intense exercise. In young persons, soreness may appear as soon as 12 hours after activity and may persist for as long as 72 hours. It seems that the older we get, the more we experience delayed and prolonged muscle soreness. This may be due to the progressive decreased permeability of our muscle cell membranes. In older adults, some soreness might not be felt until 36 hours postexercise, and may linger for as long as 96 hours. How you experience delayed muscle soreness depends on several factors, including (1) your physical condition, (2) your age, (3) whether or not you warmed up, (4) the type (what kind?), the intensity (how hard?), and duration (how long?) of the exercise you participated in, and (5) whether or not you cooled down.

Three major theories have been proposed to explain delayed muscle soreness: (1) the tissue tear theory, (2) the muscle spasm theory, and (3) the connective tissue theory. The tissue tear theory, initially suggested by Hough (1902), states that muscle soreness is caused by minute tears within the muscle itself. The greatest degree of tissue damage occurs in eccentric (downhill) loading (Armstrong, Ogilivie & Schwane 1983).

H. A. deVries (1966) and Petajan and Eagan (1968) postulate that severe exercise causes untrained muscles to remain in a semicontracted state which limits their ability to recover. This contracted state is caused by continuous, localized spasm of motor units (deVries, 1986). Ischemia in the muscle results in the production of a pain substance, P, which stimulates free nerve endings. The pain intensifies the muscle spasm and a positive feedback or vicious cycle results.

The connective tissue theory was supported by Abraham (1977), who determined that hydroxyproline, a component of connective tissue, increased in subjects' urine following intense exercise. Abraham also found a high correlation between urinary hydroxyproline and perceived intensity of muscle soreness.

As with most cases in physiology, no single theory can be used to fully explain delayed muscle soreness. Residual soreness is probably caused by damage to muscle fibers and connective tissue as well as local spasms. Even though we may not be able to pinpoint its causes, we can reduce delayed muscle soreness by following these general guidelines:

1. Use extensive general and specific warm-up before you train (see appendix C). Specific warm-up is best because it increases temperature and blood flow to a local area and allows for mental rehearsal of the exercise you plan to perform.
2. Choose lighter weights; you can always increase them. Reducing the weight does little good when you've already been injured. Avoid selecting weights out of habit. Even though it's hard to do, constantly evaluate your present physical condition to determine how much weight you should handle. Remember to overload, not over-overload, your body.
3. Be sure to progress gradually regardless of your age or experience.

4. Use slow, methodical movements when you stretch or train with weights. Minimize bouncing or ballistic movements; they can easily induce muscle soreness and injury (Reid, Yeater & Ullrich 1987). Remember to be kind to your joints, especially at the beginning and end of each repetition, where muscle and connective tissues are highly vulnerable to injury.

5. Take time to cool down following your workout. Don't rush. A cool-down may be even more important than a warm-up for minimizing delayed soreness.

6. Don't sit around the day after you train intensely. Stretching, brisk walking, or light swimming will do wonders for soreness the day after a tough training session.

7. When you've overtaxed your body, you'll experience severe delayed muscle soreness. This means that significant tissue damage has occurred. Rest, ice, compress, and elevate (RICE) the afflicted area. If your soreness is asymmetrical or unilateral (i.e., occurs only on one side of your body), chances are you're compensating when training or placing stresses on your body that aren't balanced. Have an athletic trainer or other sports medicine specialist give you a complete musculoskeletal exam. Be sure they check your shoes and other important equipment to see whether alignment problems have induced your injuries. Don't return to activity until you've been cleared by a qualified sports medicine professional.

8. Periodically, have a certified fitness instructor check your exercise technique. Remember, if you use impeccable technique you'll minimize your risk of soreness and injury.

9. Light to moderate symmetrical or bilateral soreness probably means that you've exposed yourself to an appropriate load (i.e., soreness should feel the same on both sides of your body). For 24–48 hours, you may even use your soreness as a tool to help you remember which exercises work specific muscles.

10. Most isokinetic machines don't have an eccentric or negative loading option. This makes them less likely to induce delayed muscle soreness. If you're planning to run a road race or compete in some other sport (besides weight lifting), you can use isokinetic machines during the week of the event to reduce your chance of developing soreness. You can keep training with free weights or other devices as long as you handle relatively lighter weights.

Muscles in Action

Together with sensing how muscles contract and adapt, visualizing the connections between muscles and bones will improve your ability to train with weights. In this section, we'll briefly examine how body levers work, how basic hand positions may be varied to effectively use body levers, and how active movements enable you to properly stress your muscles in weight training.

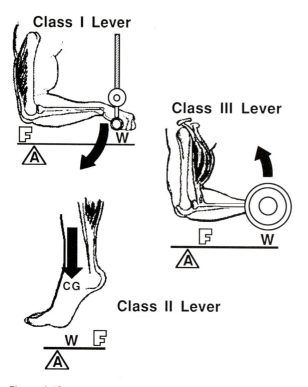

Class I Lever

Class III Lever

Class II Lever

Figure 4.12
First-, second-, and third-class levers in the human body. W is the weight or resistance, F is the force or effort exerted by the muscle, and A is the axis or fulcrum. FA is the force arm or the perpendicular distance between the line of force and the axis. WA is the weight arm or the perpendicular distance between the weight and the axis. Notice that high FA/WA ratios are only possible with class II levers. In the human body, since class II levers are rare, we usually operate at a mechanical disadvantage. Even though we're on "the short end of the seesaw" with most of our muscles, we can still generate tremendous forces and move with considerable freedom.

Body Lever Systems

A lever is a rigid bar rotating about a fixed point known as the axis or fulcrum. Nearly every bone in the skeleton can be viewed as a lever, with bones acting as rigid shafts, joints serving as axes, and contracting muscles generating forces (Wells & Luttgens 1976; Rasch & Burke 1978). The force generated by a muscle acts at the point of attachment where the muscle's tendon connects to the bone. In order for movement to occur, your muscles must generate enough force to overcome the weight you've selected.

Like other levers, levers of the human body can be placed into one of three unique categories (fig. 4.12). A class I lever has the axis located between the force and the resistance (weight). Your forearm acts like a class I lever when it's moved by your triceps. Because the triceps tendon attaches to a boney hook at the end of one of your forearm bones, the point where the force is applied is on the opposite side of the elbow axis from the resistance. When you use your forearm as a class I lever, be sure that you concentrate on stabilizing your arm and elbow axis of rotation. Only your forearm, which acts as the rigid lever, should move.

In a class II lever, the resistance is between the axis and the point where the force is applied. This type of lever is difficult to find in the human body. When you perform a calf raise, you use your foot as a class II lever (fig. 4.12). The ball of your foot (metatarsal heads) forms the axis, while the force is applied to the point where your Achilles tendon attaches to the bone of your heel (calcaneus). Your body weight plus any additional weights (like a backpack or barbell) make up the total resistance. This total resistance is transferred to your feet and acts at your ankle joints. When you generate enough force by contracting your calf muscles, you extend your ankles, overcome the resistance, and move your center of gravity (CG) upward. In chapter 6 we'll see that any unnecessary swaying during calf raises minimizes the effectiveness of these class II levers and diffuses the stress to other muscles.

The forearm acts like a class III lever when it's acted upon by the biceps and brachialis, major muscles of the anterior arm (fig. 4.12). The axis is the elbow joint. The force acts at spots where the biceps and brachialis tendons attach to bumps on both bones of the forearm. When the force exerted by the muscles overcomes the resistance, the elbow is flexed.

In chapter 3, the weight arm is defined as the perpendicular distance from the line of resistance (weight) to the axis. The force arm (FA) is the perpendicular distance from the line of the applied force to the axis. The principle of levers states that any class of lever will be in equilibrium when the product of weight and weight arm equals the product of force and force arm. If any three of these four values are known, the fourth can be calculated easily by using the equation in chapter 3:

$$F \times FA = W \times WA.$$

A simple calculation with a class III lever system might make the above equation clearer. Let's say that you grab a 30-lb dumbbell with one hand and bend your elbow so that it's at a 90° angle. Just like the class III lever pictured in figure 4.12, your forearm should be parallel, while your arm should be perpendicular to the ground. The perpendicular distance between the weight and your elbow axis (WA) is about 12 inches. The perpendicular distance between the line of force and the axis is about 3 inches. How much force do you think you'll have to generate with your biceps and brachialis to balance the dumbbell?

$$F \times FA = W \times WA$$
$$F \times 3 = 30 \times 12$$
$$F \times 3 = 360$$
$$F = 120 \text{ lb}$$

You'd be required to generate 120 lb of force in order to balance the dumbbell at a 90° angle. Hopefully, this example makes it obvious that a class III

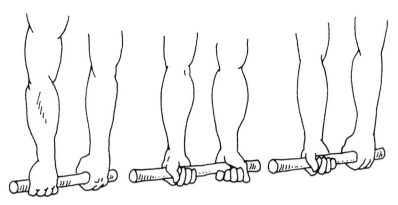

A. Pronated grip B. Supinated grip C. Alternate grip

Figure 4.13
Common handgrips used in weight training. *A*, pronated grip; *B*, supinated grip; and *C*, alternate grip.

lever requires a force (effort) greater than the weight (resistance) to balance the system. This is a true example of a mechanical disadvantage. It is mechanically advantageous to have a long force arm and short weight arm or a high FA/WA ratio. By glancing at the levers in figure 4.12, you can see that high FA/WA ratios are only possible with class II levers (Rasch & Burke 1978). Since these types of levers are uncommon in the human body, in most cases we operate at a mechanical disadvantage. Nevertheless, we're still able to generate tremendous forces with many of our body levers. We also have the distinct advantage of having joints that can move with incredible freedom through a wide range of motion.

Use lever systems to your advantage when you train with weights. To maximize the stress on a particular muscle during a single-joint-action exercise, concentrate on stabilizing the axis of rotation. Remember that an axis of rotation for a particular exercise may be your neck, shoulder, elbow, wrist, lower back, hip, knee, or the ball of your foot. Before you begin an exercise, be sure you focus on the axis of rotation and the muscles the exercise is designed to develop. By stabilizing an axis, you'll maximize the tension within your muscles and reduce your chance of injury.

Basic Hand Positions

A variety of handgrips are used in weight training so that body lever systems can isolate specific muscle groups. The three basic hand positions are pictured in (fig. 4.13). In all three cases, your thumbs and fingers should be firmly secured around the bar. If your hands are sweaty, remember to wipe them off with a towel before you grip the bar. Occasionally, the bar may need a bit of wiping.

Circumduction

Abduction
Adduction

Flexion

Extension

Supination

Pronation

Rotation
(about long axis)

Figure 4.14
Common active movements.

You **pronate** an object by putting it on its face, in a prone position. Hand pronation is the action of turning your palms downward or away from your body. You can assume a pronated grip by placing your hands with your palms facing away from your body so that you can't see them (fig. 4.13a). This is the most common handgrip in weight training and is used for all sorts of pressing and pushing movements, including the bench press, military press, and triceps extension. It's also used in the pull-up. Some people use a "false" pronated grip by placing their thumbs near their other fingers instead of wrapping or locking them completely around the bar. Although you might see this grip used for bench pressing, it's best to avoid it. A false grip is especially dangerous for overhead pressing, since it increases the chance that the bar may slip and cause severe head and neck injury.

Supination involves putting something on its back, or in the case of the hands, turning them so that the palms face upward and toward the body (fig. 4.14). A friend of mine always reminds his students, "Why, it's easy to remember supination. To hold a cup of soup, you must be supinated." A palms-up or supinated position is used in exercises such as the biceps curl and chin-up (fig. 4.13b).

Exercises like the dead lift and shoulder shrug are often performed with an alternate handgrip, in which one hand is supinated while the other is pronated (fig. 4.13c). Since this type of grip is the most stable grip, it's also commonly used for spotting.

Active Movements

In order to work, a muscle must cross a joint—a hinge where two bones meet. At both of its ends, a muscle is tightly glued by its tendons to bones. When secure, these attachments ensure that we can move freely and perform work by using our body levers. Either of the two boney segments to which a muscle is attached can serve as a lever, based on which segment is stabilized. This provides us with a virtually unlimited repertoire of complex limb movements ranging from a strikingly powerful kick in karate to a smooth and graceful arabesque in ballet.

In sciences like anatomy, kinesiology, and biomechanics, each isolated movement of a limb or other body part is described with reference to a particular joint. Flexion is a decrease, while extension is an increase in the joint angle of an axis. Using proper terminology, an isolated action is described as movement of a limb or lever at its corresponding joint axis. For example, the hard part (concentric phase) of a curling movement would be described as flexion of the forearm at the elbow or flexion of the leg at the knee. Often, the wording is shortened by naming only the joint involved. For example, we'll describe the above curling movements as elbow flexion or knee flexion.

We discussed supination and pronation when we talked about handgrips. You **adduct** a limb when you move it toward the median plane or midline of your body (fig. 4.14). You **abduct** it by moving it away from your midline. **Circumduction** involves moving a limb around the circumference of a circle, while **rotation** indicates that a limb is being moved about its long axis. These are just a few simple movements you can do by contracting your muscles.

Common movements require the contraction of many muscles simultaneously. Even when you train with weights, you perform multi-joint exercises that involve a variety of muscles and levers. For example, to perform a leg press, you must extend your thighs at the hips at the same time that you extend your legs at the knees. To execute a bench press, you must horizontally flex your arms at the shoulders and extend your forearms at the elbows. Needless to say, describing some movements can be almost as complex as performing them.

Summary

Beginners who sense how their muscles work, communicate, and adapt have a much easier time training. Muscles contain cardiac, smooth, or skeletal fibers. Cardiac fibers make up the heart, a nourishing pump, while smooth muscles line vessels and the digestive tract. Skeletal muscles are unique because they can be controlled. A skeletal muscle fiber is a cell that contains hundreds to thousands of threadlike structures called myofibrils. In turn, each myofibril contains thousands of actin and myosin microfilaments. The organized stacking of actin and myosin creates stripes or bands which are visible with a microscope. Actin is like two twisted strings of beads with active sites along every turn of the twist. Myosin is made of a thick stalk and cross-bridges with globular heads that are attracted to the active sites on actin. During a relaxed state, the active sites are covered.

Muscle contraction is triggered by nerve impulses that start in the motor cortex, the barklike outer edge of the frontal brain. After higher motor nerves carry the impulse down the spinal cord, lower motor nerves conduct the impulses directly to the muscle fiber. The muscle fiber cell membrane becomes leaky to sodium and depolarizes or reverses its charge. Transverse (T-) tubules carry this impulse deep within the fiber to calcium storage sacs. Calcium is dumped into the fiber fluid and causes actin to change its shape so that the active sites are no longer covered. The myosin globular heads attach to the active sites. Actin slides in along the myosin and contraction takes place. Before relaxation occurs, energy must be regenerated and calcium pumped back into the storage sacs.

In coordinating muscle actions, the cerebellum acts like the conductor of an elaborate orchestra. Muscle spindles and Golgi tendon organs help regulate muscle length and tension, respectively. Special spinal cord circuitry allows muscles to communicate. Muscles on the front and back, and right and left sides of the body communicate with each other. Reciprocal inhibition ensures that when agonists contract, antagonists relax to make movements easier. Supersetting agonists and antagonists helps minimize total workout time.

When muscles and bones are stimulated by strength training, they hypertrophy. With detraining, muscles and bones atrophy or decrease in size and strength. Hyperplasia or an increase in fiber cell number is difficult to verify because fiber sampling and counting procedures have not been refined. Hyperplasia may be triggered by high levels of growth hormone. There are three major skeletal muscle types distinguished by staining: (1) slow, (2) intermediate, and (3) fast. Slow fibers are red, have a high-oxidative capacity, and are fatigue resistant. They are especially good at using fat to provide energy for prolonged aerobic events. Fast fibers are white, have a high-glycolytic capacity, and are easily fatigued. They use immediate muscle stores and glycogen (stored sugar) when they are recruited for high-force, short-duration activities. Although fibers are largely genetically endowed, they can be dramatically affected by intense training. Muscle fibers adapt specifically to the stresses imposed upon them. With consistent endurance training, both slow and fast fibers increase their endurance capabilities. With consistent strength training, fibers increase their anaerobic capacity and become more like fast fibers.

Acute soreness occurs during or immediately following intense activity and is caused by poor blood flow and lack of oxygen. Delayed muscle soreness is experienced some 24–48 hours following activity and is likely due to muscle and connective tissue damage. Eccentric contractions are associated with delayed muscle soreness. Delayed muscle soreness may be reduced by using warm-up and cool-down stretches, gradual progressions, and proper technique.

The human body contains three different types of levers based on the position of the force (effort), axis (fulcrum), and weight (resistance). Class III levers, in which the force is between the axis and the weight, are the most common. Most body lever systems operate at a mechanical disadvantage. The principle of levers states that any lever system can be balanced when the product of weight and weight arm equals the product of force and force arm. To effectively engage body lever systems, three handgrips are used: (1) pronated "palms-down" grip, (2) supinated "palms-up" grip, and (3) alternate grip. Active and passive movements are defined with reference to a particular joint. Flexion is a decrease, whereas extension is an increase in a joint angle. Abduction is movement away from, while adduction is movement toward the body's midline or median plane. Other simple movements include circumduction, rotation about a long axis, pronation, and supination. Complex skills require that many muscles contract in synchrony.

Fundamental Training Principles

5

This chapter highlights the basic principles and guidelines needed to design and implement a comprehensive fitness plan. We'll review the key ingredients required for enhancing health-related fitness: warm-up, aerobics, weight training, and cool-down. We'll discuss major variables that can be manipulated in an exercise program: mode, intensity, duration, and frequency. We'll also examine the American College of Sports Medicine's (ACSM) guidelines for achieving optimal fitness and body fat together with a step-by-step procedure for creating a personal exercise prescription.

Throughout the chapter we'll emphasize overall program balance so that you will seek to improve each area of health-related fitness. We'll also stress the concept of program balance in weight training, which means selecting complementary exercises to balance the development of anterior-posterior and superior-inferior muscles. You'll learn how to apply the full range of motion (FROM) principle in a safe and effective way to increase strength as well as flexibility.

To give you a feeling for what happens with training and detraining, we'll discuss the principles of homeostasis, overload, reversibility, specificity, individuality, and variation. Finally, we'll examine periodization or cyclic training so that you can vary your program, reduce boredom, facilitate improvements, and minimize your chance of overtraining.

Hopefully, the guidelines and training principles presented in this chapter will help you design a balanced program, establish and achieve realistic goals, and maintain a high level of fitness for the rest of your life.

Total Program Balance

Without a doubt, weight training is the most effective way to increase strength. While strength is important, it's only a part of your health-related fitness (see chapter 1). You'll achieve total program balance and be more inclined to enhance all areas of health-related fitness if you reserve time for (1) warm-up, (2) aerobics, (3) weight training, and (4) cool-down (fig. 5.1).

Warm up and cool down each time you exercise to lubricate your joints and muscles and to minimize the risk of soreness and injury. Use both general and specific warm-up and cool-down. You may want to review details about warm-up and cool-down in chapter 2 along with the Basic Dozen warm-up/cool-down routine in appendix C.

Figure 5.1
A balanced program includes warm-up, aerobics, weight training, and cool-down to enhance all areas of health-related fitness.

As a general rule for developing good cardiovascular fitness, devote at least as much time to aerobics as you do to weight training. You can do aerobic and weight training exercises on the same day or on alternate days depending on the muscles you plan to work and the limitations of your schedule. To maximize your increases in strength, it's best to do strength and endurance training for similar muscles on separate days (Sale et al. 1988).

What key ingredients are needed to ensure total program balance?

Program Variables

In designing a physical fitness plan, you can vary the mode (what kind?), the intensity (how hard?), the duration (how long?), and the frequency (how many?) of your exercise.

Mode

The mode or type of exercise you choose for each component of your fitness plan will vary based on a variety of factors. For your aerobic component, the mode you select might be walking (jogging), swimming, cycling, cross-country skiing, hiking, dancing, or another continuous activity. Swimming or walking could be the mode of choice if you happen to be overweight or have problems with your joints.

You might choose isotonic, isokinetic, or isometric weight training as the mode of exercise for improving strength, but your choice depends largely on the equipment available at your facility. As mentioned in chapter 2, it's important to check with a sports medicine physician to see which modes of exercise you can perform safely.

Multi-Joint-Action (MJA) versus Single-Joint-Action (SJA) Exercises

Based on the muscles it uses, an exercise mode may be classified in a general way as either multi-joint-action (MJA) or single-joint-action (SJA). Some large muscles traverse and act upon more than one joint and are called multi-joint muscles. Endurance exercises like jogging, swimming, and cycling are called multi-joint-action exercises because they rely on the synchronous contraction of many large multi-joint muscles. Although the squat and bench press are multi-joint exercises, most weight training movements are single-joint exercises designed to isolate specific muscles. The leg extension and triceps extension are complementary SJA exercises for the MJA squat and bench press (fig. 5.2).

Make MJA exercises the cornerstone of your total fitness plan. View SJA exercises as complementary or accessory movements that help round out your program. This priority system will ensure that you will achieve an optimal level of cardiovascular fitness and percentage body fat.

Intensity

The intensity of an exercise is its level of difficulty. Some researchers like to define intensity as the power output during training or the work per unit of time. However, a definition like this ignores important individual characteristics including age, gender, health, fitness, and nutritional status. Intensity is highly individualized: the exact same exercise may be easy for one person and excruciating for another. How you perceive intensity is based primarily on your fitness level and familiarity with the specific exercise.

For most types of exercise (other than resistive movements), training heart rates can be used to estimate intensity. For weight training, the percentage of one-repetition maximum (%1-RM) for each exercise provides a reasonable estimation of intensity. If you're a beginner, do low-intensity training during the first two to three months of your program so that you adjust gradually and reduce your risk of soreness and injury.

Multi-Joint Exercises

Bench Press   Squat

Triceps Extension   Leg Extension

Single-Joint Exercise

Figure 5.2
Multiple- (MJA) versus single-joint-action (SJA) weight training exercises. *A.* The MJA squat works hip, thigh, and lower back muscles, whereas the SJA leg extension isolates frontal thigh muscles. *B.* The MJA bench press works muscles in the chest, frontal shoulder, and posterior arm, while the SJA triceps extension isolates the posterior arm. Make MJA exercises like the squat and the bench press the cornerstone of your weight training program.

In effect, the intensity of an exercise limits its duration. That is, the harder you train, the more difficult it is to continue the exercise. Thus, high-intensity activities are usually of short duration, whereas low- to moderate-intensity activities can be prolonged.

Over-Distance Training versus Interval Training

Athletes who compete in running, swimming, cycling, and other continuous, rhythmical events use two basic types of training to vary their exercise intensity: (1) over-distance training and (2) interval training. Over-distance training involves long, easy- to moderately-paced sessions, while interval training uses short, intense exercise bouts interspersed with brief rest periods. By using interval training, athletes can simulate high-intensity performances of competition (Brooks & Fahey 1984). Whether interval or over-distance training is used depends on the relative fitness of the athlete and the proximity of scheduled competitive events.

Figure 5.3
By using a light weight you can do a high number of repetitions and improve your local muscular endurance. By choosing a heavy weight (> 75% of 1-RM), you limit the number of repetitions you can do and enhance muscular strength. Remember to use a light to moderate weight for several weeks before you move on to heavier exercise sets.

Generally, athletes over-distance train during an early base period, but gradually include more interval training as competition nears. Seven to ten days prior to competition, athletes taper or decrease the total amount of work they perform during their training sessions. Later, in the section on periodization, we'll describe how workout intensity can be logically varied to maximize increases in strength.

Muscular Endurance versus Strength Training

Exercise intensity in weight training is varied by using (1) muscular endurance training and (2) strength training (fig. 5.3).

To train for muscular endurance, choose a relatively light weight so you can do a high number of repetitions ($\geq$ 10–12). This will help tone your muscles without substantially increasing their strength or size.

After you've completed a few weeks of training, you can test your local muscular endurance by counting the maximum number of repetitions you can do with

50% 1-RM. (If you don't know your 1-RM, estimate it by using appendix E.) Make sure that your technique is perfect for each repetition.

Muscular endurance weight training differs from cardiovascular endurance or aerobic training. Muscular endurance weight training improves the local endurance of specific muscles that you work, but does little to improve the endurance of your heart. You may be able to tone your muscles with this type of weight training, but you won't be able to see them unless you lose subcutaneous fat (see chapter 1, Myth 6: Spot Reduction). Compared to muscular endurance weight training, aerobic exercises are two to three times more efficient for decreasing body fat (Hempel & Wells 1985).

To train for strength, select a moderate to heavy weight ($\geq$ 75% 1-RM). This will limit the number of repetitions you can do. Berger (1962b,c) suggests that 4–8 repetitions per set is an ideal range for maximizing strength gains. It's probably best to shoot for the low end of this repetition schedule (4–6 reps/set) and do multiple sets (4–6) of an exercise.

Strength training, also called conventional weight training, relies on the overload principle, which we'll discuss in a later section. By strength training, you can expect to increase the strength and size of your muscles. As mentioned in chapter 1, dramatic increases in size occur mainly in young males because of their high circulating levels of testosterone.

Periodically, you can measure your strength gains by doing one-repetition maximum (1-RM) or higher-repetition maximum (4- to 8-RM) tests. During your first several weeks of training, don't attempt higher-intensity (1- to 2-RM) lifts; they require considerable skill and increase the likelihood of injury. Before doing a maximum lift, make sure that you satisfy criteria for safe maximum testing (see appendix D). During the early phases of your program, predict your maximum to determine the appropriate training intensity for each exercise (see appendix E).

Most athletes use a combination of muscular endurance and strength training to vary exercise intensity and to peak for performance. We'll examine these variations later in the chapter in the section on periodization.

Describe how endurance athletes use over-distance and interval training to prepare for competition. Contrast muscular endurance with cardiovascular endurance training.

Duration

The duration of an exercise is how long it's performed. Total workout duration is the product of the number of exercise sets and the time per set. The greater the number of repetitions of a particular exercise, the longer the duration. Also, the greater the number of sets, the longer the duration. Workout duration and intensity are usually inversely related. Later in the chapter we'll see that by making high-intensity workouts of short duration, we can avoid overtraining.

Don't confuse total weight room duration or time with total workout time. We've all said or heard, "I worked out three hours today" when we really mean "I spent three hours in the weight room today, but trained for a total of 30 minutes." After you're accustomed to training, try to be as efficient as possible. Be sure to focus on exercise quality rather than quantity.

Frequency

Frequency can refer to the number of times you train per week or the number of sets you perform per exercise. During the early phases of your program do low-frequency training. To minimize your risk of soreness and injury, start by working out two to three times per week and do no more than two to three sets of ten to twelve exercises.

Guidelines for Developing and Maintaining Fitness

To help us develop and maintain optimal levels of cardiovascular fitness and body fat, the American College of Sports Medicine (ACSM) has established the following exercise guidelines:

1. Mode of activity (What kind?): Any activity that uses large muscle groups, that can be maintained continuously, and is rhythmical and aerobic in nature, e.g., running-jogging, walking-hiking, swimming, skating, bicycling, rowing, cross-country skiing, rope skipping, and various endurance game activities.
2. Frequency of training (How often?): 3–5 days per week.
3. Intensity of training (How hard?): 60%–90% of maximal heart rate reserve or 50%–85% of maximal oxygen uptake (VO_2max).
4. Duration of training (How long?): 15–60 minutes of continuous aerobic activity. Duration is dependent on the intensity of the activity, thus lower intensity activity should be conducted over a longer period of time. Because of the importance of the "total fitness" effect and the fact that it is more readily attained in longer duration programs, and because of the potential hazards and compliance problems associated with high-intensity activity, lower to moderate intensity activity of longer duration is recommended for the nonathletic adult (American College of Sports Medicine 1978, vii–x).

Weight training is one of the few activities that can satisfy ACSM requirements for heart rate, but not for oxygen consumption (i.e., heart rates fall between 60%–90% of maximal heart rate reserve while VO_2's are less than 50% of VO_2max) (Hempel & Wells 1985). Even though you may feel you've had a complete workout by training with weights, be sure to take time to exercise aerobically.

Radial artery

Figure 5.4

Monitoring your heart rate is a good way to evaluate your exercise intensity, but you need some point of reference, namely, your own resting heart rate. Take your pulse by lightly placing your index and middle finger over the radial artery, which extends through a spongy area on the thumb side of your wrist. An average resting heart rate is 72 b/min, while normal values range from 60–100 b/min. Most endurance athletes have bradycardia or low resting heart rates (< 60 b/min). Tachycardia is when heart rates are greater than 100 b/min. Heart rates are influenced by many factors, including the menstrual cycle, caffeine, nervousness, sleep, illness, and previous activity.

Designing Your Aerobic Fitness Program

To help you design your own aerobics plan, we'll look at a program tailored for a thirty-year-old female subject with a resting heart rate (RHR) of 70 beats per minute (b/min).

Take your resting pulse when you are completely relaxed, preferably just after you wake up following a good night's sleep (fig. 5.4). Use your index and middle finger to palpate (Latin meaning to touch) a radial artery on the thumb side of your wrist or a carotid artery on either side of your thyroid cartilage (Adam's apple). Be sure not to palpate both carotids or to press too hard because you may trigger a reflex that slows your heart, decreases blood flow to your brain, and induces blackout (carotid is Greek for deep sleep). Take at least three measurements so that you can use the average for later calculations.

You can estimate your maximal heart rate (MHR_{est}) by using your age and the following equation:

$$MHR_{est} = 220 - AGE.$$

The estimated maximal heart rate for our sample subject is

$$MHR_{est} = 220 - 30$$
$$MHR_{est} = 190 \text{ b/min.}$$

You can calculate your training heart rate range (THRR) by using the following equation developed by Karvonen, Kentala, and Mustala (1957):

$$THRR = .6 \text{ to } .9 \text{ of } (MHR_{est} - RHR) + RHR.$$

We'll make a few simple calculations to find the training heart rate range for our subject:

$$THRR = .6 \text{ to } .9 \text{ of } (190 - 70) + 70$$
$$THRR = .6 \text{ to } .9 \text{ of } (120) + 70$$
$$THRR = (72 \text{ to } 108) + 70$$
$$THRR = 142 \text{ to } 178 \text{ b/min.}$$

To satisfy the ACSM guidelines for exercise intensity, our subject should perform a continuous aerobic exercise so that her heart rate stays between 142 and 178 b/min. Obviously, if she's a beginner, she'd like to work at the lower end of this range for the first few weeks and progress gradually until she's more accustomed to exercising. Her safe, gradual progression is mapped out in table 5.1. From the table, we can see that to satisfy her requirements for weeks 1 through 3, she'd have to exercise aerobically three times per week for 15 minutes at a training heart rate of 142 b/min. Remember, the exercise duration is above and beyond time spent on warm-up, weight training, and cool-down and does not include water breaks!

Table 5.1 Sample Personalized Aerobic Exercise Progression Chart

Weeks	Intensity (% MHRR)	Training Heart Rate Range (beats/min)	10-Sec Count (beats)	6-Sec Count (beats)	Duration (min)	Frequency (times/wk)
1–3	60	142	23–24	14	15	3
4–8	60–65	142–148	24–25	14–15	15–20	3–4
9–16	65–70	148–154	25–26	15	20–25	3–4
16–24	70–75	154–160	25–27	15–16	25–30	4
24–rest of your life[a]	70–80	154–166	25–28	15–17	30–40	4–5

Note: Values are for a clinically healthy, untrained female (age = 30 years) with a resting heart rate (RHR) of 70 beats per minutes (b/min) and a body fat of 26%. During the first three weeks, her appropriate training intensity is 60% of her maximal heart rate reserve (%MHRR) or 142 b/min. If her heart rate exceeds 23-24 beats in 10 sec or 14 beats in 6 sec, she should reduce the exercise intensity. Frequency at the beginning of her program is low according to ACSM guidelines to minimize her risk of injury and encourage compliance. Don't start an exercise program without proper medical clearance and a thorough fitness appraisal.

Table compiled from a variety of sources, including the Community Health Improvement Program Fitness Appraisal Packet by J. L. Lettunich, J. D. Seelbach and V. P. Lombardi, 1984–1987.

[a]Resting heart rate usually decreases with endurance training, while maximal heart rate decreases with age. To ensure your safety, reestablish your guidelines every four to six months. Remember that consistency, not intensity, is the key to maintaining fitness for a lifetime.

To make it easy to adjust your exercise intensity, calculate the number of beats you should get in a 10- or 6-second interval. Ten-second and 6-second exercise heart rates for our female subject are presented in table 5.1.

Every few minutes, check your heart rate to be sure you're in your target range. If you have difficulty monitoring your heart rate while exercising, pause momentarily to make your assessment.

Remember that exercise doesn't have to hurt to help. In fact, by exercising at a "conversational" pace you train special fat-burning enzymes more so than when you exercise at an exhaustive pace. You'll also be able to maintain the exercise for a longer period, decrease your chance of injury, and increase the likelihood that you'll enjoy training for the rest of your life.

Weight Training Program Balance

Anterior-Posterior and Superior-Inferior Balance

It's important to balance your total fitness plan by choosing a variety of activities to enhance your aerobic fitness, strength, muscular endurance, and flexibility. It's also essential that you balance exercises within your weight training and flexibility programs. You can do this by picking complementary movements that balance the development of anterior-posterior (front-of-body/back-of-body) and superior-inferior (upper body–lower body) muscles. Even though it's easy to focus on muscles that you like, balanced development should always be your top priority.

When you increase the strength of an agonist over its complementary antagonist, you create imbalances that may reduce flexibility and predispose your muscles and joints to injury (Burkett 1970). Sprinters and hurdlers who have strong quadriceps but relatively weak hamstrings are plagued by posterior thigh pulls more than any other injury (Ciullo & Jackson 1985). Many of these injuries can be prevented by implementing balanced weight training and flexibility programs that emphasize weaker and tighter muscles.

How strong should an agonist be compared to its complementary antagonist? This is a difficult question since strength varies with a muscle's size, points of attachment, innervation, fiber distribution, and nutrient stores. Testing velocity also makes a difference. For example, the hamstring/quadriceps strength ratio varies from .62 at slow isokinetic speeds (30°/sec) to .87 at fast isokinetic speeds (300°/sec) (Morris et al. 1983). When strength is measured on an isotonic device, most persons' hamstrings are usually 50%–60% as strong as their quadriceps (Klafs & Arnheim 1981). It may be best to keep the strength of your hamstrings at 80% of your quadriceps to maintain proper balance and reduce the risk of pulls (Ciullo & Jackson 1985).

Figure 5.5
The body builder's syndrome. As a beginner, you'll be tempted to spend most of your time developing muscles that you can see. Even the way equipment and mirrors are set up in most weight rooms will divert your attention from posterior-inferior muscles. Design your program to balance complementary muscles to reduce the risk of malalignment, inflexibility, and injury.

The Body Builder's Syndrome

Beginners are often so excited about their programs that they focus exclusively on body changes they can verify in a mirror. Invariably, they place major emphasis on anterior development. This is understandable since most mirrors give us views only from the front. Take a moment to look at the mirrors in your weight room. They're probably half-sized or blocked by dumbbell racks so that your view of your lower body is almost entirely obstructed. This directs your focus not only anteriorly, but also superiorly. It's easy to fall prey to this body builder's syndrome, a type of tunnel vision that causes you to ignore your posterior-inferior muscles (fig. 5.5).

Concern for developing your biceps and chest muscles (often a major goal of males) may be warranted, but it's more important that you seek to balance

Anterior - Posterior Balance

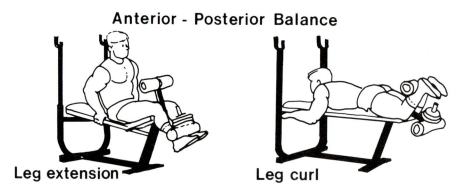

Leg extension　　　　　　　**Leg curl**

Superior - Inferior Balance

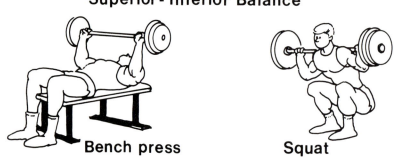

Bench press　　　　　　　**Squat**

Figure 5.6
Sound weight training programs include complementary exercises designed to balance anterior-posterior and superior-inferior muscles. Match multi-joint upper body exercises like the bench press with multi-joint lower body exercises like the squat. Complement single-joint leg extensions with single-joint leg curls.

these muscles by placing equal emphasis on your triceps, upper back, and lower body. Your desire to tone the inside of your thighs and triceps (often a major concern of females) may be justified. However, if you work your inner thigh, you must work your outer thigh; if you train your triceps, you must also train your biceps. Before you know it, you must work your whole body to provide for balance and symmetry.

Always remember to complement upper body exercises with lower body exercises. Match movements that work the front of your body with those that work the back. Be objective and strive to develop muscles that you can't see. Balance is the key—anterior-posterior, superior-inferior (fig. 5.6). By balancing your program, you'll lower the risk of malalignment, inflexibility, and injury.

Fundamental Training Principles

Full Range of Motion (FROM) Principle

In chapter 3 you learned that muscles are strengthened only through the range that they are worked. This is why isometrics are less effective than isotonics or isokinetics. By moving carefully through the full range of motion (FROM), from full extension to full flexion for each exercise, you'll enhance the strength as well as the flexibility of your muscles.

Make sure that you concentrate on being kind to your joints throughout the range of motion. Be especially sensitive as you approach a fully extended or fully flexed position, since this is where joints are most susceptible to injury.

Occasionally, competitive athletes do limited-range movements to work through sticking points or to practice specific phases of an exercise. Examples of partial-range exercises are (1) lock-outs for bench presses or squats and (2) hang cleans or high pulls from blocks for the Olympic lifts. Limited-range exercises are fine, provided that they're not the primary focus of a workout. When athletes do limited-range exercises, they do similar full-range movements to ensure that they will maintain their flexibility.

If you are conditionally cleared, you may be required to do some movements through a limited range to avoid aggravating an injury. Check with a sports medicine physician or physical therapist about rehabilitation.

Homeostasis

To shed some light on how bodies adapt to weight training and other stressors, let's examine the concept of homeostasis. Homeostasis means *like standing,* though it's a highly dynamic, rather than static, process. It is the body's ability to maintain constant conditions in the internal environment (the fluid in which cells bathe). Seventy-five trillion (75×10^{12}) cells communicate with one another by using nerves and hormones to maintain this steady state (Guyton 1986). This is an incredible, arduous task, even at rest. Just imagine how much more extraordinary this process is during exercise.

Although there are thousands of homeostatic balances that are maintained to sustain life, the most important ones are grouped in the following general categories: (1) water balance, (2) ionic balance, (3) acid-base (pH) balance, (4) gas (O_2, CO_2) balance, (5) temperature balance, and (6) biochemical or metabolic balance (Evonuk 1980). Each balance is closely regulated by a process called negative feedback that works much like a home thermostat. However, unlike a home thermostat, our bodies' negative feedback systems rely on input from a multitude of sources. Given that effective doses of hormones are in millionths, billionths, or trillions of a gram, it's evident that these systems are also remarkably sensitive. You can find out more about homeostasis by referring to the physiology texts by Guyton (1986) and Fox (1987) cited in the reference section.

The Overload Principle

The overload principle is a key principle of training. According to Greek legends, Milo, a famous athlete during the sixth century B.C., was the first person to have used the overload principle. To increase his strength progressively, Milo was said to have carried a baby bull across his shoulders every day until the bull grew to maturity (Young 1984; Brooks & Fahey 1984; Todd 1985). Like Milo, we can trigger body adaptations by introducing stimuli to overload or gently disturb our homeostasis.

Selye proposed in his general adaptation syndrome (GAS) that adaptation takes place in three distinct phases: (1) alarm reaction, (2) resistance development, and (3) exhaustion (Selye 1976). Exercise is a stimulus or stressor that acts to disrupt homeostasis. When the body senses a disturbance (e.g., exercise), it initiates an alarm reaction (phase 1) by sending out urgent nervous and hormonal messages. These signals help us survive in life-threatening, fight-or-flight situations. The heart beats vigorously to circulate nutrients and chemical signals, pupils dilate to help us see clearly, and muscles become supercharged with glucose to prep them for rapid action.

Unlike machines, our bodies have the amazing capacity to adapt (phase 2) to appropriate and consistently applied stimuli. Over a period of several weeks, the same exercise becomes less of a disturbance to homeostasis and no longer elicits an alarm reaction. As we saw in chapter 4, our muscles, like other tissues, adapt specifically to the stresses imposed upon them. High-repetition, low-resistance exercises enhance local muscular endurance but do little to improve strength. If the stress we administer is too great or haphazard, injury or exhaustion occurs (phase 3).

Although most people focus on resistance as their primary overload variable, logical overloads can be introduced by carefully manipulating any of the major exercise variables: (1) mode, (2) intensity, (3) duration, and (4) frequency. The slightest variation in any exercise variable may be all the overload you need to trigger further adaptation. For example, after you've been consistent with training, you may find that you rarely experience soreness after bench pressing but can easily induce it by doing chest flies.

Avoid Over-Overload

Unfortunately, the overload principle is often misinterpreted as meaning over-overload. The quickest way to induce injury and discourage yourself is by over-overloading your joints and muscles. If you use excessive loads, your body won't adapt but will become exhausted (phase 3) or injured.

Avoid emphasizing increases in strength at all cost. Be safe and logical in planning your exercise progression. Realize that even moderate resistance training programs (30%–40% 1-RM) can induce significant increases in strength (Duchateau & Hainaut 1984). Intersperse your heavy workouts with light training sessions to give your body a chance to recuperate and adapt. By gradually upping the weight you handle (5 to 10 lb) over a period of a few weeks, you'll build strength and confidence and reduce the risk of soreness and injury.

What major exercise variables can you adjust to apply the overload principle to your training program? Compare the effects that might occur as a result of underload, overload, and over-overload.

Principle of Reversibility

The principle of reversibility or deconditioning states that when you stop exercising, your muscles and bones decrease their strength. Your other body systems also detrain when you limit or cease training. Deconditioning is most obvious in astronauts who subsist in a weightless environment, in bedridden or casted patients, or in former athletes who are no longer active. While it's a good idea to take breaks from training to provide for physical and psychological rest, your fitness will decrease if you stop exercising for a period of longer than one to two weeks.

Fiber Types Detrain at Different Rates

Fibers within a muscle atrophy or decondition at different rates. The most rapid deconditioning occurs in slow (Type I) fibers. Since strength can be maintained longer than muscular endurance during a period of deconditioning, rehabilitation programs should also focus on developing muscular endurance (Brooks & Fahey 1984).

Principle of Specificity

The specificity principle states that our bodies adapt specifically to the mode, intensity, duration, and frequency of exercise we engage in. These specific adaptations take place not only in muscles, but also in the heart, vessels, nerves, skeleton, and other organs and tissues.

According to the specificity principle, the best way to improve your ability to execute a particular skill is to practice that skill exactly. For example, if you want to train your neuromuscular system for pole vaulting you can best achieve this goal by practicing pole vaulting. This is not to say that weight training won't help improve your strength for pole vaulting, but that practicing pole vaulting is the best way to improve this specific skill.

The specificity principle implies that training programs should be designed with specific goals in mind. A program for a beginning weight trainer should be quite different from that of a weight lifter who is preparing for competition. Similarly, weight training programs for cyclists, long-distance runners, kayakers, and volleyball players should be designed with the specific sport kept in mind.

The specificity principle, like the overload principle, is often misinterpreted. You've probably seen distance runners or sprinters practicing running form with dumbbells, basketball players jumping with leg weights, or baseball players swinging weighted bats. The theory is that practicing a sport's skill with added resistance makes that skill without resistance easier. This is a misapplication of the specificity principle, since timing is the most important factor in performing a skill.

Although mimicking a particular sport's movement in the weight room can be safe with some isokinetic devices, it's usually risky with most isotonic devices. Almost all injuries during exercise are the direct result of sudden movements (Allman 1976). Explosive-type isotonic weight training is associated with a high dropout rate (55%) and a high incidence (30%) of head and neck pain (Reid, Yeater & Ullrich 1987). Even high-speed exercise on an isokinetic machine designed to mimic the vertical jump is associated with a high frequency (63%) of lower back pain and injury (Brady, Cahill & Bodnar 1982). Regardless of the system that you use, the most critical factor for safety is proper technique.

If you'd like to improve your strength for a specific sport: (1) analyze the muscles involved in the particular sport, (2) strengthen those specific muscles by isolating them with controlled isotonic or intermediate-velocity isokinetic training, and (3) integrate muscle actions by devoting considerable time to that sport's skill acquisition and improvement.

Even if you design your weight training program to strengthen specific muscles for a particular sport or skill, be sure to include complementary exercises so that you'll achieve anterior-posterior and superior-inferior balance.

In what ways might our understanding of the theory of specificity affect the nature of pretraining warm-up?

Specificity of Training Velocity

At what velocity should you train to improve your strength and power for a specific sport? This is a difficult question to answer. Research on isokinetic exercise is hard to interpret because most programs have been short-term (4–8 weeks) and have used a wide range of training velocities (0–288°/sec). Some researchers have expressed peak force values relative to joint angle while others have not. Additionally, there are problems associated with high-speed isokinetic testing and with generalizing from one training device to another (see chapter 3, Isokinetic Exercise).

Early studies indicated that it was best to train at fast velocities since strength appeared to increase only at or below the velocity at which training took place (Moffroid & Whipple 1970; Pipes & Wilmore 1975; Lesmes et al. 1978). However, these "fast" training velocities (108°–180°/sec) were actually slow to intermediate given maximal power outputs of untrained persons and elite athletes (240°–288°/sec) (Perrine & Edgerton 1978; Gregor et al. 1979; Kanehisa & Miyashita 1983b). One study indicated that fast (300°/sec) or mixed fast (300°/sec) and slow (60°/sec) training was superior to slow (60°/sec) training alone

(Coyle et al. 1981). However, recent studies have demonstrated that slow (60°–96°/sec) to moderate (180°/sec) training velocities are optimal for increasing strength at a variety of speeds (Caiozzo, Perrine & Edgerton 1981; Kanehisa & Miyashita 1983b). If you're an athlete and want to improve your strength at high speeds, then high-velocity isokinetic training may be for you. However, you may not improve your strength at low to intermediate velocities (Caiozzo, Perrine & Edgerton 1981; Kanehisa & Miyashita 1983b).

As the speed of a movement increases, the tension developed within a muscle decreases (Hill 1922; Fenn, Brody & Petrilli 1931). Nearly twice as much work is performed at an isokinetic velocity of 60°/sec compared to 300°/sec (Coyle et al. 1981). Isotonic speed resistance training may not create sufficient tension in muscles to elicit a training effect (Brooks & Fahey 1984). Amino acid uptake by muscle, which is positively correlated to the rate of muscle protein synthesis, increases according to the intensity and duration of muscle contraction (Goldberg 1972). By using a slow (60°/sec) to intermediate (96°/sec) training velocity, you can maximize the tension in your muscles, increase strength over a wide range of velocities, and minimize the risk of injury (Hill 1922; Fenn, Brody & Petrilli 1931; Caiozzo, Perrine & Edgerton 1981; Kanehisa & Miyashita 1983b; Brooks & Fahey 1984; Reid, Yeater & Ullrich 1987).

Name a sport of your choice. How can the principle of specificity be correctly applied to practice for that sport? How is the principle often misinterpreted?

Principle of Individuality

The principles of individuality and specificity are closely linked. When considering the specificity of a particular exercise, we must look at three things: (1) the exercise conditions, (2) the environmental conditions, and (3) the individual's characteristics. The conditions of the exercise are determined by selecting the mode, intensity, duration, and frequency. In most cases, especially when exercising outside, you have little control over the environmental conditions such as temperature, humidity, and wind velocity. These factors can dramatically alter your body's adaptation to a particular exercise.

The single most important factor that influences adaptation is individuality. Each of us adapts uniquely to the stress of exercise based on age, gender, nutritional status, and biological rhythms. These factors must be considered when selecting an exercise stimulus. The identical exercise stimulus may be appropriate at one time but entirely inappropriate at another. For example, exercise altogether may be inappropriate if you're ill or haven't slept recently.

Realize that the changes you'll experience due to training will be different from those of others. It's best to avoid competing with anyone but yourself. Remember that you have the last word about training. Listen to your body. Only you know exactly how you feel and how your body will respond to the stress of exercise.

Periodization or Cyclic Training

You can avoid overtraining by using periodization or cyclic training. By mapping out training cycles you can vary stimuli and maximize your adaptation. Periodization involves five phases or macrocycles that are based on preparing for an athletic event: (1) base phase, (2) load phase, (3) peak phase, (4) taper phase, and (5) recovery or off-season phase (Brooks & Fahey 1984). Within each phase, microcycles are used to vary workout intensity (table 5.2).

Obviously, you can use periodization in training even though you don't intend to compete in an athletic event. Cyclic training can help you (1) avoid maintaining the status quo in your muscles, (2) induce adaptation by logically disturbing your body's homeostasis, and (3) give your body adequate time for rest and recovery. In most cases, disturbances don't have to be dramatic; they might involve only minor changes in your exercise routine (e.g., working a particular muscle group from a different angle with a dumbbell or cable exercise).

Before starting cyclic training, you should complete an extended base or conditioning phase of at least three to four months. During this period, your training time should be devoted to perfecting exercise technique. After you begin to cyclic

Table 5.2 Sample Weight Training Periodization Plan

| Variables | Macrocycle | | | |
	Base	Load[a]	Peak	Recovery
Approximate duration in weeks	6–8	6–8	3–4	2–4
Percentage of 1-RM	60–70	70–80	80–95[b]	60
Number of sets per exercise	3–4	4–6	2–5	2–3
Repetitions per set	8–12	4–8	1–5	8–10
Sample days	M-W-F,	M-W-F,	M-W-F,	M-TH,
% Variation	60–65–70	70–75–80	80–90–95	60–60
Corresponding daily repetition	M-W-F,	M-W-F,	M-W-F,	M-Th,
schedule	12–10–8	8–6–4	5–3–1 or 2	10–10
Daily microcycle intensity[c]	M-W-F,	M-W-F,	M-W-F,	M-TH,
	L-M-H	L-M-H	L-M-H	L-L

Note: See text for further explanation.

[a]A brief one-week recovery period is usually introduced between the load and peak phases. This gives time for supercompensation or manifestation of the delayed training effect. The maximum length of the load cycle should be six to eight weeks. Anything beyond this increases the risk of overtraining and injury. The peak training period may be partially extended by interspersing brief recovery cycles between load and peak phases (e.g., short load phase followed by recovery, followed by short peak phase, followed by recovery, etc.). If an extended peak phase is desired, then a lengthened off-season or recovery phase must be used prior to reinitiating the base phase.

[b]Percentage of 1-RM varies according to individual goals. Competitive weight lifters and field-event track athletes often train near 90%–95% of maximum during the peak cycle. Football and sprint-event track athletes seem to benefit the most by training at approximately 85% of 1-RM (80%–87% range during the peak phase). Handling lighter weights during training sessions reduces the risk of injury during the competitive season. Endurance-trained athletes should probably not exceed 80% of 1-RM during the peak phase.

[c]L, M, and H signify low-, moderate-, and high-intensity workouts, respectively.

train, have your technique checked about once a month by a certified instructor. This will help further refine your technique and reduce your risk of injury.

Before we discuss each separate phase of a periodization plan, we'll examine the concept of exercise volume to demonstrate how weight and repetitions can be altered to vary workout intensity.

Volume

You may have heard the term volume used by an athlete involved in track and field or weight lifting. Volume is the total work you perform when training. You can calculate training volume for a single exercise, for a whole workout, or even for an entire year. Since work equals force times distance, it's a bit cumbersome to calculate the exact work you do during a training session. This is why training volume is most often estimated.

For aerobics, volume is taken as the product of the distance (or duration) and the number of repeats (or repetitions). In weight training, volume is estimated as the product of the weight (the resistance or work load), the number of repetitions, and the number of sets. Make sure that you limit your high-intensity workouts to a low volume to reduce the risk of overtraining and injury. Table 5.3 gives a simple example of how volume and intensity should vary in a weight training program.

Table 5.3   The Relationship between Volume (V), Work Load (WL), Repetitions (R), and Number of Exercise Sets (S)

Sample Exercise	Work Load		Repetitions		Number of Sets	Exercise Volume
A. Squat						
Low WL/High V:	140 lb	×	10	×	4	= 5600 lb
High WL/Low V:	185 lb	×	2	×	4	= 1480 lb
B. Mean WL and PEI						
Sample squat sets						
Warm-up:	100 lb	×	10	×	1	= 1000 lb
Workout:	140 lb	×	10	×	4	= 5600 lb
				Total volume		= 6600 lb
Mean WL = Total V/Total R = 6600/50						= 132 lb
PEI	= Mean WL/1-RM = 132/200					= 0.66

Note: In part A, the concepts of low intensity/high volume and high intensity/low volume are presented for an individual with a hypothetical 1-RM squat of 200 lb. Part B presents a calculation of mean exercise work load (intensity) for 1 warm-up and 4 workout sets of a trainee's low-work load, high-volume squat routine. Mean exercise intensity equals the total exercise volume divided by the total number of repetitions. By dividing this value by the subject's estimated 1-RM, we calculate a proportional estimate of intensity (PEI) for all sets the subject completed. The PEI of .66 indicates that the subject trained at 66% of 1-RM for the cumulative squat sets. PEIs of .85 or above should occur only in low-volume workouts. You can make similar calculations for your entire workout. It's quite a bit easier to remember to avoid high-intensity, high-volume workouts to prevent overtraining.

Base Phase

The first cycle of a periodization plan is called the base, conditioning, preparation, or foundation phase. Typically, it lasts about six to eight weeks (if you are a beginner, extend it to at least twelve weeks). During this moderate to high-volume, low-intensity training period, focus on perfecting exercise technique. Use high repetitions (8–12) and low to moderate work loads (60%–70% of 1-RM).

This phase of training should be relaxing and enjoyable since your workouts are of a relatively low intensity. Limit the number of unique exercises that you do to 10–12 during your first time through this phase. Do a moderate number of sets (3–4) per exercise (not including specific warm-up).

To provide for adequate overload, gradually increase the weights you handle every two to three weeks. By the end of your conditioning phase, you should be anxious to move on to the more challenging load phase.

Load Phase

A load phase is designed to trigger dramatic increases in strength. It usually lasts six to eight weeks and is used to prepare athletes during the preseason for the upcoming competitive period.

You can accelerate your increases in strength by beginning a load phase. Whether you enter a load phase depends on the particular goals you've established. If you're satisfied with maintaining strength and/or muscular endurance, you may elect to continue with moderate- to high-repetition (8–12) sets. If you're mainly interested in increasing muscle tone rather than strength and size, you can increase the number of sets per exercise (up to 4–5). However, this type of program will not induce substantial increases in strength. Remember that unless you resistance overload your muscles, they won't adapt by increasing their strength.

During a load phase, you should use a moderate weight (70%–80% of 1-RM), a moderate to high number of sets per exercise (4–6), and a low to mid-range repetition schedule (4–8). You can use the low end of the exercise set range (4), especially if you are committed to perfecting exercise technique.

During a load phase, you should make moderate increases in resistance every one to two weeks. As with other macrocycles, every workout should not be intense, but should vary based on one- to two-week mini- or microcycles that rotate from light (L) to moderate (M) to heavy (H) days (table 5.2). If you're an intermediate to advanced weight trainer, you can stagger your microcycles so that you don't heavily tax two major muscle groups on the same day. For example, match an intense day for squatting with an easy day for bench pressing if your program is based on a major-minor muscle group design (see appendix H).

Many people overtrain by doing an incredible number of exercises and sets per body part. On their way to the weight room, they must get exhausted just thinking about the number of sets they have to do in their upcoming workout.

Realize that by using strict exercise technique, you can get just as much out of three sets as someone else can get out of five to seven sets. Be sure that you concentrate on the specific muscles the exercise is designed to isolate. By decreasing the number of sets per exercise, you'll give yourself a physical as well as a psychological break. You'll also be delightfully surprised when you make greater improvements by decreasing your workout volume.

Peak Phase

Since strength usually begins to diminish during the last few days of a load cycle, a brief, one-week recovery period is introduced between the load and peak phases. This gives muscles time to rebound or supercompensate above and beyond their previous levels of strength (Verkhoshansky 1979a,b; Brooks & Fahey 1984).

The peak phase is generally a three- to four-week period, primarily designed for those who are involved in athletic competition. This phase coincides with the actual performance or competitive season. For a weight lifter, the peak phase is the time during or immediately prior to competition, when maximizing strength is the primary goal. As indicated in table 5.2, workout volume is drastically reduced (2–5 sets of 1–5 repetitions), while heavy work loads are used (80%–95% of 1-RM).

Psychologically, this is often a difficult phase because athletes rarely feel as though they're performing enough sets. This is far from true due to the heavy weights they handle. To reduce the risk of overtraining, it's important to avoid introducing more sets (Brooks & Fahey 1984). Workout days should be varied from L,M,H, and back to L, with major muscle groups staggered so that no two are worked heavily on the same day.

The peak phase, designed to peak for performance, is a time for high-intensity, low-volume training. Work loads are quite high compared to previous macrocycles. If you're an intermediate or advanced weight trainer, you may choose to use the peak phase to prepare for maximum testing.

Can you define training volume and give a specific example of its appropriate relationship to intensity?

Taper Phase

The taper phase can be viewed as the final component of a peak phase. It's usually a period of seven to ten days immediately prior to competition, although for some endurance events it may last a bit longer. The taper phase is like a recovery period when athletes rest just prior to competition so they can reap the full benefits of the intense load and peak phases. If properly introduced, this incubation period maximizes adaptation and supercompensation.

If you plan to taper, reduce both the number of sets and repetitions you do the last seven to ten days before competition. Drastically limit your training at least three days before the competitive event. One to two days before competition, you may choose to go through an extremely light workout just up to the point that you sweat. This final week of low-intensity training is designed to give you time to relax physically and to focus mentally on your upcoming performance.

Recovery or Off-Season Phase

After a peak phase or competitive season, two to four weeks of low-key training will give your body a chance to relax. During this recovery phase, train two times per week by using a low to moderate intensity. Make sure that your total workout volume is also low to moderate. By the end of this period of active rest, you should be fully refreshed and anxious to start a new base or conditioning phase.

You can include a short, one-week recovery cycle between your load and peak phases to maximize your strength gains. You can also intersperse brief recovery cycles within a peak phase to prolong it during extended competitive periods.

Summary

Total program balance can be achieved by taking time for (1) warm-up, (2) aerobics, (3) weight training, and (4) cool-down. The exercise mode (what kind?), intensity (how hard?), duration (how long?), and frequency (how many?) can be varied in a fitness program. An exercise mode may involve aerobic, resistive, multi-joint, or single-joint movements. Fitness programs should be based on multi-joint exercises. The intensity of an exercise refers to its level of difficulty, which may be perceived differently based on an individual's genetic characteristics and previous training. Athletes who endurance train vary intensity by using over-distance and interval training, while those who weight train vary intensity by using strength and muscular endurance training. Muscular endurance training emphasizes low-resistance, high-repetition sets to tone, rather than hypertrophy muscles. Strength training relies on high-resistance, low-repetition sets to effect dramatic increases in strength. The duration of an exercise is how long it is performed. Exercise quality is more critical than quantity. Frequency can refer to the number of training sessions per week or the number of sets per exercise.

The American College of Sports Medicine has established guidelines for achieving and maintaining an optimal level of fitness. Continuous aerobic exercises that work major muscles should be performed three to five times per week, for fifteen to sixty minutes at 60%–90% of maximal heart rate reserve.

Program balance in weight training is achieved by doing exercises that develop anterior-posterior (front-of-body/back-of-body) and superior-inferior (upper body–lower body) muscles. Most weight trainers fall prey to the body builder's syndrome, which directs their focus to anterior-superior muscles. To decrease the risk of malalignment, inflexibility, and injury, strive for anterior-posterior and superior-inferior balance.

Exercises should be performed through the full range of motion (FROM), from full extension to full flexion. To reduce the risk of injury, be kind to the joints, especially at the beginning and end of each movement.

Homeostasis is maintenance of the body's internal environment. In order to trigger adaptation, homeostasis must be gently disturbed. According to Selye's general adaptation syndrome (GAS) our bodies react to stressors in three phases: (1) alarm reaction, (2) resistance development, and (3) exhaustion. The overload principle states that the body adapts to appropriately applied stimuli and that logical increments in work load are needed to further strength gain. If exercise stresses are too great or administered haphazardly, the body breaks down and injury occurs. Over-overload can be avoided by implementing strict exercise techniques and cyclic training. The principle of reversibility states that the body decreases its functional capacity when a stimulus is removed. The most rapid deconditioning occurs in slow fibers. The specificity principle states that the body adapts uniquely to the mode, intensity, duration, and frequency of exercise. To improve a particular skill, it must be practiced precisely. The specificity principle implies that training programs should be designed with particular goals in mind. Programs for beginning weight trainers should be different from those of competitive weight lifters or other athletes. The conditions of the exercise, the environment, and characteristics of the individual must be considered in designing a specialized program. The principle of individuality states that each person adapts uniquely to a particular exercise stress.

Training volume is the total work performed during exercise and should vary inversely with intensity. Periodization or cyclic training involves five basic phases in which stimuli are varied to maximize adaptation: (1) base or conditioning phase, (2) load phase, (3) peak phase, (4) taper phase, and (5) recovery or off-season phase. The base phase lasts approximately six to eight weeks and is used to establish a foundation with high-repetition (8–12), low-intensity sets (60%–70% of 1-RM). To stress exercise technique, beginners should extend their base phases to at least ten to twelve weeks. During a six- to eight-week load phase, work loads (70%–80% of 1-RM) and sets per exercise (4–6) are increased, while repetition schedules (4–8) are decreased. The load and peak phases are usually interspersed with a short one-week recovery period to allow for maximal adaptation and supercompensation. The peak phase lasts about one month and involves an increased work load (80%–95% of 1-RM) together with a decreased number of repetitions (1–5) and exercise sets (2–5). Tapering is a drastic reduction in training intensity and duration just prior to competition. A recovery or early off-season period should provide for both physical and psychological rest so that athletes are rejuvenated before they begin a new conditioning phase.

Beginning Weight Training

6

It's sad to say that most who train with weights give little thought to program planning or exercise technique. Countless hours are wasted by those whose only goal is to lift as much weight as possible. It's not surprising that weight rooms are filled with clients who are discouraged by nagging injuries and lack of progress.

Program design and exercise technique are the key ingredients for safe and effective training. These two important topics are the focus of this chapter. We'll start by taking a look at beginning weight training programs along with specific guidelines for workout frequency, resistance selection, repetition schedules, and rest intervals. We'll spend the remainder of the chapter examining the Basic Dozen weight training exercises. These twelve classes of complementary movements will help you achieve balanced muscular development and tone. The Basic Dozen are the foundation for beginning as well as intermediate and advanced weight training programs.

The major muscles worked by the Basic Dozen are given in common (lay) and equivalent anatomical terms. Mini form checks are included as quick and easy references to help verify that you are using proper technique. Exercise techniques are then described in detail. Important areas to warm up and notes concerning spotting are given for each exercise. Contraindications are presented as a guide for appropriate exercise selection for those who are conditionally cleared. To help you troubleshoot and further refine your form, special sections called Coaches' Corners have been included. These highlight common mistakes made by beginners along with pertinent points used in teaching the particular movement.

I hope this chapter gives you the tools needed to design your own program and enjoy training in a safe and effective way for the rest of your life.

Weight Training Program Design and Emphasis

Sound weight training programs are based on a division of the body into several symmetrical parts or regions. By designing your program to highlight specific body regions, you'll make it much easier to balance your anterior-posterior and superior-inferior muscles.

Anatomists commonly divide the body into the following major parts: (1) lower extremity (hip, thigh, leg, and foot), (2) thorax (chest), (3) upper extremity (shoulder, arm, forearm, and hand), (4) back, (5) pelvis, (6) head, (7) neck, and (8) abdomen. Since the foot, hand, pelvic, and head regions don't contain large skeletal muscles that require training beyond that achieved in normal daily activity, exercises which work these areas aren't usually included in typical weight training programs (programs for athletes involved in ballet, soccer, or racquet sports may be exceptions).

To provide for balance, your program should be designed to work each of the following regions: (1) lower extremity (hip, thigh, and leg), (2) chest, (3) shoulder, (4) back (upper and lower), (5) arm, (6) forearm, (7) neck, and (8) abdomen. To make things simple, we'll divide the exercises that work these regions into three major categories: (1) lower body movements, (2) upper body movements, and (3) lower back and abdominal movements. Exercises that work the abdomen and lower back bridge the gap between those that work the upper and lower body.

Most people think that weight training works only superficial muscles. However, body regions contain superficial and deep bones, muscles, nerves, vessels, and other vital tissues. As we've mentioned before, you can tone or hypertrophy your muscles, strengthen your bones, and even train your nerves by exercising with weights. Later in the chapter when we talk about exercises working specific muscles, don't forget that other tissue components beside muscle are also being stressed. Remember that tissues adapt specifically to the mode, intensity, duration, and frequency of exercise.

The Basic Dozen

The Basic Dozen are twelve groups of complementary exercises that work major muscles in each of the regions outlined above. Table 6.1 lists each of the Basic Dozen exercise categories together with the corresponding regions and muscles that they work. In most cases, the exercises are grouped together because they work the same or similar muscles. For example, the squat, front squat, and leg press are grouped together as category 1 exercises because they work common muscles in the hip, thigh, and lower back regions.

You can balance your weight training program by performing at least one exercise from each of the Basic Dozen categories listed in table 6.1. Exercise options are built into the Basic Dozen so you can (1) minimize boredom by doing alternative exercises, (2) work the same or similar muscles from a slightly different angle to trigger adaptation during stagnant training periods, and (3) choose safe and effective alternative exercises if you are conditionally cleared.

Table 6.1 Body Regions and Specific Muscles Worked by the Basic Dozen Weight Training
Exercises

Exercise	Body Regions[a]	Specific Muscles[b]
1a. Squat	Lower extremity and	Hip, thigh, and lower back
b. Front squat	back	Hip, thigh, and lower back
c. Leg press		Hip and thigh
2a. Leg extension	Lower extremity	Front of thigh
b. Lunge		Hip, thigh, and back of leg
3a. Leg curl	Lower extremity	Back of thigh
b. Lunge		Hip, thigh, and back of leg
4a. Calf raise (knees straight)	Lower extremity	Back of leg (plantar flexors: gastrocnemius)
b. Calf raise (knees bent)		Back of leg (plantar flexors: soleus)
5a. Bench press	Chest, shoulder, and arm	Chest, front of shoulder, and back of arm
b. Supine chest fly		Chest and front of shoulder
6a. Upright row	Shoulder, arm, forearm, neck, and chest	Front and middle of shoulder, front of arm, forearm, and neck
b. Parallel dip		Front of shoulder, back of arm, and chest
7a. Military press (standing)	Shoulder, arm, and neck	Front and middle of shoulder, back of arm, and neck
b. Behind-the-neck press (seated)		Shoulder, back of arm, and neck
8a. Lat pull	Back, chest, shoulder, arm, and forearm	Upper back, chest, back of shoulder, front of arm, and forearm
b. Bent-over row		Upper back, back of shoulder, front of arm, and forearm
c. Pull-up		Upper back, chest, back of shoulder, front of arm, and forearm
9. Triceps extension	Arm and forearm	Back of arm and forearm
10. Biceps curl	Arm and forearm	Front of arm and forearm
11. Back extension	Back and lower extremity	Lower back, hip, and back of thigh
12. Sit-up (knees bent)	Abdomen	Abdominal

[a]Body regions that are affected by the entire group of exercises listed under the same number in column 1.
[b]Lay terminology for specific muscles that are worked by each of the exercises listed in column 1.

In column 2 of table 6.1, body regions worked by a group of exercises are listed in the order that they are emphasized. For example, the bench press mainly strengthens muscles in the chest, but also works muscles in the shoulder and arm regions. The Basic Dozen provide for balanced development by focusing on muscles in all of the regions listed previously: (1) the lower extremity (hip, thigh, and leg), (2) chest, (3) shoulder, (4) back (upper and lower), (5) arm, (6) forearm, (7) neck, and (8) abdomen. Notice that each of these major regions appears first in column 2 of table 6.1 with the exception of the forearm (6) and neck (7). While exercises that isolate the forearm and neck are not usually included in beginning weight training programs, many upper body movements do engage muscles in these areas. Every time you grab a bar you use forearm muscles. They are especially active when you perform biceps curls, triceps extensions, lat pulls, bent-over rows, and pull-ups. You recruit neck muscles during the upright row, military press, behind-the-neck press, and sit-up. If you play football, soccer, handball, or racquet sports, you may want to do isolated work for your neck or forearms.

Program Design for the Basic Dozen

Exercises that make up the Basic Dozen have been carefully selected to help you achieve balanced muscular development and tone. Note in table 6.1 that the exercises are listed in a special order proceeding from larger to smaller muscles. Doing the exercises in this sequence may help elevate and maintain your heart rate for more overall conditioning.

The most difficult and often neglected lower body exercises come first in the Basic Dozen, while common favorites such as the biceps curl and triceps extension are scheduled later. This priority listing will help you focus on inferior-posterior development and avoid falling prey to the body builder's syndrome (see chapter 5, fig. 5.5). Although abdominal and lower back movements are listed last in the Basic Dozen, you may want to perform them first with other exercises in your warm-up routine (especially before squatting). You can also easily incorporate these movements into your cool-down (see appendix C).

The special order of the Basic Dozen facilitates supersetting, which you can use to reduce your total workout time (see chapter 4, fig. 4.8). Exercises that you can superset include the (1) squat and bench press (for a quick, exhausting workout), (2) leg extension and leg curl, (3) bench press and lat pull, (4) upright row and dip, (5) military press and lat pull, (6) military press and upright row (for a rugged shoulder workout), (7) triceps extension and biceps curl, and (8) sit-up and back extension (or other abdominal and lower back work). You can use other combinations as long as you alternately work agonistic and antagonistic or upper and lower body muscles.

For a change of pace you can vary the order of the Basic Dozen (especially when you are supersetting), but be sure to complete multi-joint foundation exercises before moving on to single-joint refinement exercises. For example, do squat/front squat/leg press sets before you do polishing movements like the leg extension and the leg curl.

View the squat (1a) and the bench press (5a) as the key exercises of the Basic Dozen. Heavily emphasize these multi-joint movements; they are the cornerstone of your program. When there is little time for training, your primary goal should be completing your sets of squats and bench presses.

The lunge (2b and 3b) is listed as an alternative to both the leg extension and leg curl since it works muscles in the front and back of the thigh. This exercise is especially valuable when leg extension–leg curl machines are heavily used or unavailable.

The upright row (6a) and parallel dip (6b) are listed together as group 6 because both are good multi-joint movements. Both engage the shoulder muscles; in addition, the upright row works the biceps and neck, whereas the dip works the triceps and chest. These antagonistic exercises may be supersetted or alternated every other workout for variety. As an alternative, you may choose to do dips with your chest or triceps work and superset your upright rows with military or behind-the-neck presses. We'll describe these and other Basic Dozen exercises in detail later in the chapter.

Workout Frequency

Before you begin training, attend a facility orientation session to familarize yourself with new equipment and surroundings. When starting (or restarting) the Basic Dozen plan, you should work out two times per week during a two- to three-week accommodation period. During this time, focus on warming up, selecting an appropriate resistance, perfecting exercise technique, and cooling down. Try to spread out your training sessions so that you have two to three days of rest between workouts (e.g., train on Monday and Thursday, Tuesday and Friday, or Wednesday and Saturday). This initial low-frequency period will reduce your risk of injury and soreness and will give your body time to adapt gradually. After this accommodation period, you can do the Basic Dozen three times per week provided that you have at least one day's rest between workouts.

Exercise Sets

Complete two to three sets from each group of Basic Dozen exercises during your initial accommodation period (these sets should be above and beyond your specific warm-up sets). So that you'll emphasize superior-inferior balance from the very beginning, you may want to do three sets of each foundation exercise (i.e., the squat and the bench press) and two sets of each refinement exercise (i.e., the rest of the Basic Dozen).

Unless you are conditionally cleared (see chapter 2, Medical Clearance), do at least one exercise from each group of the Basic Dozen listed in table 6.1. Since consistency is critical in establishing your program, it's best to focus on the first exercise listed in each group until you finish the accommodation period. Later, you can choose a variety of options to complete three sets from each Basic Dozen group. For example, you can finish three sets of the exercises listed in group 1 (squat/front squat/leg press) by doing three sets of squats *or* two sets of squats and one set of front squats *or* one set each of the squat, front squat, and leg press. While many combinations are possible, your goal should be to complete three sets from each category of the Basic Dozen during each workout.

Resistance, Repetition Schedules, and Rest Intervals

During the accommodation period, perform two to three sets of 8–12 repetitions of the Basic Dozen. Be sure that you use a relatively light weight. Beginners often say, "But I don't even know where to start!" Table 6.2 has been included to help you select an appropriate trial resistance for each of the Basic Dozen. Remember, when in doubt, always choose on the light side. Don't let table 6.2 limit the resistance you handle if you happen to be a strong beginner or intermediate trainee.

Table 6.2   Resistance Selection Guidlines for the Basic Dozen Weight Training Exercises

Exercise	Trial Resistance for Females (lb)	Trial Resistance for Males (lb)
1. Squat	20–25	50–70
Front squat	15–20	40–60
Leg press[a]	120–150	180–210
2. Leg extension[b]	10–20	40–60
Lunge[c]	8–12	15–25
3. Leg curl[b]	10–20	30–50
4. Calf raise (straight knee)[d]	80–120	120–160
Calf raise (bent knee)[b]	25–50	50–75
5. Bench press	20–25	60–90
Chest fly[e]	8–12	15–20
6. Upright row	15–20	40–50
Parallel dip[f]	0	0
7. Military press	15–20	40–60
Behind-the-neck press	10–15	35–55
8. Lat pull[b]	20–40	50–80
Bent-over row	15–25	40–50
Pull-up[f]	0	0
9. Triceps extension[b]	10–20	30–50
10. Biceps curl	15–20	35–50
11. Back extension[f]	0	0
12. Sit-up (knees bent)[f]	0	0
Twist[f]	0	0

Note: Trial resistances are for medically cleared, 20-year-old female and male novices with average body weights of 110.3 lb (50 kg) and 154.4 lb (70 kg), respectively. Unless indicated otherwise, resistances were used to complete three sets of 8–12 repetitions with free weights. Remember, when in doubt, choose on the light side.
[a]Top steps of a Universal leg press or comparable device.
[b]Universal or similar stationary machine.
[c]Dumbbells were used to improve balance. Weights indicated for each dumbbell.
[d]Bottom steps of a Universal leg press or comparable machine.
[e]Dumbbells or cables. Weights indicated for each dumbbell or weight stack.
[f]Only body resistance was used.

Following the accommodation period, your instructor may ask you to complete a 1-RM test for the bench press and leg press. If you're training on your own, you may want to test yourself on a stationary circuit machine. Knowing your 1-RMs makes it easier to determine an appropriate training resistance (e.g., 60–70% of 1-RM for base training). Make sure that you satisfy the requirements for maximum testing before you do a 1-RM test (see appendix D). Remember that it is safer to predict your 1-RM (see appendix E).

If you plan to train for strength, keep the rest time between exercise sets between three to five minutes to give muscles time to replenish their immediate energy stores. If you are more concerned with toning muscles and developing local muscular endurance, you can gradually reduce your rest time to as little as one minute, 30 seconds, or 15 seconds between sets. You can also use supersetting to minimize rest and total workout time (see chapter 4, fig. 4.8).

Now that we've talked about the Basic Dozen program, let's take a detailed look at each of the Basic Dozen.

Lower Body Exercises

Squat (1a)

Common Terminology for Muscles Exercised (1) Hip, (2) front of thigh, (3) back of thigh, (4) inside of thigh, and (5) lower back.

Equivalent Anatomical Terminology (1) Gluteal group, (2) anterior thigh (most notably, the quadriceps group), (3) posterior thigh (hamstring group), (4) medial thigh (adductor group), and (5) erector spinae (sacrospinalis).

Mini-Form Check (1) Place feet with slight toe-out a bit wider than shoulders, (2) pronate hands on bar, comfortably wider than shoulder-width, (3) position bar low on shoulders off of neck, (4) contract abdominals, (5) straighten back, (6) focus eyes above, (7) slowly lower hips until thighs slightly beyond parallel to floor, (8) pause, (9) drive up with head and chest "to the sky," (10) breathe continuously.

Exercise Description Due to its multi-joint-action nature, the squat is often called the pillar of strength exercise for the lower extremity. If you squat in a strict fashion, you'll be assured of strengthening and toning most of the muscles in your lower body. You can also use the squat (unlike the leg press) to develop substantial lower back strength.

Practice squatting without weights before moving on to weighted sets. The safest way to do squats is by using a power/squat rack with safety support devices. Adjust and secure the support brackets so that the weight bar is positioned about 4–6 inches below your shoulders (just below the level of your armpits). If the squat rack has adjustable bottom safety bars, position and fasten them so they support the weight bar when your thighs are just beyond parallel to the ground. Be sure that the collars are secured on the weight bar before you begin training. Ask your instructor or an experienced friend to spot during the exercise.

Proper bar placement is essential. Place your hands in a pronated grip about 4–6 inches ouside of your shoulders (to review different handgrips, see chapter 4, Basic Hand Positions, and fig. 4.13). Stabilize the bar low on your shoulders and upper back so that it rests below a shelf formed by the spine of your scapulae (shoulder blades) (fig. 6.1a). Some people use towels or special cylindrical bar pads when they squat. Usually this indicates that the bar has been positioned improperly (too high on the shoulders and neck). As a beginner, you'll probably need to work on shoulder flexibility so that you'll feel comfortable positioning the bar in its proper, low position (extra muscle padding also helps!). By placing your thumbs over the bar in a "false" grip, you can help alleviate some stress on your wrist and shoulder joints (fig. 6.1b).

Never look down at the ground while squatting. To help avoid sudden plunging or nose diving when you squat, focus your eyes at a point "in the sky" (fig. 6.1a, b). Later, when you've improved technique and balance, you may choose to look straight ahead.

Place your feet with a slight toe-out, a bit wider than your shoulders (fig. 6.1b, c, d). To protect your lower back, contract your abdominals and keep your back flat throughout the exercise. With eyes focused above, lower your hips in a controlled fashion toward the ground as if sitting in a low chair (fig. 6.1d). Keep your heels in contact with the floor. Pause when your thighs are just beyond parallel to the ground. When viewed from the (lateral) side, your hips should move slightly back during the eccentric (easy) phase. After you pause deliberately, drive your head and chest "to the sky" and return to the starting position (fig. 6.1c). Exhale during the hard part and inhale during the easy part. If this seems difficult, just remember to breathe continuously throughout the exercise.

Important Areas to Warm Up Muscles of the medial thigh (adductors) are most frequently pulled in squatting. Use general adductor stretches (see appendix C, stretch 2 and 3) and extensive specific warm-up (squat/front squat/leg press) to decrease your risk of injury. Remember, specific warm-ups are best for increasing blood flow.

The lower back is said to be the weak link in the squat. Before you squat, warm up your lower back and gluteal muscles by performing slow, controlled back extensions. Use abdominal exercises to help tighten the midsection prior to squatting. We'll look at these movements later in the chapter.

Spotting For a review, you may want to reread the section on spotting in chapter 2. When you are spotting, be sure to protect your own back by contracting your abdominals, flattening your back, and using hips and thighs to do the work.

If you are the only available spotter, stand directly behind the trainee. If there's another experienced spotter, stand on one side of the lifter to provide assistance. When extremely heavy lifts are attempted, get a third spotter to stand directly behind the lifter.

A

C

B

D

Figure 6.1

The squat is the pillar of strength exercise for the lower extremity because of its multi-joint-action nature. *A.* Focus eyes at a point above and use a pronated grip with your hands about 4–6 inches outside your shoulders. Be sure that the bar is low off your neck. *B.* Notice the symmetry in this photo. The subject's feet are slightly wider than shoulder-width apart and his eyes are focused "to the sky." *C.* Starting position for the squat. *D.* Slowly lower your hips until thighs are slightly beyond parallel to the ground. After a deliberate pause, return to the starting position by driving your head and chest "to the sky." Remember to keep your heels on the floor and to breathe continuously.

If you are spotting from behind, guide the trainee to and from the bar support brackets. Don't release the bar until the lifter gives the "okay" or until the bar is safely secured in the rack. Squat with the trainee as he or she proceeds through the movement. If the lifter has difficulty when you are spotting from behind, place your hands on the upper abdominal area and help drive the head and chest "to the sky." If you are one of the spotters on either side of the bar, track the bar with your hands clasped. Should problems arise, grasp the bar, drive it upwards, and secure it in the rack.

Contraindications If you have a history of low back or hip injuries, chondromalacia patellae (early degeneration of cartilage on the undersurface of the kneecap), or other lower body problems, it may be best for you to avoid squatting. Some people with previous low back injuries can successfully engage in alternative exercises like the leg press. Don't squat without the approval of a sports medicine physician.

Coaches' Corner During the eccentric (easy) phase of the squat, you may have problems balancing and keeping your heels on the floor, especially if you have tight calf muscles or Achilles tendons. However, avoid squatting with boards or plates beneath your heels. This substantially alters the movement and increases your risk of injury; boards or plates can easily slip. Also, don't use benches or chairs to limit the depth of your squat as this increases the risk of back compression fractures. What, then, should you do to help maintain balance and keep your heels planted?

Practice squatting by performing several sets without weight. To help maintain an upright position during these practice sets, cross your forearms, put your hands on your shoulders and your elbows "to the sky." Check your stance to make sure that your feet are slightly wider than shoulder-width with a slight toe-out. As you lower your hips, have someone check to see that your knees are over the balls of your feet. Be sure to contract your abdominals and keep your back flat throughout the exercise. Carefully sit back and concentrate on keeping your heels on the floor. Take extra time to work on your calf, hamstring, and adductor flexibility (see appendix C, stretches 2, 3, and 5) and above all, be patient! Soon you'll find that you've developed good squatting technique because of your attention to detail.

Some orthopedic surgeons cringe at the thought of going beyond parallel during squats. Unless you have a previous lower body injury, are predisposed to lower body injuries, or abuse exercise techniques, you'll improve lower body strength and flexibility by squatting. As soon as you abuse your technique in order to handle more weight, you'll induce injury. Don't bounce, especially at the bottom of the movement. Bouncing places knuckle-shaped bumps on the lower thigh bone (femoral condyles) and kneecap (patella) in a dangerous position relative to each other. When you bounce, forces are no longer working to hold your joints together, but are essentially acting to pull them apart. This vulnerable openness of your knee joints increases the risk of injury. When you concentrate on controlling your descent and pausing at the bottom of the movement, you reduce the potential for injury and enhance the effectiveness of this valuable exercise.

Front Squat (1b)

Common Terminology for Muscles Exercised (1) Hip, (2) front of thigh, (3) back of thigh, (4) inside of thigh, and (5) lower back.

Equivalent Anatomical Terminology (1) Gluteal group, (2) anterior thigh (most notably, the quadriceps group), (3) posterior thigh (hamstring group), (4) medial thigh (adductor group), and (5) erector spinae (sacrospinalis).

Mini-Form Check (1) Place feet with slight toe-out a bit wider than shoulders, (2) use standard or crosspronated grip to secure bar (see exercise description), (3) position bar off of neck on platform made by frontal shoulders, (4) lift elbows high, (5) contract abdominals, (6) flatten back, (7) focus eyes above, (8) slowly lower hips until thighs slightly beyond parallel to floor, (9) pause, (10) drive up with head and chest "to the sky" (11) breathe continuously.

Exercise Description The front squat is nearly the same as the squat. The major difference is that you put the bar in front of, rather than behind your head.

When you do front squats, you can use a variety of hand positions. The military press position is the easiest and is ideally suited for beginners (fig. 6.2a). If you are more advanced, you may feel comfortable placing your hands over the top of the bar in a crossed (fig. 6.2b) or standard parallel fashion (fig. 6.2c).

If you don't have access to a rack, clean (lift) the bar to the starting position by using your hips, thighs, and legs instead of your lower back. A beginner's technique for cleaning is described in the section on the military press. Once you've developed adequate lower back strength by using nonballistic movements, you may want to try the competitive lifter's cleaning technique described in appendix I.

After you clean the bar (fig. 6.2a), carefully position it far enough away from your neck, yet high enough on your deltoids (shoulders) to provide for adequate support. Lift your elbows high so that your deltoids form a platform to support the bar (fig. 6.2b, c). Regardless of the grip you use, keep your elbows elevated throughout the exercise to prevent the bar from sliding off your deltoid platform. Place your feet slightly wider than your shoulders, focus your eyes above, and contract your abdominals. Just as in squatting, slowly lower your hips as if sitting in a low chair until your thighs are slightly beyond parallel to the floor (fig. 6.2c). Pause deliberately at the bottom of the movement, then drive your head and chest up to return to the starting position.

Important Areas to Warm Up As with squats, it's easy to pull muscles of the medial thigh (especially the adductor magnus) during front squats if you don't do adequate general and specific warm-up. Be sure to highlight stretches 2 and 3 in appendix C along with lots of specific warm-up prior to front squatting.

A

B

C

Figure 6.2

The front squat. *A.* The standard military-press hand position may be the easiest to start with. *B.* Advanced, crossed and pronated hand position. *C.* As with the squat, your feet are slightly wider than your shoulders, abdominals contracted, back flat, and eyes above. Notice that the elbows are elevated in order to maintain the deltoid platform.

Spotting When a squat/power rack is used, spotting techniques for the front squat and squat are identical. If the bar is cleaned from the floor and you are the only spotter, stand at a safe distance facing the lifter. Use a pronated grip outside of the lifter's grip, squat with the lifter, and grasp the bar from above if problems occur. Limit your spotting to less than your own 1-RM and rely on your hips, thighs, and legs, not your lower back.

If another spotter is present, each of you should stand on either side of the trainee. Track the bar with your hands and guide the lifter through the movement. If the lifter loses his or her balance, grab the bar, and return it safely to the floor or squat/power rack.

Contraindications The contraindications for the front squat are nearly identical to those for the regular squat. Avoid this exercise if you have a lower back or lower extremity injury. If you've had previous shoulder injuries you may be limited to performing the leg press as an alternative exercise. Check with a sports medicine physician prior to front squatting.

Coaches' Corner It is safer and easier to learn front squats before squats because (1) less weight is used (about one-half to two-thirds of that used for squats), (2) there is a greater sense of controlling the bar, (3) there are less problems with shoulder inflexibility or bar placement being uncomfortable, and (4) with the bar in front of the head, it's easier to sit back on the heels and remain upright. Also for light weighted front squats, squat/power racks are not required since the bar can be cleaned directly from the floor to the starting position. This is a distinct advantage especially when racks are heavily used or unavailable.

The most common mistakes in the front squat are (1) improper initial bar placement, (2) failure to keep the elbows elevated, and (3) dropping or bouncing, rather than controlling, during the eccentric phase.

If you don't have well-developed shoulder muscles, you may find that it's most comfortable to use the military press position. When you increase your shoulder strength and "padding" and become more familiar with the movement, you'll find that it's easier to use the other hand positions (fig. 6.2b, c).

Unlike the leg press, the squat and the front squat work lower back muscles. An additional advantage of the front squat is that a variety of hand grips may be used. Often subjects with casted forearms or hands cannot perform squats, but can execute front squats safely and comfortably. (Leg presses are recommended if a subject cannot control the free bar because of inadequate grip strength.) Even though the front squat is an acceptable alternative, remember that the squat is the best exercise for increasing lower body strength.

Before and during the performance of squatting exercises, what safety precautions should be observed? In what situations might front squats be preferred over squats?

Leg Press (1c)

Common Terminology for Muscles Exercised (1) Hip, (2) front of thigh, (3) back of thigh, and (4) inside of thigh.

Equivalent Anatomical Terminology (1) Gluteal group, (2) anterior thigh (most notably, the quadriceps group), (3) posterior thigh (hamstring group), and (4) medial thigh (adductor group).

Mini-Form Check (1) Adjust and lock seat or body-support board for full-range work, (2) plant hips, (3) with slight toe-out, position feet a bit wider than shoulders on foot platform or upper steps, (4) put hands at waist, (5) contract abdominals, (6) flatten back, (7) focus eyes straight ahead, (8) press platform up with feet and turn grips outside to release safety supports (if inverted leg press), (9) slowly flex hips and knees until thighs beyond parallel to foot platform or steps, (10) keep paper-thin distance between plates (if machine with weight stack), (11) pause, don't bounce, (12) smoothly extend hips and knees, (13) pause, slightly short of full extension, (14) breathe continuously.

Exercise Description If you are fully cleared, the leg press should be your third choice from the multi-joint, lower body exercises in group 1. Even though it works nearly the same muscles as the squat and the front squat, it only lightly taxes muscles in the lower back. The leg press may be the best exercise for you if you are conditionally cleared due to previous low back problems (see chapter 2, Medical Clearance).

There are many different types of leg presses. In this section we'll focus on describing the inverted (vertical) leg press, although with a few minor changes, you'll be able to do leg presses on Universal, Nautilus, or any other comparable device. Unlike other machines, inverted leg presses require that you do the eccentric (easy) phase first.

Verify that the device you are using is working properly and adjusted for full-range work. Though you'll find that different machines require unique adjustments, all involve adjusting the seat or support board to account for differences in thigh (femur) length, leg (tibia) length, and flexibility. To get the most from leg presses, you must be aligned so that you can move through the full range of motion. With an inverted leg press, you are lined up properly when (1) your hip axes are in line with the foot platform and (2) your thighs are at least parallel to the foot platform and comfortably close to your chest in the terminal eccentric position (fig. 6.3c).

Make sure you lock the seat or platform in place before you start exercising. Throughout the movement, keep your hips planted firmly. Place your feet on the foot platform with a slight toe-out and a bit wider than your shoulders (fig. 6.3a). If working on a Universal or Nautilus leg press, put the balls of your feet between midway and two-thirds of the way up on the top steps or foot pads. Place your hands at your waist or lightly grip the handgrips if they're present. Focus your

A

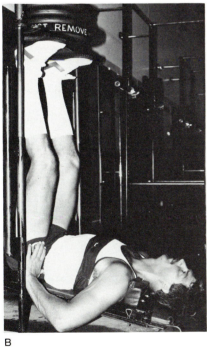

B

C

Figure 6.3

A. During the leg press, your feet should be slightly wider than shoulder width to ensure balanced development. *B.* Starting and/or terminal concentric position for the inverted leg press. Keep your eyes focused above, hands at your waist, hips directly beneath the platform, and knees slightly flexed to decrease posterior joint capsule stress. *C.* Move carefully through the full range of motion to the terminal eccentric position.

eyes straight ahead and contract your abdominals to protect your lower back. If working on an inverted leg press, your knees should be nearly extended in the starting position (fig. 6.3b). Slowly lower the weight to the terminal eccentric position (fig. 6.3c). If you are on a Universal or Nautilus leg press, keep a paper-thin distance between the plates so that your muscles, rather than the weight stack, bear the brunt of the weight. After pausing deliberately, extend your hips and knees smoothly (from fig. 6.2c to b). Don't "pop"! Remember to be kind to your joints, especially at the beginning and end of each repetition. Stop slightly short of full extension to minimize stresses on your knee joints (fig. 6.2b).

Important Areas to Warm Up As with the squat and front squat, use general and specific lower extremity stretches before you perform this exercise (see appendix C, stretches 1–5).

Spotting One advantage of the leg press is that it requires little or no spotting. Occasionally, spotting is used for eccentric (negative) or heavy concentric (positive) work on Universal, Nautilus, or similar machines. Be sure to ask for spotting if you need help moving heavy plates to and from inverted leg presses.

Contraindications If you have a history of low back problems you may find that the leg press is an ideal way to increase your lower body strength. Frequently, persons who've had knee surgery or knee conditions (e.g., chondromalacia patellae) can't tolerate squats or front squats, but feel quite comfortable doing inverted leg presses. However, don't take chances. If you've had a hip, knee, ankle, or foot problem, check with an orthopedic surgeon, physical therapist, or athletic trainer before doing leg presses.

Coaches' Corner If you use leg presses as an alternative exercise, don't forget to supplement your workout with isolated lower back work.

A common sight in many weight rooms is a novice attempting to use the entire weight stack on a typical leg press machine. To overcome this excessive resistance, the trainee positions the seat as far back as possible, lifts his or her hips completely off the support board and bangs the plates between repetitions. To maximize your benefits, adjust the seat for full-range work, plant your hips, proceed smoothly, and avoid touching the plates between reps.

Compared to most circuit-type leg presses, inverted leg presses maximize the range of motion and minimize knee joint stress. If you do leg presses on a Universal or comparable device, use the upper rather than lower steps to reduce the stress on your knees and to increase the stress on your hamstrings. Use the lower steps only for calf raises.

With an inverted leg press you can change the position of your feet to vary the distribution of stresses on your muscles. While you can also change your stance with the squat and front squat, it's safer and easier with an inverted leg press. By putting your feet high, so that your heels are in line with the center of the foot platform, you more heavily stress your hips and hamstrings. By positioning the balls of your feet low on the foot platform, you place less emphasis on your hips and hamstrings and more on your quadriceps. A wide stance stresses adductor (inner thigh) muscles, whereas a narrow stance emphasizes lateral (outer) thigh and hip muscles. You can more thoroughly isolate your hip and thigh muscles by doing specialized abduction and adduction exercises.

As a beginner, start by using a standard stance with your feet slightly wider than your shoulders to ensure balanced development. After you finish your initial conditioning period, you can make slight changes in your stance to vary the stress on your muscles.

Your stance during leg presses can affect the muscles you stress. What muscles are emphasized by putting your feet wide? narrow? high? low?

Leg Extension (2a)

Common Terminology for Muscles Exercised (1) Front of thigh.

Equivalent Anatomical Terminology (1) Anterior thigh, most notably the quadriceps femoris group (rectus femoris, vastus lateralis, vastus intermedius, and vastus medialis).

Mini-Form Check (1) Sit upright on body-support pad, (2) place hands at side and lightly grip support platform or handgrips, (3) contract abdominals, (4) flatten back, (5) focus eyes straight ahead, (6) throughout movement, point toes powerfully toward face, (7) slowly extend knees, (8) pause, (9) slowly flex knees to return to starting position, (10) keep paper-thin distance between plates, (11) pause, (12) breathe continuously.

Exercise Description The leg extension is a polish or refinement exercise for muscles of the anterior thigh. When performed with strict technique, this exercise develops and tones one of the largest and most powerful muscle groups in the body, the quadriceps femoris (literally, four-headed muscle of the thigh).

If you are using a Universal or similar machine, sit up relatively straight to protect your back and use your hands to grip the body-support board lightly (fig. 6.4a). If the machine you are using is adjustable (e.g., Nautilus), adjust and secure the seat to account for the length of your thigh. Lean your head and upper body firmly back into the body-support board. Align your knee joints with the axis of rotation of the machine so that the back of your knees are touching the edge of the body-support board (fig. 6.4a). Curl your feet beneath the leg extension roller pads so that your toes point toward your face. (If there are two sets of pads on the machine, the lower ones are the extension pads and the upper ones are the curl pads.) Fix your eyes on a point straight ahead. Elevate your chest, contract your abdominals, flatten your back, and plant your hips firmly (fig. 6.4a). Free the plates from the weight stack, pause, then extend your knees in a slow, controlled fashion (see chapter 2, Special Techniques for Circuit or Stationary Machines). Concentrate on pointing your toes toward your face, especially during the last 10–15° of extension. If you don't do this, you won't fully tax the vastus

A   B

Figure 6.4

The leg extension develops the quadriceps. *A.* In the starting position, plant your hips, contract abdominals, flatten back, focus eyes straight ahead, point toes toward your face, and place hands lightly on the bench for support. *B.* To work your vastus medialis, it's critical that you extend fully during the last 10–15°. By forcefully pointing toes toward your face, you'll increase the intensity of your quadriceps' contraction. Notice that the subject's back remains in the same relative perpendicular position in both *A* and *B*. This indicates that she's avoided swaying backward to recruit extraneous muscles to complete the movement.

medialis, the medial (innermost) muscle of the quadriceps group (fig. 6.4b). After pausing deliberately at the top of the movement, slowly return to the starting position. Between repetitions, keep a paper-thin distance between the plates to ensure that your thighs bear the brunt of the weight.

Important Areas to Warm Up By doing squats or other multi-joint, lower body exercises first, you'll prewarm your thighs and knee joints. If you do leg extensions before other lower body work (e.g., for rehabilitation), use quadriceps stretches and low-resistance, specific warm-up to increase the blood flow to your frontal thighs (see appendix C, stretch 3). You can also superset leg extensions with leg curls to relax and stretch antagonists while working agonists. If your hamstrings or calves are tight, do an extra set or two of warm-up stretches just before leg extensions to reduce the risk of pulling a muscle (see stretches 2 and 5, appendix C). This is especially critical if you plan to do heavy resistance sets.

Spotting A spotter is not needed for leg extensions, but can assist with negative resistance (eccentric only) training or with the last 10–15° of extension during heavy resistance sets. An experienced spotter can help point out poor technique and can always provide encouragement during difficult sets.

Contraindications If you have a thigh, knee, leg, ankle, or foot problem, you may not be cleared for leg extensions. However, isokinetic and isotonic leg extensions and leg curls are used extensively in rehabilitating knee injuries. During the early phases of knee rehabilitation, patients may do limited-range exercises called short arcs or terminal extensions to improve vastus medialis strength. Once they've gained a pain-free range of motion in their afflicted limb, patients are cleared for isotonic leg extensions. If you've had a lower body injury, check with a sports medicine specialist before doing this exercise.

Coaches' Corner The leg extension is one of the most abused lower extremity exercises. In order to handle heavy weights, many novices thrust their hips forward, bang the weights, and recruit extraneous muscles. This rarely strengthens the quadriceps, but is a foolproof way to develop nagging knee pain.

The most common mistakes with the leg extension are failing to (1) fully extend, (2) point the toes toward the face, (3) pause at the top of the movement, and (4) move smoothly through the eccentric phase. Remember that by practicing strict exercise technique, you'll maximize the tension in your muscles and trigger the most rapid increases in strength.

Throughout the exercise, resist the tendency to lift your hips up and bring your trunk forward. This is difficult because the rectus femoris (one of the muscles of the quadriceps), crosses both the hip and knee joints and acts to extend the knee and flex the hip. Some newer machines (e.g., Nautilus leg extension) provide for a greater range of motion due to the greater flexion of the knee joint in the starting position. They also have an angled back-support board to support the back and place the rectus femoris on more of a stretch. Even though this may help support your lower back, it doesn't completely alleviate the action of the rectus femoris at your hip. By lying down, you can place the rectus femoris on stretch, but you'll also put an incredible strain on your lower back. Within limitations of current machine design, the best you can do is try to plant your hips firmly and stabilize your trunk throughout the exercise. Limit the weight if your technique begins to fail. Don't forget to emphasize hamstring exercises like leg curls to achieve anterior-posterior balance.

Lunge (2b)

Common Terminology for Muscles Exercised (1) Hip, (2) front of thigh, (3) back of thigh, (4) inside of thigh, (5) calf, and (6) lower back.

Equivalent Anatomical Terminology (1) Gluteal group, (2) anterior thigh (most notably, the quadriceps group), (3) posterior thigh (hamstring group), (4) medial thigh (adductor group), (5a) gastrocnemius, (5b) soleus, and (6) erector spinae (sacrospinalis, primarily acting to stabilize the trunk).

Mini-Form Check (1a) Grasp dumbbells with grip midway between pronation and supination and position at side *or* (1b) grasp bar using comfortable pronated grip and place on shoulders off of neck, (2) stand upright with feet slightly wider than shoulders, (3) contract abdominals, (4) flatten back, (5) focus eyes straight ahead, (6) take controlled step forward until thigh slightly beyond parallel, (7) front knee should be over ball of foot in terminal eccentric position, (8) keep back knee relatively straight, (9) pause, (10) take controlled slide-step back, (11) repeat with opposite side, (12) breathe continuously.

Exercise Description The lunge is a multi-joint lower body exercise that is an excellent alternative to the leg extension and leg curl. It's exceptional for toning hip and frontal thigh muscles, but also works medial (inner) thigh, hamstring, and calf muscles. Lunges are especially valuable when leg extension–leg curl machines are heavily used or unavailable.

The lunge is relatively hard to do because it requires considerable balance. Recruit a seasoned spotter to help when attempting your first sets. Try lunges without weight to get a feel for the balance involved. When you feel comfortable about adding resistance, start out with hand-held dumbbells. By using dumbbells instead of a barbell, you'll lower the center of gravity of the system (you and the weight you handle) and improve your ability to balance.

In the starting position, stand with your feet shoulder-width apart, eyes straight ahead, and abdominals contracted (fig. 6.5a). Hold the dumbbells with your hands facing medially and your elbows relaxed. Focus eyes straight ahead, contract the abdominals, and keep your back flat throughout the exercise. Being sure not to overstride (fig. 6.5d), start by taking a smooth step forward with your nondominant side. Lower your hips so that your front thigh is slightly beyond parallel and your front knee is directly over the ball of your foot (fig. 6.5b and c). Your front foot should be straight ahead and your back knee relatively extended so that you stretch hip flexor muscles on the back side (tight hip flexors are often the culprit in low back pain). Pause deliberately, then push off the ball of your front foot and slide it back to the starting position. To complete a single repetition, repeat the same movement with your opposite side (fig. 6.5c).

Eventually, your strength may increase to the point that dumbbells are limiting. Once you've developed good technique, try using a barbell. The safest way to do lunges with a barbell is to use a power/squat rack. Secure the adjustable bar-support brackets below the level of your shoulders (at about level of your armpits) to the front vertical bars of the power/squat rack (see fig. 6.1). If a rack is not available, clean the bar to the military press position (see fig. 6.13), then carefully jerk it overhead without leaning backward. Just as you did for the squat, position the bar just below the shelf near the ridges of your shoulder blades (spines of your scapulae). You might be able to place the bar a bit higher if you have well-developed neck and shoulder muscles. Repeat the exercise with each side as described for dumbbells.

A

B

C

D

Figure 6.5

The lunge is an excellent exercise for developing the hip and thigh regions. Dumbbells help lower the center of gravity of the system (trainee + resistance) and make the exercise easier. *A.* In the starting position hold the dumbbells with your palms facing in. Stand with feet shoulder width, abdominals contracted, and eyes straight ahead. *B.* Slide one foot forward and lower hips until front thigh is just below parallel and front knee is directly above the ball of the foot. After pausing deliberately, return to the starting position (*A*). *C.* Repeat with opposite side. *D.* An example of overstriding during the lunge. Notice that the front knee is not over the ball of the foot as in (*B*) and (*C*).

Important Areas to Warm Up Since you'll usually do lunges after squats and other multi-joint lower body exercises, your muscles will be prewarmed. Nevertheless, it's easy to pull adductor, hamstring, or gluteal muscles, especially if you are sore. If you are tight or sore, do extra general and specific warm-up before you do lunges (see appendix C, stretches 1–5). Do 8–12 controlled reps without weight before doing weighted sets.

Spotting It's easy to lose your balance during the push-off (concentric or return) phase of the barbell form of this exercise. One spotter directly in front or two spotters on either side of a lifter can help provide assistance throughout the movement.

As a single spotter, stand directly in front of the trainee about four feet away. Pronate your hands and position them just above the bar and the lifter's shoulders. Mirror the movements of the trainee by stepping backward as the trainee steps forward and forward as the trainee returns to the starting position. The lifter can make it easier for you to spot by stepping to a point midway between your feet. Interfere as little as possible, but be extremely alert because loss of balance is common. In the severe case, you may have to grab the bar close to the trainee's shoulders to redirect his or her path. When squat/power racks are not available and the trainee can't clean the barbell, you may help with proper bar placement.

If you are one of two spotters, stand about one to two feet from the side of the lifter with your hands together. Track the barbell with your hands and mirror the movement of the lifter by stepping directly to the side without crossing over your feet. Position your feet wide, contract your abdominals, and bend your knees to protect your lower back.

Contraindications If you've had a hip, thigh, knee, leg, ankle, or foot problem you may not be cleared for lunges. Persons with chondromalacia patellae (degeneration of the cartilage under the kneecap) or previous knee ligament or cartilage damage can usually tolerate leg extensions and leg curls better than lunges. Check with a sports medicine physician before doing this exercise.

Coaches' Corner Even though you'll work first without weight and then use dumbbells, you'll probably lose your balance a few times. Generally, this is caused by stepping out too far (fig. 6.5d) or forgetting to keep your back straight and eyes focused ahead. You can improve balance by focusing your eyes at a spot on the wall and by using a controlled, half rather than full stride.

Leg Curl (3a)

Common Terminology for Muscles Exercise (1) Back of thigh and (2) calf (minor involvement).

Equivalent Anatomical Terminology (1) Posterior thigh (hamstring group) and (2) gastrocnemius.

Mini-Form Check (1) Lie prone on body-support pad so kneecaps are clear of edge, (2) position head straight and plant chin and pelvis, (3) lightly grasp handgrips or body-support pad at side or in front, (4) check to see that clothes, hair, and hands are clear of cables and plates, (5) contract abdominals, (6) flatten back, (7) point toes toward face, (8) free the weight stack, (9) slowly flex knees fully while keeping hips planted, (10) pause, (11) slowly extend knees to return to starting position, (12) keep paper-thin distance between plates, (13) breathe continuously.

Exercise Description The leg curl is often neglected, yet it is the most beneficial exercise for balancing posterior and anterior thigh muscles. It works the hamstrings and also recruits the gastrocnemius, the large calf muscle that crosses the ankle and knee joints.

To do leg curls, lie face down on a leg extension/leg curl or comparable machine. If there are two sets of roller pads, put your legs under the upper set so that your kneecaps are 1½″ to 2″ clear of the edge of the body-support pad. Your partner can verify this distance by placing two to three fingers' width between the top of your knees and the edge of the pad. This positioning should ensure that your knee joints are aligned with the machine's axis of rotation (fig. 6.6a). Alignment is important because your kneecaps move during the exercise. If you put your knees on or near the edge of the support pad you can increase compression forces and the risk of knee injury.

Throughout the exercise, plant your hips and pelvis into the body-support pad to protect your lower back. This is difficult to do, especially on older model machines with flat body-support boards. Since most of the posterior thigh muscles cross the hip and knee joints, we tend to lift our hips when we flex our knees. Newer devices with angled body-support boards place the hamstrings on more of a stretch, but still don't completely alleviate the problem (see Coaches' Corner). Regardless of the type of machine you use, contract your abdominals and lengthen your back, especially during the hard (concentric) part of the exercise.

Free the plates from the weight stack (see chapter 2, Special Techniques for Circuit or Stationary Machines). Slowly flex your knees and pause for a full second at the top of the movement (fig. 6.6b). Without letting the plates touch, extend your knees smoothly to a point just short of full extension. On most machines (e.g., Universal) you can verify your position by watching the plates as you exercise. With practice, you'll sense exactly when the plates are within a fraction of an inch of the weight stack. By not letting the plates touch between reps, you'll constantly stress your hamstrings instead of periodically relieving them when the weight stack bears the brunt of the weight.

Important Areas to Warm Up You'll probably do leg curls after other lower extremity work; thus, your hamstrings will be prewarmed. If you have tight hamstrings or calves, you may want to do additional general and specific warm-up before moving on to moderate to heavily weighted sets (see appendix C, stretches 2 and 5).

A

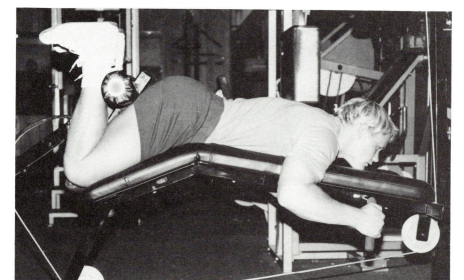

B

Figure 6.6

The leg curl is a must for posterior thigh development. This newly designed, angled leg curl machine helps to decrease lower back stress. *A.* Starting position with knees two- to three-fingers' distance from the edge of the body-support pad, abdominals contracted, back flat, chin and pelvis planted, and toes pointed toward the face. *B.* Flex your knees in a smooth, controlled fashion. After pausing deliberately, slowly return to the starting position (*A*), but don't let the plates touch the remaining weight stack.

Spotting Spotting on the leg curl may be beneficial for those who have trouble going through the full range of motion or those who desire to perform negative (eccentric) work.

If you are asked to spot, stand at the lifter's feet about two to three feet from the end of the curling pads. Lightly press at the ankles as the trainee completes the hard part of the exercise. You'll notice that if you press the roller pads instead of the ankles, the lever arm will move through the last part of the range of motion without the lifter's legs. Remember to help as little as possible so that the trainee's muscles bear the brunt of the weight. If you are asked to do negative or eccentric resistance spotting, lightly press down on the roller pads as the subject returns to full extension (the starting position). Be careful in spotting eccentric work as you can easily induce muscle pulls. Ask for feedback about the level of difficulty, but minimize idle chatter to avoid disrupting the lifter's concentration.

Contraindications You should avoid leg curls if you have a pulled hamstring or calf muscle, kneecap (patellar) problem, hyperextended knee, or low back condition. When in doubt, consult your physician, physical therapist, or athletic trainer.

Coaches' Corner You may have seen people lift their hips high off the support pad during the hard part of the leg curl. Although it's unlikely, some have suggested that this practice maximizes tension in the hamstrings. By lifting your hips during leg curls, you place undue stress on your lower back. Although difficult, try to plant your hips, contract your abdominals, and flatten your back throughout the exercise.

Some newer machines (e.g., by Flex and Universal) have angled body-support boards so that the hips remain elevated and flexed throughout the exercise. This stretches the hamstrings or fixes them more fully where they attach to the hips so they can be isolated better. Although they are not perfect, these preflexed devices also help reduce lower back stress (fig. 6.6).

Since your hamstrings will probably lag behind your quadriceps, place special emphasis on leg curls to bridge this gap.

Lunge (3b)

See previous exercise description for the lunge (2b).

Calf Raise (4a and b)

Common Terminology for Muscles Exercised (1) Back of leg (calf).

Equivalent Anatomical Terminology (1a) Superficial posterior leg muscles or triceps surae (gastrocnemius and soleus) and (1b) deep posterior leg muscles (tibialis posterior, flexor digitorum longus, and flexor hallucis longus).

Mini-Form Check (1a) Place bar or support pads on shoulders off of neck (if standing calf raise) *or* (1b) assume seated position with knee-thigh pads over lower thighs (if seated calf raise), (2) position balls of feet on edge of foot platform, (3a) keep knees near full extension (to highlight gastrocnemius) *or*

(3b) keep knees flexed at constant angle (to highlight soleus), (4) focus eyes straight ahead, (5) contract abdominals, (6) flatten back, (7) slowly dorsiflex (stretch fully), (8) pause, (9) slowly plantar flex (contract fully), (10) breathe continuously.

Exercise Description Beginners often ignore calf raises and posterior leg development. Calf raises can dramatically improve strength for plantar flexion (toe raising), which is needed for any activity that involves walking, running, or jumping.

Although it works some small muscles, the calf raise mainly works two large muscles of the calf, the gastrocnemius and soleus. The larger, more surface gastrocnemius (Greek for stomach- or belly-shaped muscle of the leg) has two parts or heads, each shaped like a stomach. Together with the more slender and deep soleus (Latin for flatfish), the gastrocnemius makes up the triceps surae (three-headed calf). Since the gastrocnemius crosses the knee joint whereas the soleus does not, each of these muscles can be isolated by varying the angle of the knee joint.

By keeping your knees relatively straight during calf raises, you put your gastrocnemii on stretch and rely on them more heavily. When your knees are bent at a constant angle, your "gastrocs" are corrugated or loose, which makes them fairly inactive. Thus, while straight-knee calf raises mainly work the gastrocnemii, bent-knee calf raises primarily stress the solei.

You can do calf raises with different types of equipment including standing or seated calf machines. When special machines aren't available, all you need is a stable step and a barbell. In this section we'll take a brief look at two of the most common types of calf raises: (1) the straight-knee calf raise on a circuit-type machine and (2) the bent-knee calf raise on a seated calf machine.

Straight-knee calf raises are often done at Universal leg press stations like the one pictured in figure 6.7. Although we'll describe the exercise on this machine, with a few slight modifications you'll be able to do calf raises on many other devices.

Start by securing the seat in the farthest back position. Plant your hips firmly, focus your eyes straight ahead, and contract your abdominals to protect your lower back. If handgrips are available, grasp them lightly; if not available, place your hands at your waist. Press the weight up by pushing with your feet on the bottom steps. Keep your knees just short of full extension to avoid stressing the back of your knee joints (otherwise, you'll tax your posterior joint capsules, important supporting structures of the knees). Put the balls of your feet just over the edge of the bottom steps to allow for full-range work. Slowly lower the weight by pointing your toes toward your face (dorsiflex) (fig. 6.7a). This controlled stretch is critical. After you pause deliberately for one to two seconds, point your toes away from your face (plantar flex) so that you powerfully contract the calf muscles (fig. 6.7b). Pause and repeat repetitions without using gravity or momentum to your advantage. By avoiding rapid or bouncing movements, you'll

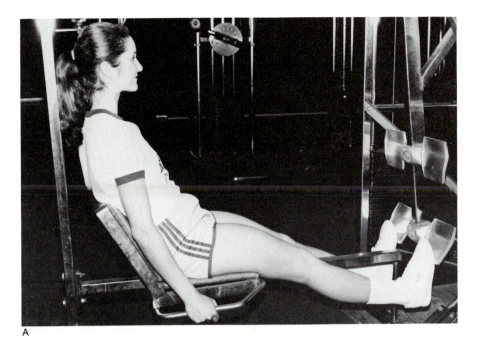

A

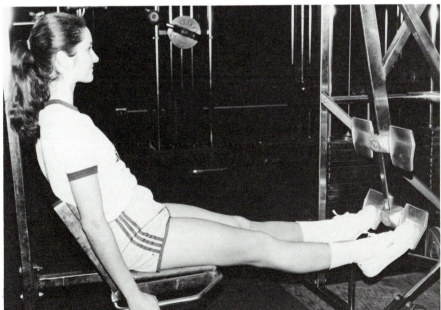

B

Figure 6.7

Do your first straight-knee calf raises on a Universal or other stationary device. Use the lower rather than the upper steps to improve body alignment and to maximize the stretch of calf muscles. *A.* Lightly grasp handgrips, focus eyes ahead, contract abdominals and fully stretch calves (dorsiflex). *B.* Point toes (plantar flex) powerfully yet smoothly to contract calf muscles completely.

minimize the risk of injury and maximize your calf development. As with other exercises, exhale during the hard part and inhale during the easy part. Above all, remember to breathe continuously.

To do seated (bent-knee) calf raises, you must first adjust the position of the knee-thigh pads according to the length of your legs (tibia). Most newer models can be adjusted easily by placing a standard weight key through a bore on a sliding metal sleeve attachment. The knee-thigh pads should be as low to the floor as possible so that you can stretch fully at the bottom of the movement. To start exercising, point your toes (plantar flex) while you push the weight support bar forward (fig. 6.8b). Once you've done this, sit up straight, focus your eyes ahead, contract your abdominals, and lightly grasp the outside of the knee-thigh pads (fig. 6.8c). Stretch fully at the bottom of the movement, pause deliberately, then point your toes so that you contract your calf muscles powerfully (fig. 6.8d). To maximize the tension in your calves, exaggerate stretching and avoid bouncing or leaning backward.

Important Areas to Warm Up Use controlled general and specific warm-up for both the gastrocnemius and soleus before you do calf raises (see appendix C, stretch 5a and b). Walking with exaggerated plantar and dorsiflexion can also help to loosen stubborn posterior leg muscles.

You can easily aggravate your Achilles tendons and tibialis posterior muscles (associated with shin splints) by doing calf raises, especially if you are involved in long-distance running, ballet, basketball, or volleyball. During a single training session for each of these sports, you may do hundreds to thousands of calf raises with your body weight. When your training time for sports increases, decrease the resistance and number of calf raises that you do in the weight room. Concentrate on extensive warm-up and cool-down. If you do experience soreness, remember to rest, ice, compress, and elevate (**RICE**) the afflicted area and consult an athletic trainer or sports medicine physician.

Spotting Spotting for calf raises is not needed unless free weights are used. Attentive spotting can help make free-weight calf raises safe and effective. Two spotters on either side of the barbell or one spotter directly behind the lifter will maximize safety during free-weight lifting.

If you are asked to be a spotter when a rack is not available, you might need to help the lifter position the bar on his or her shoulders. Be sure to use your hip and thigh muscles to do the work. Once the bar is positioned, stand close enough to provide help but far enough away so that you are not distracting. Track the lifter throughout the range of motion. If loss of balance occurs, grab the bar with a pronated grip and drive the lifter to an upright position.

Be sure to use stationary calf raise machines rather than free weights when spotters are not available.

Contraindications Avoid calf raises if you have Achilles tendonitis, shin splints, or sore arches. Other knee, leg, ankle, or foot problems may keep you from doing this exercise. Even shoulder injuries make it difficult to do standing calf raises. When in doubt, contact a sports medicine specialist.

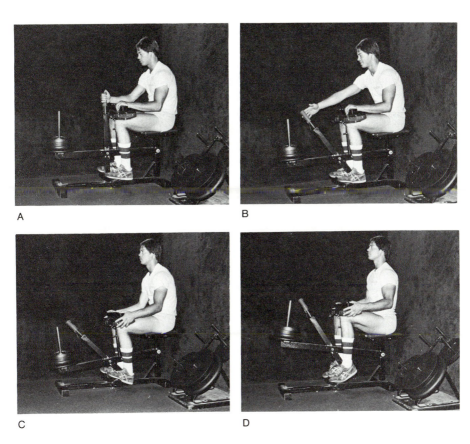

A

B

C

D

Figure 6.8
The bent-knee calf raise stresses the soleus, although the gastrocnemius is also partially engaged. *A.* Adjust the knee-thigh pad to allow for full-range work. *B.* Point your toes (plantar flex) and push the support bar forward so that your calves bear the brunt of the weight. *C.* Move your heels toward the ground to assume the fully stretched starting position. *D.* Powerfully point your toes (plantar flex) to drive through the concentric phase. Be sure to pause deliberately at both ends of the movement.

Coaches' Corner When you do calf raises, resist the temptation to sacrifice your form for weight. The most common errors are thrusting the hips forward, extending the knees, and bouncing or swaying to handle excessive weight. To maximize calf development, move smoothly and deliberately through the entire range of motion. Be sure that you pause for a full one to two seconds at both the top and bottom of the movement.

When using a free bar or a Nautilus multipurpose, standing calf raise, or inverted leg press machine, move only in a vertical plane. Don't let your range of motion be limited by the height of the platform or support board. Properly adjust and stabilize boards or platforms to avoid touching your heels to the floor between reps. By doing this you'll place the brunt of the weight on your posterior leg muscles.

Practice calf raises on a stationary machine before trying the free-weight version of the exercise. Try dumbbells first, then barbells. Grasp dumbbells so that your hands face medially as if you are doing lunges (see fig. 6.5a). If using a barbell, position the bar on the shelf beneath the spine of your scapulae like you did for squatting (see fig. 6.1a). If your shoulders and neck are well developed you may feel comfortable placing the bar a bit higher.

Be especially careful when you plan to do calf raises with a barbell. Verify that the platform is fully secured. Injuries often occur when free-weight calf raises are done with poorly fixed 2″ × 4″ boards, logs, or other homemade devices. The balance needed to do calf raises with free weights is difficult enough without adding an unstable support structure. Secure the bar with collars and use a spotter to maximize your safety.

Even when equipment is limited, you can always find safe and effective ways to do calf raises. You may be able to do calf raises by slightly modifying military press or bench press stations on circuit machines. If you don't have machines or free weights, you can do "donkey" calf raises by resting your forearms on a table or bench and having your partner sit on your hips (not on your lower back).

Upper Body Exercises

Bench Press (5a)

Common Terminology for Muscles Exercised (1) Chest, (2) front of shoulder, and (3) back of arm.

Equivalent Anatomical Terminology (1) Pectoral group (pectoralis major and minor), (2) anterior deltoid, and (3) triceps brachii.

Mini-Form Check (1) Lie on bench and make a tripod with feet, buttocks, and head stabilized, (2) grasp bar with wide pronated grip, 4″–6″ wider than shoulders, (3) don't track bar—keep eyes "at the sky", (4) contract abdominals and flatten back, (5) slowly lower bar to chest, (6) at bottom of movement, elbows should be directly beneath bar and forearms perpendicular to floor, (7) pause bar high on chest, but avoid sliding to neck, (8) drive bar up to return to starting position, (9) be kind to the joints at top of movement, (10) pause deliberately, (11) breathe continuously.

Exercise Description The multi-joint bench press is the pillar of strength exercise for the upper body. Together with the squat, the bench press is a cornerstone of sound weight training programs. It highlights chest, frontal shoulder, and rear arm muscles. The bench press also activates the long head of the biceps, which crosses both the shoulder and elbow joints.

If the bench you'll be using has adjustable bar-support uprights (e.g., like those made by AAI, formerly AMF), position them according to the length of your upper limbs. The key is to place the uprights so that you do as little work as possible to assume the starting position. To measure yourself for correct positioning, put an unweighted bar in the uprights. Lie on the bench and grab the bar using a wide grip, about 4″–6″ wider than your shoulders. After you extend your elbows to lift the bar, your wrists should be in line with the bottom of the U made by the uprights. If you lunge off the bench to move the bar to the starting position, you've positioned the uprights too high. If you move the bar vertically more than an inch or two to assume the starting position, you've positioned the uprights too low. Readjust and secure the uprights to maximize your safety and comfort. Even though adjustable, spring-loaded bench presses have many advantages, they must be used carefully. If you aren't sure how to use the equipment in your facility, ask an instructor. When bench pressing, always have a spotter nearby to ensure safety.

To do the bench press, lie down and make a tripod with your body by planting your (1) feet, (2) buttocks and (3) head plus shoulders (fig. 6.9a). Your tripod should never move during the exercise. Grasp the bar firmly by using a pronated grip about 4″–6″ wider than your shoulders. Your hands are positioned properly if your forearms are directly beneath the bar and perpendicular to the ground when the bar touches your chest (fig. 6.9c). Contract your abdominals and flatten your back to protect your lower back. To avoid straining your neck, don't track the bar with your eyes, but fix them on a point "in the sky" (fig. 6.9b). Focusing on this point will also help you *think through* rather than *be limited by* the bar.

From a point directly overhead, lower the bar to a spot high on your chest (above the nipple line if you're a male, slightly higher if you're a female). Control the bar so it doesn't slide to your neck. By touching the bar relatively high on your chest and keeping your elbows directly beneath the bar (away from your side), you'll fully stress your pectoral muscles instead of your triceps. Don't bounce or recoil the bar off of your chest, but rather pause it deliberately to (1) avoid recruiting extraneous muscles, (2) reduce the risk of injury, and (3) maximize your gains in chest strength (fig. 6.9b). Press the bar to the original position in a controlled yet powerful fashion. Remember to be smooth, especially at the beginning and end of the movement, to decrease forces on your shoulder, elbow, and wrist joints.

Important Areas to Warm Up Pectoral and frontal shoulder muscles are vulnerable to pulls during heavy bench presses. To prevent muscle strains, use both general (see appendix C, stretch 9) and specific warm-up (e.g., wide grip push-ups or light weight bench presses). Specific warm-up is the most effective. Do at least 1–2 sets of high-repetition (10–12), low-resistance (35%–50% of 1-RM) bench presses before moving to heavier sets.

Spotting Usually one or two spotters are used for free-weight bench presses. If you are the only spotter, stand in a crouched position about six inches from the lifter's head. Be close enough to help, yet far enough away to avoid distracting the lifter. (Don't stand directly over the lifter or with one thigh forward as this is quite distracting.) If the trainee wants a lift-off, use an alternate grip to grasp

A

B

C

Figure 6.9

The bench press is the pillar of strength exercise for the upper body due to its multi-joint nature.
A. Get set for the starting position by making your feet, hips, and head and shoulders form a
tripod that never moves during the exercise. *B.* Bring the bar to a point high on your chest
during the eccentric (easy) phase. Focus eyes directly on a point "in the sky" to avoid tracking
the bar and to reduce risk of neck injury. *C.* Your elbows should be directly beneath the bar and
forearms perpendicular to the ground at the bottom of the movement. By using a relatively wide
handgrip you'll more fully stretch pectoral and anterior deltoid muscles and reduce the work
done by your triceps.

the bar and smoothly guide it to the starting position (see chapter 4, Basic Hand Positions, and fig. 4.13). To maximize safety, always use an alternate grip to help the lifter complete the movement. Be sure to contract your abdominals and use your hips and thighs to do the work, not your lower back. Don't touch the bar unless it's absolutely necessary. A slight pull in the wrong direction or even hand-waving can disrupt the lifter's concentration and timing, and thwart a successful attempt.

If you are one of two spotters, stand about one to two feet away from one side of the bar. Before spotting heavier lifts, practice spotting lighter lifts so that you learn to synchronize your movements with another spotter. Clasp your hands, track the bar, and squat as the lifter lowers the bar to his or her chest. Sometimes three spotters are used for extremely heavy lifts with one spotter standing at the lifter's head and the other two on either side of the bar. Spotting may be helpful but is not required for those who perform bench presses on stationary circuit devices.

Contraindications If you've injured your chest, shoulder, arm, elbow, forearm, wrist, or hand, get a sports medicine specialist's approval before doing bench presses. Neck and low back problems can also be aggravated by bench presses, especially when poor technique is used. In the Coaches' Corner, we'll talk about using alternative exercises to reduce joint stress.

Coaches' Corner The bench press is one of the most abused strength-training exercises. Beginners and intermediate lifters are often so concerned with the weight they handle that they completely ignore the form. Many will do anything to improve their 1-RM, including arching their backs, placing their feet on benches, or thrusting their trunks toward bars that appear to be virtually immovable.

Remember that you can't maximize the tension in pectoral muscles by using poor technique and diffusing the stress to other muscles and bones in the body. You'll only increase the risk of injury and minimize gains in strength. Concentrate on maintaining your tripod, contracting your abdominals, and focusing your eyes at a point on the ceiling. Guide the bar smoothly and pause deliberately at both ends of the movement. If strict with your technique, you'll maximize safety as well as gains in strength.

By using a stationary bench press machine, you can decrease the risk of back injuries. If you have relatively short legs or are limited to using a high bench, you may need additional support to protect your lower back. Elevate your feet by placing them on two stable blocks, wooden boxes, or platforms. When these support devices are not available, put your feet on the bench to reduce back strain. However, don't put your feet on a bench when using free weights or you'll reduce stability and increase the risk of being injured (i.e., you'll eliminate one of the three components of the tripod). When you try to modify an exercise, always keep safety in mind.

You'll find that you can reduce shoulder, elbow, or wrist stress by (1) varying the width of your grip, (2) altering the incline of the bench, or (3) using an alternative system (e.g., machines versus dumbbells or barbells). For example, you may be able to tolerate light, close-grip (two-thumbs' distance) bench presses despite the fact that you can't do regular bench presses following recovery from an A-C (acromion-clavicular) separation. If you can't grip a bar (even if you are casted), you may be able to maintain your chest strength by working on a stationary chest fly machine ("pec deck"). Above all, when you aren't sure what alternatives are appropriate, ask an athletic trainer, physical therapist, or sports medicine physician.

Many lifters disregard proper form in executing the bench press. What is the motivation that prompts this mistake, and what are the common errors that increase the risk of injury?

Supine Chest Fly (5b)

Common Terminology for Muscles Exercised (1) Chest and (2) front of shoulder.

Equivalent Anatomical Terminology (1a) Pectoral group (pectoralis major and minor), (1b) serratus anterior, and (2) anterior deltoid.

Mini-Form Check (1) Grasp dumbbells with mid-pronated/supinated grip, (2) carefully assume supine position with dumbbells close to chest, (3) make tripod with feet, buttocks, and head stabilized, (4) focus eyes "at the sky," (5) contract abdominals and flatten back, (6) move dumbbells to position directly overhead, (7) keep elbows constantly flexed at an angle 30°–45° short of full extension, (8) slowly lower dumbbells in arclike fashion to floor until chest comfortably stretched, (9) keep elbows out and wrists in, (10) pause, (11) controlled fly, not press-up—"hug the big oak tree," (12) pause deliberately at top of movement, (13) breathe continuously.

Exercise Description The supine chest fly can be used as an alternative or supplement to the standard bench press. The major difference between the two exercises is that the chest fly eliminates the action of the triceps and primarily stresses the muscles of the chest and anterior shoulder. Thus, it is more of a pure chest movement than the bench press and is highly effective for enhancing pectoral development. The chest fly, like the bench press, also activates the long head of the biceps, which crosses both the shoulder and elbow joints.

To do a press, you must extend your elbows and engage the triceps muscles in the back of your arms. You don't do this when performing a fly, but instead maintain your elbows at a constant angle. When you do flies, your elbows should be locked at an angle of about 30°–45° throughout the entire exercise. This will help reduce elbow joint strain and will tax your chest muscles rather than your triceps.

Start by checking to see that the dumbbells you plan to use are stable. If your dumbbells are adjustable, make sure weights on either side are balanced before you secure the collars. Even with fixed-weight dumbbells, injuries can occur due to poor joint welding. If the bench you're using is adjustable, secure it in the full-down or supine position.

Squat down and grab the dumbbells by using a half-pronated/half-supinated grip (see chapter 4, fig. 4.13). Move to the starting position by sitting, then carefully lying back on the bench. If the dumbbells are relatively heavy, have a spotter hand them to you after you lie down. Assume a tripod position identical to that used for the bench press with your (1) feet, (2) buttocks, and (3) head plus shoulders stabilized (fig. 6.10a). Your tripod should never move during the exercise. To protect your neck and lower back, fix your eyes "to the sky" and contract your abdominals.

Extend your elbows just before aligning them in the starting position. Turn your elbows outside toward your head (partially abduct your arms) while keeping your hands and wrists inside. Move your hands to a point just below the level of your chin. Position your elbows about 30°–45° short of full extension. Keep them there throughout the range of motion as though they were casted (fig. 6.10a, b). Carefully lower your arms so that you fully stretch your pectoral muscles and then pause (fig. 6.10b). By moving only your arms, smoothly drive the dumbbells through an arc to the original starting position (fig. 6.10a). Avoid pressing the dumbbells up to minimize the action of your triceps. You may find that chest flies are easier when you follow the advice of a wise Southern coach: "Just pretend like you're hugging a big oak tree!"

Important Areas to Warm Up As with bench presses, chest flies place chest and shoulder muscles in a vulnerable position. Due to the balance they require, dumbbells further increase the risk of injury. Make sure you use general (appendix C, stretch 9) and specific warm-up (light weight push-ups, bench presses, and chest flies) to help prevent pulls. Practice your technique extensively before you increase the weight. Always do at least one to two light weight warm-up sets before moving on to heavier weighted sets.

Spotting In most cases, if problems arise, all the lifter has to do is return the dumbbells to the floor. Unless heavy weights are used, only a single spotter is needed for chest flies. Spotting is not required but may be helpful for those doing chest flies on stationary machines.

As a spotter, stand one to two feet from the lifter's head. Carefully hand the dumbbells to the lifter and help him or her assume the starting position. Verify that the lifter's elbows are out at a constant angle and the wrists are in. Spot from a position below the arms by pressing up lightly with your hands in a supinated position. At the end of a set, help the lifter return the dumbbells to the floor. When spotting, stay in a crouched position with your knees bent and abdominals contracted to protect your lower back.

Contraindications The contraindications for the chest fly are similar to those for the bench press. If you've had a chest, shoulder, arm, elbow, forearm, wrist, hand,

A

B

Figure 6.10

The supine chest fly is an excellent supplement or alternative to the bench press. *A.* Assume a starting tripod position with your feet, buttocks, and head + shoulders stabilized, and your eyes focused at the ceiling. Throughout the entire exercise, maintain your elbows at a constant angle as though they were casted. *B.* Slowly move to a fully stretched position. After a deliberate pause, smoothly return to the starting position (*A*).

low back, or neck injury, contact a sports medicine specialist before doing chest flies. Injuries to the sternum (breastplate) or clavicle (collarbone) are easily irritated by chest flies.

Coaches' Corner Chest flies and other dumbbell movements are relatively difficult to do. First try doing chest flies on Universal, Nautilus, or other pec-deck machines. Once you feel fairly comfortable with the movement on one of these tracked devices, try doing chest flies with light weight dumbbells.

Use light weights during the first several weeks. Focus on keeping your elbow joints at a constant angle throughout the range of motion. Be sure you are doing a pure fly instead of a combination fly-press. By doing pure flies, you'll ensure proper isolation and dramatically enhance the development of your chest.

Upright Row (6a)

Common Terminology for Muscles Exercised (1) Front and middle of shoulder, (2) front of arm, (3) back of forearm, and (4) neck.

Equivalent Anatomical Terminology (1) Anterior and middle heads of the deltoid, (2) biceps brachii and brachialis, (3) brachioradialis (most notably), (4a) posterior neck muscles (trapezius and levator scapula), and (4b) anterior neck muscles (most notably, the sternocleidomastoid).

Mini-Form Check (1) Place feet slightly wider than shoulder width, (2) squat down and grasp bar on floor by using pronated, two-thumbs' distance grip, (3) move to upright position by using hips, thighs, and legs rather than lower back, (4) flex knees at a constant angle, (5) contract abdominals and flatten back, (6) focus eyes straight ahead, (7) fully extend elbows, (8) raise elbows high to lift bar smoothly, keeping it close to chest, (9) pull to a point high beneath chin, (10) pause deliberately, (11) slowly return to starting position, (12) pause before next rep, (13) breathe continuously.

Exercise Description The upright row is a good multi-joint upper body exercise that works the shoulders, upper back, and neck.

Stand close to the center of a barbell, with your feet slightly wider than your shoulders. Squat down and grip the bar at its center by using a two-thumbs' distance, pronated grip (fig. 6.11a). Stand by using your hip, thigh, and leg muscles rather than your lower back (see chapter 2, Use Lower Body Muscles in Lifting, and fig. 2.5).

Once you are in an upright position, rebend your knees and keep them at a constant angle throughout the exercise. Remember to do this any time you do an exercise in the standing position (see chapter 2, Bend Knees and Contract Abdominals When Standing, and fig. 2.6). By keeping your knees and hips flexed and abdominals contracted, you'll reduce the stress on your lower back.

Once you are in the proper starting position, lift your elbows as high as possible and scrape the bar across your chest. Keep your abdominals contracted and don't rock forward or backward. At the top of the movement, the bar should be

A   B

Figure 6.11

The upright row is an excellent shoulder and trapezius developer. *A.* In the starting position, feet should be slightly wider than shoulders, abdominals contracted, eyes focused straight ahead, and hands secured with a two-thumbs' distance grip on the bar. *B.* Move smoothly through the concentric phase by scraping the bar across your chest to a point high beneath your chin.

close to your neck, directly beneath your chin (fig. 6.11b). Pause at this point, then lower the weight smoothly to return to the starting position. Extend your elbows fully at the bottom of the movement, but avoid bouncing or recoiling. By pausing for a full second at both the bottom and top of the movement, you'll maximize the tension developed in your shoulder and neck muscles. As with all resistance movements, remember to breathe continuously throughout the exercise.

Important Areas to Warm Up Deltoid and neck muscles are the most vulnerable to injury during the upright row. Forearm muscles (especially the brachioradialis) are also susceptible to irritation or pulls. Do light neck and shoulder stretches to help loosen the trapezius and deltoid muscles prior to lifting (see appendix C, stretches 10, 11, 12). Prewarm forearm muscles by doing light weight, specific warm-up sets of upright rows.

Spotting The upright row is a fairly low-risk free-weight exercise. If you are asked to spot for the upright row, stand facing the lifter about one and one-half to two feet away. Spotting is most often needed when the bar is pulled to a point high beneath the chin. Use a supinated hand position to apply light, even pressure from beneath the bar on either side of the lifter's hands. If the bar deviates or drops to one side during the lift, guide the bar in a straight path. Be sure to contract your abdominals and bend your knees to protect your own lower back when spotting.

Contraindications If you've had a recent neck, shoulder, elbow, wrist, or hand injury, you may have to avoid upright rows. Light upright rows may be included in some shoulder rehabilitation programs. However, upright rows are especially difficult for those with tendinitis in the wrist, elbow, or shoulder joints. If you've been injured recently, be sure to check with a sports medicine physician before doing this exercise.

Coaches' Corner Many people try to handle too much weight and fail to pause for a full second at the top of the movement. To compensate for the excessive weight, they swing the bar in a circular fashion, thrust their hips, straighten their knees, or stand on their toes to recruit extra muscles. As you might guess, this won't help shoulder strength and may make the back and elbows sore.

If you bounce the bar at the bottom or fail to pause at the top, use less weight until you can do the exercise in a controlled manner. Perfect technique will maximize safety as well as gains in strength.

As mentioned in chapter 2, the general rule is to inhale before you start, exhale during the hard part (concentric phase), and inhale during the easy part (eccentric phase) of an exercise. The upright row may be an exception to this rule, since exhalation may be counterproductive to thoracic cavity expansion during the hard part of the exercise. As long as you breathe continuously, use whatever breathing pattern feels the most comfortable.

Parallel Dip (6b)

Common Terminology for Muscles Exercised (1) Front of shoulder, (2) back of arm, and (3) chest.

Equivalent Anatomical Terminology (1) Anterior head of the deltoid, (2) triceps brachii, (3a) pectoral group (pectoralis minor and major), and (3b) serratus anterior.

Mini-Form Check (1) Place hands on parallel bars with palms facing medially (toward chest), (2) step or jump up (with spotter) to a supported position with elbows fully extended, (3) focus eyes straight ahead, (4) cross or stabilize feet, (5) maintain knee joints at a constant angle to avoid kicking up or using lower body muscles, (6) lower body by slowly flexing elbows until arms are beyond parallel to floor, (7) pause, (8) push up to original position by extending elbows, (9) be kind to the joints, (10) breathe continuously.

Exercise Description The parallel dip is an excellent multi-joint exercise that develops many of the same muscles as the bench press. It's most noted for developing the triceps, which provide considerable thrust during the concentric phase.

To complete a single dip you must be able to control your body weight. This requires considerable upper body strength, especially if you are carrying a few excess pounds or have long upper limbs. At first, it's wise to try only the eccentric (easy) phase of the body-resistive form of this exercise. Be sure to have a seasoned spotter assist you. The Nautilus multipurpose machine with built-in steps, weight strap, and parallel bar support is a handy device for increasing strength with eccentric-only dip movements. (A simple parallel bar with a stable step will also do.) You can also build strength for dipping by working on bench presses, triceps extensions, and military presses. Later, when you improve your upper body strength and your ability to handle your body weight, you may want to do dips with additional resistance. You can then chain dumbbells or plates to a sturdy belt that fits snugly around your waist.

When you are first starting out, secure the bar (if adjustable) in the lowest position so you can use the floor for support if needed. Otherwise, to reach the starting position, use a spotter, stable chair, or step-type device. In the starting position, your body should be perpendicular to the ground and your elbows fully extended by the strong contraction of the triceps (fig. 6.12a). Focus your eyes on a point straight ahead to avoid swaying and to help maintain an upright posture. When you are sure you have things under control, slowly and carefully flex your elbows to lower your body toward the floor. At the bottom of this eccentric phase, your arms should be slightly beyond parallel (fig. 6.12b). Pause deliberately (it may be the only thing you can do!), and then push powerfully and smoothly to extend your elbows and return to the starting position. During this concentric (hard) part, be sure to keep your knees at a constant angle to avoid thrusting, kicking, bouncing, or jerking to return to the starting position.

Important Areas to Warm Up Use lots of general and specific warm-up before you do dips to avoid injuring your chest, shoulders, and elbows (see appendix C, stretches 9, 10, and 11). Light bench presses, controlled push-ups, and similar pressing movements help prewarm muscles and joints for dipping. If you're a stronger weight trainer, you may elect to hang carefully at the bottom of the eccentric phase of the dipping movement.

Spotting Spotting for dips requires considerable strength. For some people the dip may be a muscular endurance exercise, whereas for others it may be entirely isometric. It's especially difficult to spot obese subjects or those with limited upper body strength. As a general rule, when you first begin weight training, limit your spotting to those who weigh less than you do.

To maximize safety with an inexperienced or obese subject, use an adjustable dip bar and secure it in the lowest position. To spot, position yourself directly behind the subject. Put your hands on the subject's waist and use your lower body to lift the subject to the starting position (this works best when timed with the subject's jump). Don't spot by grabbing the legs or feet; this may cause the subject to nose-dive forward. Gently push up on the waist to help the trainee resist during the eccentric phase. After the set is completed, carefully guide the subject back to the floor.

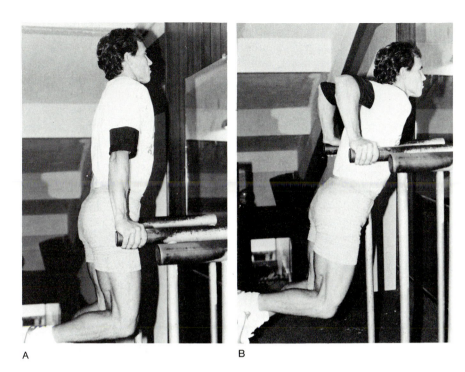

A   B

Figure 6.12
The multi-joint parallel dip works the triceps, chest, and shoulders. *A.* Start with eyes straight
ahead, abdominals contracted, and elbows locked to support your body so that it's
perpendicular to the ground. *B.* Carefully lower your body until your arms are slightly beyond
parallel to the ground. After you pause for a full second, push to extend your elbows and return
to the starting position (*A*). By keeping your knees at a constant angle throughout the
movement, you'll avoid kicking up or recruiting lower body muscles.

Contraindications If you've had a chest, sternum, shoulder, elbow, wrist, or hand
injury, you should avoid this exercise until you've been cleared by a sports medicine physician. Interestingly, some subjects with previous shoulder injuries who
can't perform bench presses can use modified dips to help maintain or improve
chest, shoulder, and triceps strength. If you're a bit overweight or don't have
considerable upper body strength, focus on bench presses, military presses, and
isolated triceps exercises. You can use (1) body-resistive, eccentric-only or
(2) more advanced, weighted eccentric-only dips to develop strength for concentric dips. Make sure you have a spotter regardless of the type of dip you plan to
do.

Coaches' Corner The dip is commonly done in a rapid, ballistic fashion. This not
only minimizes intramuscular tension and strength gain, but also dramatically
increases the risk of joint and muscle injury.

Don't be concerned with how many dips you can do, but rather emphasize your form. Use slow, methodical movements and pause deliberately at both the top and bottom of the movement. Avoid kicking or swaying to return to the starting position.

Those with less triceps' strength often lean forward to place more stress on their pectoral and anterior deltoid muscles. In contrast, those with less chest and shoulder strength lean backward to recruit their triceps more heavily. Focus your eyes straight ahead so that you stay upright and develop your muscles in a balanced way.

Even though the dip is often (invalidly) used as a measure of upper body muscular endurance, don't be discouraged if you have difficulty performing a single repetition. Choose the upright row (6a) as your first choice of the group 6 exercises. Use bench presses, military presses, isolated triceps movements, and negative dips to improve your upper body strength. By using these strength exercises and by decreasing your percentage body fat with an aerobics program, you'll learn quickly to do dips.

Military Press (7a)

Common Terminology for Muscles Exercised (1) Front and middle of shoulder, (2) back of arm, and (3) neck.

Equivalent Anatomical Terminology (1a) Anterior and middle heads of deltoid, (1b) supraspinatus, (2) triceps brachii, (3a) anterior neck muscles (most notably, the sternocleidomastoid), and (3b) posterior neck muscles (upper trapezius and levator scapula).

Mini-Form Check (1) Place feet a bit wider than shoulders, with toes straight ahead and beneath bar on floor, (2) grasp bar using pronated grip, just outside feet, (3) use lower body muscles to clean bar to starting position just above deltoids and beneath chin, (4) contract abdominals and flatten back, (5) keep knees at constant angle, (6) focus eyes straight ahead, (7) slowly extend elbows to press the bar over front of head, (8) pause, (9) slowly return to the original position, (10) breathe continuously.

Exercise Description The military press is an excellent shoulder and posterior arm developer. The anterior and middle heads of the deltoid are worked extensively by this movement, although the posterior deltoid is also used as a stabilizer.

If a power rack is not available you must clean the bar from the platform or floor to the starting position. To do this, rely heavily on your hips, thighs, and legs, not your lower back (see chapter 2, Use Lower Body Muscles in Lifting, and fig. 2.5). Put your feet directly beneath the bar so they are slightly wider than the width of your shoulders. Using a pronated grip, place your hands on the bar a bit wider than your feet. Focus your eyes on a point above and contract your abdominals to protect your lower back (fig. 6.13a). Throughout the clean, keep the bar close to your body and your elbows high and away. Slowly pull the

A

B

C

Figure 6.13
The military press is an excellent shoulder and triceps exercise. *A.* Position used to clean the weight for military pressing or front squatting. *B.* In the starting position, keep eyes straight ahead, abdominals contracted, and knees slightly flexed to protect the lower back.
C. Slowly press the weight directly overhead without changing knee joint angles to avoid recruiting lower body muscles.

bar off the ground by relying heavily on your hips and thighs. Your head, shoulders, and hips should move straight up simultaneously. When the bar passes the middle of your thighs, rapidly accelerate it by shrugging your shoulders, lifting your hips up and out, and rising up on your toes. When the bar reaches chest level, quickly rotate your elbows, bend your knees, and dip beneath the bar in one rapid, fluid motion. In the starting position, secure the bar on a platform made by your frontal shoulder and upper chest muscles (fig. 6.13b).

Once you are in the starting position, rebend your knees and contract your abdominals to protect your lower back (fig. 6.13b). With your eyes fixed on a point ahead, smoothly press the bar directly over the front of your head. When you've fully extended your elbows, pause momentarily to control the weight. It's critical at this point that you focus on contracting your abdominals to protect your lower back. Pressing the weight straight overhead rather than posteriorly will help minimize lordosis and further protect your lower back (fig. 6.13c). Slowly lower the weight to return to the starting position (fig. 6.13b). Pause deliberately at the bottom of the movement so that you don't recruit other muscles or use momentum to help with subsequent repetitions.

Important Areas to Warm Up Be sure to loosen trapezius and shoulder muscles with light neck and shoulder stretches prior to doing military presses (see appendix C, stretches 11 and 12). Also warm up your triceps, abdominals, and erector spinae to minimize your risk of elbow and lower back injuries (see appendix C, stretches 6, 7, and 10).

Spotting Like the dip, the free-weight military press is a difficult exercise to spot. It's more dangerous since a bar is pressed directly overhead. To ensure safety for you and the lifter, limit your spotting to weights that you can press by yourself.

As a single spotter, stand directly in front of the subject about one to two feet away. To assist with the lift, place your hands inside the subject's grip as though you were doing the exercise. Press lightly from beneath the bar if the lifter can't complete the repetition without help. Guide the bar in a straight path if it deviates or drops to one side. Be sure to contract your abdominals and bend your knees to protect your back while spotting. For heavier lifts, two spotters may stand on either side of the lifter and track the bar during the movement.

Contraindications The contraindications for the military press are similar to those for the upright row. If you've recently injured your neck, shoulder, elbow, wrist, or hand, consult a sports medicine specialist before you do this exercise.

Coaches' Corner At first you may have difficulty cleaning the bar to the starting position. (The more you practice, the better you'll be.) Ask a spotter if you need help placing the bar over your deltoids.

Most back strains and sprains occur when an underdeveloped, unprepared, or overloaded spine is suddenly and violently extended, particularly when rotation is also involved (Cantu 1980). When you first learn to clean, de-emphasize the forward hip thrust, backward head action, and massive contraction of the back and neck muscles used for the competitive clean. By doing this you'll minimize the risk of back injury. When you've increased your lower back strength and mastered the beginner's technique for the clean, you may want to try the competitive clean so that you can lift heavier weights (see appendix G).

It's tempting to extend the hips and knees to help lift the bar overhead. Once you have the bar in the starting position, contract your abdominals and keep your knees flexed at a constant angle. By doing this, you'll place the brunt of the weight on your shoulders instead of your hips and thighs.

Although the military press primarily stresses the anterior and middle heads of the deltoid, the posterior head of the deltoid must also contract for balancing purposes. When all three heads of the deltoid contract simultaneously, the arm is abducted anteriorly (moved toward the front) rather than in a plane parallel to the body. This is because the anterior deltoid overpowers the weaker posterior deltoid. Don't forget to work the back of your shoulders to achieve anterior-posterior balance. Variations of the military press involve the seated military press, which limits the use of the lower body, and the behind-the-neck press, which places more stress on the middle deltoid, posterior deltoid, and posterior neck muscles (especially the upper fibers of the trapezius). After you've had considerable practice with military presses, focus on behind-the-neck presses and complementary exercises like the bent-over row to emphasize your posterior deltoids. By doing this, you'll counterbalance dominant anterior muscles developed by bench and military presses.

Behind-the-Neck Press (7b)

Common Terminology for Muscles Exercised (1) Middle, back, and front of shoulder, (2) back of arm, and (3) neck.

Equivalent Anatomical Terminology (1a) Middle, posterior, and anterior heads of the deltoid, (1b) supraspinatus, (2) triceps brachii, (3a) posterior neck (trapezius and levator scapula), and (3b) anterior neck (most notably, the sternocleidomastoid).

Mini-Form Check (1) Sit on stable support bench, (2) plant feet firmly on floor, (3) grasp bar on support rack with pronated grip slightly wider than shoulders, (4) free bar from rack with aid of spotter, (5) rest bar low on shoulders off neck to assume starting position, (6) contract abdominals and flatten back, (7) focus eyes straight ahead, (8) control press-up until elbows fully extended, (9) pause, (10) slowly return to starting position, (11) pause deliberately before next rep, (12) breathe continuously.

Exercise Description The behind-the-neck press is nearly identical to the military press. The only difference is that the bar is pushed up from behind the neck rather than in front of it, placing more stress on the trapezius and the middle and posterior heads of the deltoid.

When you do behind-the-neck presses from a seated position, you minimize the tendency to recruit lower body muscles. However, you also increase the risk of lower back compression injuries. Even though it's easy to feel relaxed when in a seated position, be sure to concentrate on contracting the abdominals and flattening the back so that you reduce low back stress. It's been estimated that vertebral stresses in the lower back can be reduced by about 30% by the supportive action of the abdominals (Morris, Lucas & Bressler 1961; Morris 1973).

Take care not to bounce the bar off your cervical vertebrae when returning to the starting position. Always use a spotter to minimize your risk of injury. The behind-the-neck press is pictured in figure 6.14. For further details about this exercise see the Coaches' Corner and the Exercise Description for the military press (7a).

Important Areas to Warm Up If you don't do complementary neck exercises, you'll be especially vulnerable to neck pulls during this movement. Be sure to do lots of general and specific warm-up before you do behind-the-neck presses (see appendix C, stretches 10, 11, and 12). Do light weight neck exercises, upright rows, and behind-the-neck presses to help loosen stubborn trapezius muscles.

Spotting If a rack is not available, you may have to help the lifter clean the bar and place it in the starting position behind his or her neck. To ensure safety when you are the only spotter, limit your spotting to weights you can handle by yourself.

When a rack is available, you'll mainly be needed to help guide the weight off the rack and return it to the rack after the subject completes the set. As a single spotter, you should stand directly behind the subject about one to two feet away. Depending on the height of the rack and your position relative to the lifter, you may use a pronated, supinated, or alternate grip when spotting. You may have to apply light pressure on the bar to help the trainee complete a repetition at the end of a set. If you let the bar travel downward during the hard (concentric) phase, you've waited too long to help. As with other spotting, ensure that the bar flows in a continuous, uninterrupted fashion during the concentric part of the movement.

If you are one of two spotters needed during heavy resistance lifting, stand about one to two feet from either side of the bar. With your hands clasped, track the bar during the entire movement. If the lifter needs help, lift up lightly on the bar to match the pressure applied by the other spotter. Be sure to practice working with another spotter by spotting light sets before heavier sets.

Contraindications Avoid this exercise if you have neck, back, shoulder, arm, elbow, wrist, or hand injuries. If you've been injured recently, contact a sports medicine professional for alternative exercises for rehabilitation.

Coaches' Corner You may have problems assuming the starting position. When you don't have a rack, limit your sets to relatively light weights until you've become experienced at cleaning the bar. Since the bar is always near your head and neck during this exercise, be smart and safe by recruiting an attentive spotter.

A

B

Figure 6.14

Compared to the military press, the behind-the-neck press shifts the brunt of the work posteriorly to the middle and posterior heads of the deltoid and upper fibers of the trapezius. *A.* Place feet at shoulder width, contract abdominals, focus eyes ahead, and rest the bar on the shoulders off of the neck. *B.* Press smoothly through the concentric phase to a point straight overhead.

In figure 6.14 the subject is doing the exercise by facing away from the uprights of an AAI adjustable bench press. Some prefer to face the uprights and back out to assume the starting position. Either way is fine as long as you have a spotter behind you to help if problems occur. If it's hard to get the bar off the rack, you may have the rack adjusted too high. As with any exercise that involves the use of a support structure, the secret is to position it so that you minimize the work you do to assume the starting position.

You may have seen people do behind-the-neck presses through a limited range. Invariably, this common error in technique is used to handle excessive weight. Since work is force through a distance, partial movements limit the work muscles do as well as their development through a functional range of motion. Be sure to contract your abdominals and pause the bar low on your shoulders at the bottom of the movement. By working slowly through the entire range, you'll maximize your shoulder flexibility and strength as well as your safety.

The posterior emphasis provided by the behind-the-neck press is a distinct advantage since most popular upper body exercises highlight the anterior deltoids. When you do shoulder work, emphasize behind-the-neck presses to help strengthen lagging posterior muscles and to balance your anterior development.

Which exercises are recommended for development of the neck, shoulder, and posterior arm muscles? Can you list the guidelines to follow when these exercises are performed in a standing position?

Lat Pull (8a)

Common Terminology for Muscles Exercised (1) Upper back, (2) chest, (3) back of shoulder, (4) front of arm, and (5) back of forearm.

Equivalent Anatomical Terminology (1a) Latissimus dorsi, (1b) teres major, (1c) rhomboid group (major and minor), (1d) trapezius (mainly middle fibers), (2) pectoral group (acts mainly as stabilizer), (3a) posterior deltoid, (3b) infraspinatus, (3c) teres minor, (4a) biceps brachii, (4b) brachialis, and (5) brachioradialis together with other forearm muscles.

Mini-Form Check (1) Kneel or sit directly beneath the bar, (2a) use a wide pronated *or* (2b) shoulder-width pronated *or* (2c) shoulder-width supinated handgrip on the bar, (3) focus eyes straight ahead, (4) contract abdominals and flatten back, (5) free plates from weight stack—don't let them touch while exercising, (6) stabilize body position—spotter or external support device may help, (7) fully extend elbows, (8a) smoothly pull bar behind head to point low on upper back to avoid neck (only wide pronated grip) *or* (8a, b, c) smoothly pull bar in front of head to point high on chest (all grips), (9) pause deliberately, (10) slowly return bar to starting position with elbows fully extended—avoid bouncing or jerking, (11) pause, (12) breathe continuously.

Exercise Description The "lat" or latissimus dorsi pull is an excellent multi-joint exercise that mainly develops upper back muscles. Although the pectoral (chest) muscles are activated during lat pulls and other climbing-type movements, they work mainly as stabilizers to balance the action of the latissimus dorsi. Lat pulls, like bent-over rows and pull-ups work posterior muscles that complement anterior muscles worked by the bench press.

You can do lat pulls by kneeling or sitting at a Universal, Nautilus, or similar station. As illustrated in figure 6.15a, at most lat stations you should be directly beneath the bar when you hold it so that the attached cable is perpendicular to the ground. (The Nautilus combination duo-torso arm II station is one of the few exceptions.)

By varying your handgrip, you can emphasize or de-emphasize specific back muscles. In figure 6.15 the subject is using a wide handgrip to place more stress on muscles in the middle part of his upper back (rhomboids and trapezius) and less stress on muscles in the lateral part of his upper back (latissimus dorsi). If you use a wide pronated handgrip, you can pull the bar either behind or in front of your head. You must pull the bar in front of your head to a point high on your chest when you use a shoulder-width grip, close grip, or supinated grip.

Make sure your shoestrings, shoes, warm-ups, and hair are clear of cables and weight stacks before you start exercising. Once you've freed the weights from the weight stack, stabilize your body with the aid of a spotter (or machine thigh-support pads, if available). Focus your eyes straight ahead, contract your abdominals, and fully extend your elbows. If you're using a wide (pronated) handgrip, slowly pull the bar to a position low on your shoulders to avoid hitting the back of your neck (fig. 6.15b). By pulling the bar in front of your head to a position high on your chest, you shift stresses more anteriorly (fig. 6.15c). Regardless of the grip or pull you use, be sure to touch the bar gently and pause it deliberately before you return to the starting position. Extend your elbows fully at the top of the movement, but don't let the plates touch the weight stack. You want to keep constant tension on your muscles throughout the range of motion. Remember to be kind to your joints. By pausing at the end of both the hard and easy parts, you'll reduce forces on your shoulder and elbow joints and limit the recruitment of extraneous muscles.

Important Areas to Warm Up General warm-up that includes controlled side stretches may be helpful (see appendix C, stretch 8), but specific warm-up is best for preventing injuries during the lat pull. Use shoulder shrugs (see appendix C, stretch 11) to loosen taut trapezius and rhomboid muscles. Light resistance movements on a rowing machine, as well as static pulling or hanging from a pull-up bar (with a spotter), may also help loosen stubborn lat muscles.

Spotting On a stationary machine, you can easily do lat pulls without the aid of a spotter, especially if the machine has an adjustable seat and thigh-support pads to help stabilize your body. However, it's nice to have a spotter when these support devices aren't available, particularly when you handle a resistance greater than or equal to your own body weight. If there are no spotters around, you can keep your body in a relatively stable position close to the floor by powerfully

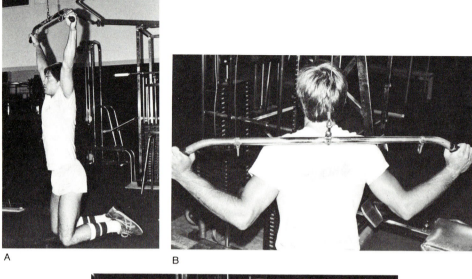

Figure 6.15
You can do latissimus dorsi pulls using different handgrips at a variety of stations. *A.* Start with your body directly beneath the bar so that the attached cable is perpendicular to the ground. If you use a wide handgrip you may choose to pull the bar either *B,* behind your head to a point low on your shoulders or *C,* in front of your head to a point high on your chest.

contracting your abdominal muscles. On some machines (e.g., Universal), you can further maximize your stability by carefully wrapping your legs around the lower portion of the machine beneath the weight stack. If you plan to do this (when no spotters are available), be sure to keep your hair, clothes, shoes, and shoe strings clear of the path of all plates and cables. Don't place heavy plates or dumbbells over your lower body to maintain your position. These can easily slip and induce injury.

If you are asked to spot someone for the lat pull, stand directly behind the trainee about one to two feet away. Hold the trainee down by placing your hands gently at the base of the neck and shoulders. Use lateral rather than medial pressure so as not to reduce circulation to the head and neck. If the lifter pulls the bar behind the head, watch out! The bar can easily come crashing down on your hands, wrists, or fingers. Protect your lower back by bending your knees and contracting your abdominals.

Contraindications Avoid this exercise if you have neck, back, shoulder, elbow, wrist, or hand injuries. Lat pulls may also aggravate strained chest muscles that are active during the first part of the movement.

Coaches' Corner The lat pull is a heavily abused exercise. The most common errors are (1) moving the bar rapidly through a partial range of motion, (2) jerking the bar at the bottom and/or top of the movement, and (3) bouncing up and down off the floor, while crashing the plates between repetitions. These abusive styles not only place tremendous stress on the elbows and shoulders, but also accelerate wear and tear of the machines.

As with any exercise, the form—not the weight—is critical. Use a light enough weight so that you can move the bar slowly and methodically through the full range of motion. Pause deliberately at both ends of the movement.

Contrary to what you may have heard, the best way to develop the lats is by using a shoulder-width rather than a wide handgrip. The latissimus dorsi is a powerful adductor and extensor of the arm. It's heavily activated in such movements as the downstroke of swimming, climbing, and hammering (Gardner, Gray & O'Rahilly 1975). When you use a pronated wide handgrip (as in fig. 6.15), you force the bottom angle of your shoulder blade toward the outside (i.e., abduct the inferior angle of your scapula). This puts the muscles in the middle of your upper back (the rhomboids and trapezius) on a greater stretch. In contrast, by using a pronated shoulder-width grip, you place more stress on the large, triangular-shaped latissimus dorsi muscles.

By pulling the bar in front of your head to a point high on your chest you place more stress on the pectoral muscles. When you use a supinated (palms up) grip, you work more of the frontal arm (biceps and brachialis) and less of the rear forearm (brachioradialis). By pulling the bar behind your head (pronated wide grip only) to a point low on the shoulders, you more heavily stress the back of the shoulders (posterior deltoid and infraspinatus) and the middle of your back (rhomboids and middle fibers of the trapezius).

If you are a beginner, make the lat pull your first choice of group 8 exercises in the Basic Dozen (lat pull/pull-up/bent-over row). Later, when you gain more upper body and lower back strength, you can include pull-ups and bent-over rows to add variety to your back routine.

Bent-over Row (8b)

Common Terminology for Muscles Exercised (1) Upper back, (2) back of shoulder, (3) front of arm, and (4) back of forearm.

Equivalent Anatomical Terminology (1a) Rhomboid group (major and minor), (1b) trapezius (middle and upper fibers), (1c) latissimus dorsi, (1d) teres major, (2a) posterior deltoid, (2b) infraspinatus, (2c) teres minor, (3a) biceps brachii, (3b) brachialis, and (4) brachioradialis together with other forearm muscles.

Mini-Form Check (1) Put feet, slightly wider than shoulders, directly beneath bar on floor, (2) grasp bar by using wide pronated grip with hands 4″–6″ wider than shoulders,(3) don't watch the bar—focus eyes straight ahead, (4) keep knees flexed at constant angle, (5) contract abdominals, (6) flatten back and stabilize near parallel to floor, (7) slowly pull bar in vertical line toward chest, (8) keep elbows high and away from side, (9) pause high on chest, (10) control return to starting position, (11) be kind to the joints, especially at bottom of movement, (12) breathe continuously.

Exercise Description The bent-over row is an excellent multi-joint exercise for developing upper back and posterior shoulder muscles. Compared to the lat pull and pull-up, the wide-grip bent-over row is the best exercise for working the posterior deltoids. It may help to imagine the bent-over row as being the exact inverse or complement to the bench press. The bench press develops the (1)"anterior" chest, (2) anterior shoulder, and (3) posterior arm, while the bent-over row works the (1) "posterior" back, (2) posterior shoulder, and (3) anterior arm.

To do bent-over rows, place your feet slightly wider than the width of your shoulders with toes about 1″–2″ away from the barbell. Grab the bar by using a pronated grip 4″–6″ wider than your shoulders. If your grip is correct, at the top of the movement your forearms should be perpendicular to the floor. (You can get a good idea of where to place your hands by doing the movement without weight.) Keep your knees at a constant angle and contract your abdominals to protect your lower back. Free the bar from the floor just enough so that your back, shoulder, and lat muscles are on stretch. To maximize the tension in your muscles, don't let the bar touch the floor throughout the rest of the exercise. Slowly move the bar in a perpendicular (*not circular*) motion from the floor to a point high on your chest. Pause the bar for a full second, then slowly return it to the starting position.

During the exercise, avoid bobbing your head up and down. Try to keep your back stabilized in a plane near parallel to the floor (fig. 6.16a, b). To increase stress on the posterior deltoids, keep your elbows away from your body and high above the floor (fig. 6.16b).

Important Areas to Warm Up Use general stretches to loosen upper and lower back muscles before you do bent-over rows (see appendix C, stretches 7, 8, 9, and 11). You may also choose to do low-intensity back extensions, rows, lat pulls, or pull-ups to further warm your muscles.

A

B

Figure 6.16

View the bent-over row as the exact inverse or complement to the bench press. *A.* Assume the starting position, free the bar from the floor. Be sure to keep knees bent to protect your lower back. *B.* Smoothly pull the bar from the floor through a perpendicular plane to a point high on your chest. Pause deliberately before you return to the starting position.

Spotting Since the bent-over row is quite safe to do yet difficult to spot, it's usually done without a spotter. For heavier lifts (which should be avoided by beginners due to increased low back stress), two spotters may stand on either side of the bar. As a spotter, you should assume a low squat position with your knees bent and abdominals contracted to protect your back. Clasp your hands together and track the bar during the movement.

Contraindications If you have a back, shoulder, elbow, wrist, or hand injury, check with a sports medicine specialist before you do bent-over rows. If you have low back syndrome and are conditionally cleared for participation, avoid bent-over rows as they may further aggravate your problem. Do lat pulls to fulfill your group 8 exercise requirement for the Basic Dozen.

Coaches' Corner The bent-over row is the best exercise for developing muscles that are antagonistic to those worked by the bench press. If you do this exercise as much as you do bench presses, you'll be virtually assured of achieving balanced development of your upper body.

As with most rowing movements, bent-over rows allow for a wide range of handgrips. When you use a relatively wide handgrip, you more heavily activate the rhomboids, trapezius (mainly the middle fibers), and posterior deltoids. By using a close handgrip (less than shoulder-width), you accentuate development of the latissimus dorsi. Since the posterior deltoids are often completely ignored in training programs, it's best to emphasize wide-grip rather than narrow-grip bent-over rows.

A major disadvantage of bent-over rows is the added stress they place on the vulnerable lower back region. Be sure to avoid this exercise if your lower back is a bit tender.

Don't put your forehead on a table or bench while performing bent-over rows; this could place your cervical spine in a precarious position. As with most exercises, it's best to stabilize your body by contracting your muscles rather than by using extraneous support devices.

The most common errors in bent-over rowing are (1) working through a limited range of motion, (2) failing to pause the bar high on the chest, and (3) jerking the weight from the floor to the chest by using the erector spinae muscles. By stabilizing your back, moving through the full range of motion, and pausing the bar high on your chest, you'll maximize your safety and strength gains.

Pull-up (8c)

Common Terminology for Muscles Exercised (1) Upper back, (2) chest, (3) back of shoulder, (4) front of arm, and (5) back of forearm.

Equivalent Anatomical Terminology (1a) Latissimus dorsi, (1b) teres major, (1c) rhomboid group (major and minor), (1d) trapezius (middle and lower fibers), (2) pectoralis major, (3a) posterior deltoid, (3b) teres minor, (3c) infraspinatus, (4a) biceps brachii, (4b) brachialis, (4c) coracobrachialis, and (5) brachioradialis along with other forearm muscles.

Mini-Form Check (1a) Grasp stable high bar with shoulder-width grip (pronated or supinated) *or* (1b) wide grip about 6″ outside shoulders (pronated only), (2) use spotter or stable bench to assume starting dead-hang position, (3) feet should not touch floor to allow for full elbow extension, (4a) slowly pull up so that chin is over bar and chest touches bar (wide pronated grip or shoulder-width pronated or supinated grip) *or* (4b) taking care to avoid neck, slowly pull up so that shoulders and upper back touch bar (wide pronated grip only), (5) don't kick up or thrust during concentric phase, (6) pause for a full second count, (7) slowly return to fully extended starting position, (8) pause deliberately and repeat, (9) be kind to the joints, especially at bottom of movement, (10) breathe continuously.

Exercise Description There are many muscles brought into play in a climbing movement like the pull-up. The pull-up is an excellent overall upper body exercise. It mainly works the primary adductors and extensors of the arm—the latissimus dorsi and teres major—which are fused together tightly at their tendons. Other major muscles worked by the pull-up common to the lat pull are the rhomboids, trapezius, biceps brachii, and brachialis. During the initial phases of the climbing action, the pull-up engages the pectoralis major more so than the lat pull. As with other group 8 exercises, the pull-up can be done with different handgrips to stress specific muscles.

Use a spotter, a sturdy platform, or a chair to assume the starting position. Start from a dead-hang position with your elbows fully extended and your eyes focused straight ahead (fig. 6.17a). Without swaying, thrusting, or jerking, pull your chest or upper back to the bar by extending your shoulders and flexing your elbows. Once you touch your chest or upper back to the bar, pause deliberately for a full second count (fig. 6.17b), then return slowly to the starting position (fig. 6.17a).

Important Areas to Warm Up General side and back stretches may help (see appendix C, stretches 8, 9, and 11), but specific low-resistance lat pulls and bent-over rows are best for warming up muscles prior to pull-ups.

Spotting If you are a beginner, have an instructor or experienced lifter spot you for pull-ups. Spotting for pull-ups requires substantial upper and lower body strength and is quite difficult, especially for larger persons. It may help to limit yourself to spotting those who weigh less than you do.

To spot for pull-ups, stand behind the trainee. Place your hands on the back of his or her waist and lift up to help the trainee assume the starting position. Don't let go until the lifter's hands are fully secured. You'll probably need to help the most during the very end of the concentric phase (this is the most difficult position to reach). Some spotters grab the feet or legs, but as with spotting dips, this may cause the trainee to fall forward into the bar.

Use your lower body to do the work in spotting. Try not to get too far underneath the trainee as this will force you to arch your back. Above all, be sure to bend your knees and contract your abdominals to protect your lower back.

A   B

Figure 6.17
The pull-up is an excellent multi-joint exercise for developing overall upper body strength. Use a spotter or have a platform nearby when you first try the exercise. *A.* Start with your elbows fully extended and your feet off the ground. A pronated, shoulder-width handgrip will accentuate development of your latissimus dorsi and teres major muscles. *B.* By totally relying on your upper body, pull through the hard part until your chin is high over the bar. Pause for a full 1–2-second count, then slowly return to the starting position (*A*).

Contraindications If you are a beginning weight trainer or happen to be carrying a few extra pounds, you may want to avoid pull-ups until you've developed enough upper body strength to handle your own body weight. Do lat pulls or bent-over rows to satisfy the requirements for group 8 of the Basic Dozen. If you've had a hand, wrist, elbow, shoulder, neck, back, or chest injury, check with a sports medicine specialist before you do pull-ups.

Coaches' Corner The most common mistake in doing pull-ups is failing to start from a dead-hang position before each repetition. Beginners often compensate for their lack of upper body strength by kicking, thrusting, or lunging during the hard part of the exercise or by limiting their range of motion. Be sure to move smoothly and to pause both at the top and bottom of the movement.

As with lat pulls and bent-over rows, pull-ups allow for handgrip variations. Use a pronated (palms down) hand position with either a wide or shoulder-width grip. By using a shoulder-width grip, you'll more fully tax the triangular latissimus dorsi together with its counterpart, the teres major. If you pull your chest to the bar, you'll more heavily engage the pectoral muscles, which are important in climbing activities. When you use a wide grip, you have the option of pulling either your chest or shoulders to the bar. By touching the bar low on your shoulders, you'll shift the stress more to the posterior deltoid, infraspinatus, and teres minor muscles. Be sure to use a supinated (palms up) hand position only with a narrow, shoulder-width grip. This type of grip places more stress on muscles of the anterior arm (the biceps, brachialis, and coracobrachialis), but less on those of the posterior forearm (the brachioradialis).

How does varying the handgrip affect muscles that are stressed during the lat pull, bent-over row, and pull-up?

Triceps Extension (9)

Common Terminology for Muscles Exercised (1) Back of arm and (2) front and back of forearm.

Equivalent Anatomical Terminology (1) Triceps brachii (medial, lateral, and long heads), (2a) selected superficial and deep anterior forearm muscles, and (2b) the aconeus, a posterior forearm muscle.

Mini-Form Check (1a) Stand facing lat bar with feet slightly wider than shoulders (if lat station) *or* (1b) lie down on floor with head about 3″–4″ from center of bar and feet slightly wider than shoulders (if supine position with free weight), (2) bend knees, (3) contract abdominals and flatten back, (4) focus eyes straight ahead, (5) grasp bar using pronated, two-thumbs' distance grip, (6a) push bar to starting position (if lat station) *or* (6b) with aid of spotter, move bar directly overhead and lock elbows (if supine position with free weight), (7a) pin elbows to front of abdominals (if lat station) *or* (7b) force elbows inside and keep arms stable and perpendicular to floor (if supine position with free weight), (8a) position bar so forearms are slightly beyond parallel to ground (if lat station) *or* (8b) carefully lower bar toward head with help of spotter (if supine position with free bar), (9) pause, (10) smoothly press bar until elbows are fully extended, (11) gradually return through eccentric phase, (12) breathe continuously.

Exercise Description Free-weight triceps extensions are difficult to master. If you're a beginner, try your first triceps extensions at a Universal lat or similar station. The cables, chains, and cams on stationary devices will keep you on the right track as you practice your first movements. Once you've had considerable practice on a stationary machine, try doing triceps extensions with barbells or dumbbells. We'll look at both machine and free-weight forms of the exercise in this section.

To do the exercise at a lat station, stand facing the bar about one to one and one-half feet away. Grasp the bar by using a pronated, two-thumbs' distance grip similar to that used for the upright row. Use the lat and teres major muscles to pull the bar down to the starting position (from figure 6.18a to b). Pin your elbows

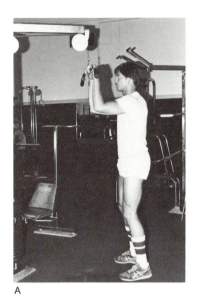

A

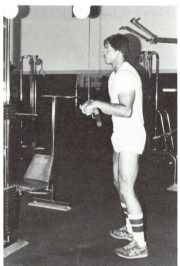

B

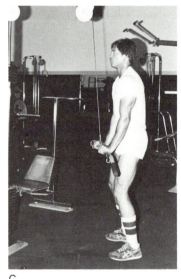

C

Figure 6.18

For your own safety, try your first few sets of triceps extensions at a Universal lat or similar station before doing them in a supine position with free weights. *A.* Get set for the starting position by using a "two-thumbs" distance, pronated grip. *B.* Pin your elbows to the front of your abdominals and focus your eyes straight ahead. Bend your knees and contract your abdominals to protect your lower back. *C.* Keep your arms perpendicular to the floor as you fully extend your elbows.

to the front sides of your waist. Once secured, your elbows and arms shouldn't move. Only your forearms and hands should move during the exercise. Bend your knees and contract your abdominals to protect your lower back. Smoothly press the bar down toward the floor by fully extending your elbows (from figure 6.18b to c). Pause for a full second, then slowly return the bar to the starting position (from figure 6.18c to b). If you let the bar travel too fast, your elbows will move up and away from your sides (fig. 6.18a). To return the bar to the original position (fig. 6.18b), you must again recruit the lat and teres muscles. This decreases the work done by the medial and lateral heads of the triceps. Flex your wrists slightly as you approach the top of the movement (fig. 6.18b), and extend them as you approach the bottom (fig. 6.18c). By doing this, you'll work your muscles through a greater range.

After you've practiced at a lat station, try doing triceps extensions in a supine position with a barbell (fig. 6.19). Be sure to have a spotter help you. Lie down on the floor so that the top of your head is about 3″–4″ from the center of a bar (fig. 6.19a). Grasp the bar by using a two-thumbs distance pronated grip like the one you used to work the triceps at the lat station. To make sure you've gripped the center of the bar, check the relative position of the knurling marks (on most bars) or the distance of your hands from the plates on either side. Have your spotter verify that your hands are equidistant from the center of the bar.

Your feet should be slightly wider than your shoulders to provide for good stability. Contract your abdominals, flatten your back, and keep your knees constantly flexed to protect your lower back. With the spotter guiding you, pull the bar over your head until it's directly over your shoulders. In this starting position, your elbows should be locked and your forearms and arms perpendicular to the ground (fig. 6.19b). Inhale as you carefully and slowly lower the bar toward your forehead (fig. 6.19c). After you pause deliberately, exhale while fully extending your elbows to return to the starting position (fig. 6.19b).

Avoid bouncing at the bottom or popping at the top of the movement—be kind to your joints. Although it's difficult to do, keep your arms perpendicular and allow only your forearms to move. If your arms do move, you diffuse the stress to muscles other than the triceps. Concentrate on forcing your elbows together, especially during the hard part of the exercise. If your elbows move laterally, your chest and shoulder muscles help reduce stress on the triceps. If you have problems stabilizing your arms, ask your spotter to hold the outside of your elbows while you exercise.

Important Areas to Warm Up The elbow joint is vulnerable during triceps movements. General triceps and shoulder stretches help reduce the risk of injury (see appendix C, stretch 10). It helps to prewarm your muscles by doing multi-joint exercises (e.g., military press, bench press, or push-up) before moving on to isolated triceps work. Light to moderate, specific warm-up sets are most beneficial.

Spotting A spotter is not usually needed for persons doing triceps extensions at lat or similar stations. However, when you are first trying the movement, a spotter

A

B

C

Figure 6.19

The triceps extension is the most difficult and dangerous when performed from a supine position. To protect yourself, always use a spotter. Supine movements generally place more stress on shoulder and elbow joints. *A.* Focus your eyes above and position your hands using a two-thumbs' distance grip. *B.* Keep feet planted, abdominals contracted, and knees bent to protect your lower back. Your arms and forearms should be perpendicular to the floor in the starting position. *C.* Carefully lower the bar toward your forehead as you force your elbows inside. The spotter has been omitted for clarity.

can pin your elbows to the front of your waist and can help guide you through the range of motion. Always have a spotter when performing supine triceps extensions with free weights.

To spot for supine triceps extensions, stand about a foot from the trainee's head. Assume a low squatting position with the abdominals contracted to protect your lower back. Using a shoulder-width pronated grip, pick up the bar and guide the trainee to the starting position (from figure 6.19a to b). Don't release the bar until the trainee's elbows are fully locked and you're given an "OK." Hold the outside of the trainee's elbows so that your forearms are beneath the bar. If the lifter loses control, your forearms will stop the bar on its path toward the lifter's head. You can also use your forearms like levers to help the trainee during the hard part of the exercise.

Contraindications Triceps extensions can easily aggravate wrist, elbow, or shoulder injuries. Elbow and shoulder injuries are most vulnerable during the supine form of the exercise. If you have a shoulder or elbow injury and are conditionally cleared for weight training, you may be able to tolerate standing triceps extensions at a lat station. When in doubt, check with a sports medicine professional before you do this exercise.

Coaches' Corner The biggest problem with this exercise is inability to isolate the triceps because the elbows and arms aren't stabilized. Many lifters try swinging the lat bar or crouching over it to gain a mechanical advantage for handling excessive weight. When "cheating" like this is used, muscles besides the triceps are recruited. It's critical to force your elbows inside and stabilize your arms throughout the exercise.

It's preferable to do supine triceps extensions on the floor rather than on a bench. When exercising on the floor, you can easily secure the bar by putting it directly over your head (onto the floor) without placing undue strain on your shoulder joints. You are also in position that's more stable and more conducive for flexing your hips and knees to reduce low back stress.

You can use a variety of devices to work the triceps, including dumbbells, E-Z curl bars, and special machines. Regardless of the device you use, remember to (1) fix your elbow axes to more fully isolate the triceps and limit extraneous muscle activity, and (2) work in a slow, controlled fashion to reduce joint forces and maximize intramuscular tension.

Biceps Curl (10)

Common Terminology for Muscles Exercised (1) Front of arm and (2) front and back of forearm.

Equivalent Anatomical Terminology (1a) Biceps brachii, (1b) brachialis, (2a) superficial anterior forearm muscles, and (2b) the brachioradialis, a posterior forearm muscle.

Mini-Form Check (1) Stand facing bar with feet a bit wider than shoulders, (2) squat down and grasp bar with supinated grip, narrower than shoulder width, (3) stand up by using hips, thighs, and legs instead of lower back, (4) pin elbows to front sides of abdominals, (5) focus eyes straight ahead, (6) contract abdominals and flatten back, (7) bend knees, (8) fully extend elbows in starting position, (9) smoothly curl barbell until elbows are fully flexed, (10) pause deliberately, (11) gradually return to starting position, (12) be kind to joints, especially at bottom of movement, (13) breathe continuously.

Exercise Description Although there are many variations, the standard biceps curl is the best exercise for anterior arm development. It activates the brachialis, a deep anterior arm muscle, and the biceps brachii, the two-headed muscle that lies above the brachialis.

Grasp a bar by using a supinated (palms-up) grip so that your hands are slightly closer than the width of your shoulders. Lift the bar from the floor by relying on your hips, thighs, and legs rather than your lower back (see chapter 2, Use Lower Body Muscles in Lifting, and fig. 2.5). To provide for good stability, focus your eyes straight ahead and keep feet slightly wider than your shoulders. Contract your abdominals and bend your knees to protect your lower back. Fully extend your elbows and pin them directly over the outside of the abdominals (fig. 6.20a). Keep your elbows in this position throughout the exercise. If they move, you'll diffuse the tension away from the biceps and brachialis to other muscles (e.g., the coracobrachialis and anterior deltoid). Once you are stabilized, slowly curl the bar toward your chest by flexing your elbows (fig. 6.20b). Keep your back in a rigid, perpendicular position relative to the floor. Thrusting your hips forward, swaying, or arching your back will increase your risk of low back injury. Pause at the top of the movement, then slowly return the bar to the starting position (fig. 6.20a).

Important Areas to Warm Up In weight training, anterior arm muscle pulls aren't that common. However, if you forcefully hyperextend during biceps curls, you may end up with extremely sore brachioradialis and biceps tendons. Specific warm-up is by far the best, especially when you plan to do curls using a Scott curl or other inclined board. Do multi-joint movements that use the biceps (e.g., lat pull, bent-over row, pull-up) before you do isolated biceps work to ensure that your muscles are adequately warmed.

Spotting If you are asked to spot for curls, stand facing the lifter about two feet away. The lifter may need help completing the last few repetitions of a set. Press lightly from beneath the bar with your hands in a supinated position. At the end of an exhaustive set, help the lifter return the bar to the floor or rack.

Contraindications If you've had an elbow or wrist injury, especially a hyperextension injury, consult a sports medicine specialist before performing this exercise. Sometimes shoulder injuries are aggravated by biceps curls. In many of these cases, the culprit is the tendon of the long head of the biceps. This tendon

A   B

Figure 6.20
The biceps curl is the best exercise for anterior arm development. *A.* Use a relatively narrow supinated handgrip with hands about 6–8 inches apart. Position feet slightly wider than shoulders, focus eyes straight ahead, contract abdominals, and bend knees to protect your lower back. By pinning elbows to the front of your abdominals, you'll make it easier to extend your elbows and tax your muscles more fully throughout the range of motion. *B.* As you exhale, only your forearms should move through the concentric phase.

crosses the shoulder joint and is quite susceptible to tendinitis when it's repeatedly stressed. If you have bicipital tendinitis avoid biceps curls and ice the inflamed area. Consult an athletic trainer, physical therapist, or sports medicine physician before you resume training.

Coaches' Corner The biceps curl is another abused exercise. Common mistakes include (1) thrusting the hips forward or arching the back to accommodate for excessive weight, (2) dropping rather than controlling the weight during the eccentric phase, and (3) working through a limited range. Remember to make form, not weight, a top priority. Reduce the resistance until your technique is perfected. Strict technique will make a world of difference.

Back Extension (11)

Common Terminology for Muscles Exercised (1) Lower back, (2) hip, and (3) back of thigh.

Equivalent Anatomical Terminology (1) Erector spinae, (2) gluteal group, and (3) hamstring group.

Mini-Form Check (1) Adjust support pads to accommodate for lower extremity length, (2) assume prone position by securing ankles beneath ankle-support pads, (3) align hip axis of rotation with edge of hip-support pad, (4) clasp hands lightly behind head, (5) slowly flex hips to lower trunk to starting position, (6) slowly extend hips to raise trunk until parallel to floor, (7) pause and repeat movement without jerking at any point through range of motion, (8) breathe continuously.

Exercise Description It's often said that the lower back is the weak link in many exercises, including the squat, dead lift, clean and jerk, snatch, and military press. Unless you do preventative exercises like the back extension, chances are you'll injure your lower back in weight training. Together with strengthening the abdominals and improving your hip flexor and hamstring flexibility, by doing back extensions you'll be virtually assured of having a healthy lower back. You'll also notice that you've eliminated your weak link and improved your functional strength for a variety of activities.

You can include back extensions with abdominal work as a part of your warm-up routine (see appendix C, exercises 6 and 7). If you are a beginner, start by doing back partial extensions on the floor. After you've developed more back strength, try full-range back extensions on a table or stationary machine.

Before you do back extensions on a circuit-type machine, adjust and secure the support pads according to the length of your lower body. (Unfortunately, some older machines don't have adjustable support pads.) Your ankles should fit directly beneath the ankle-support pads and your hips should rest in a comfortable position on the pelvic-support pad (fig. 6.21). Your alignment is correct when you feel stable and comfortable and your hip flexion (fig. 6.21a) and extension (fig. 6.21b) are not limited.

Clasp your hands behind your head and slowly flex the hips to lower your trunk to the starting position (fig. 6.21a). Pause briefly to relax and breathe normally. Slowly extend your hips, lifting your upper body slightly beyond parallel to the floor (fig. 6.21b). After a deliberate pause, carefully return to the starting position by flexing your hips to lower your trunk (fig. 6.21a). To protect your lower back, avoid ballistic movements and do all repetitions in a controlled and methodical fashion. Stop exercising if you feel a sharp pain or burning sensation in your lower back, hips, thighs, legs, or feet.

Don't use resistance until you can do two to three unweighted sets of 15–20 repetitions. Using added weight can be quite risky. You have the option of carefully positioning a dumbbell or plate directly behind your head or in front of your head close to your chest. In either case, be sure to grasp the weight securely. If the weight is behind your head, take care to avoid stressing the cervical vertebrae. If the weight is at your chest, secure it tightly, especially during the hip flexion phase (see fig 6.21a), to prevent it from sliding and injuring your chin or face.

A

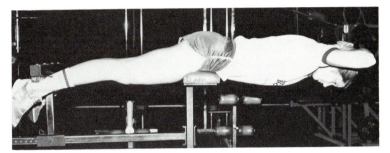

B

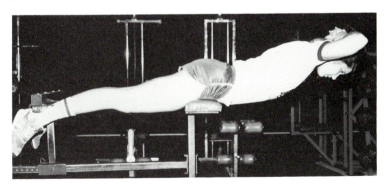

C

Figure 6.21

Provided you're fully cleared, you can use the back extension to significantly increase lower back strength. *A.* After you adjust the support pads according to your lower body length, assume a prone starting position with trunk flexed and hands clasped behind your head. Your hip axis of rotation should be directly over the body-support pad. *B.* Slowly move your upper body to a position slightly beyond parallel, pause, then carefully return to the original position (*A*). *C.* If your lower back is strong and healthy you can move a bit beyond parallel as long as you move in a slow, controlled way.

Important Areas to Warm Up Lower back and abdominal warm-up and strengthening exercises are described in appendix C (see exercises 6 and 7). If you are fully cleared, do these along with hip and thigh stretches before performing back extensions (see appendix C, stretches 1, 2, 4, and 5). Be sure to do specific warm-up prior to resistance sets.

Spotting If a back extension station is not available, a single spotter may secure your lower body while you exercise on a table or other support device.

If you are asked to spot someone for back extensions, secure the trainee's lower body by firmly pressing down on his or her ankles. You may also carefully sit down or rest your upper body on the trainee's legs.

Contraindications Back extensions and abdominal curl-ups are often used in rehabilitation programs. However, if you've had neck, back, sciatic nerve, hip, or other lower body problems, check with a sports medicine physician before you do back extensions.

Coaches' Corner The lower back is particularly vulnerable to injury because it's the only supportive structure linking the upper and lower body (Alexander 1985). By progressing through a series of safe exercises designed to strengthen lower back and abdominal muscles you can avoid injury.

If you're a bit heavy or have a weak lower back, be sure to start out by doing exercises from the floor (see appendix C, exercises 6 and 7). If you have normal back strength, do one to two sets of low- repetition (5–8) back extensions during your two to three week accommodation period. At first, go just to parallel to minimize stresses on your lumbar spine (fig. 6.21b). After you increase your strength, you can go slightly beyond parallel provided that you move slowly (fig. 6.21c).

After your accommodation period, do two to three sets of 10–15 reps of back extensions. Be sure you can handle your own body weight easily before you add resistance.

When a back extension station is not available, all you need is a spotter and a solid table or bench. You can create a back extension station by positioning a table beneath an adjustable bar on a power/squat rack.

Avoid "good mornings" (forward bends or hip flexions with straight knees) or "straight-legged" dead lifts; these exercises place undue stress on the ligaments and disks in the lower spine (Gardner, Gray & O'Rahilly, 1975). Develop considerable back strength before you attempt power cleans, clean and jerks, or snatches (appendix G). Jesse (1977) recommends that no athlete be permitted to engage in hyperextension exercises or lift greater than 40% of their body weight overhead until they've done forward flexion, rotation, and lateral flexion exercises for spinal muscles for a full year.

Athletes who participate in gymnastics, weight lifting, and football have the greatest risk of low back injury (Alexander 1985). Most back injuries occur when an underdeveloped, unprepared, or overloaded spine is subjected to a sudden violent extension, especially when rotation is also involved (Cantu 1980). One of the primary causes of low back pain in athletes is failure to develop strength and flexibility in rotational muscles of the lower back and abdomen (Allman 1982). Multiplanar movements that emphasize rotation, along with the body acting as its own stabilizer, may be quite helpful in preventing and rehabilitating back injuries (Jesse 1977; Saudek & Palmer 1987).

Like most other weight training exercises, the standard back extension works muscles in a single plane. If you want to improve your midsection strength for athletics, do controlled, twisting back extensions and sit-ups.

Sit-up (12)

Common Terminology for Muscles Exercised (1) Abdominal and (2) hip flexor.

Equivalent Anatomical Terminology (1a) Rectus abdominis, (1b) external oblique, (1c) internal oblique, (2a) iliopsoas, (2b) rectus femoris, and (2c) sartorius.

Mini-Form Check (1a) Lie down on floor with feet unanchored *or* (1b) adjust and secure inclined board in lowest position for anchored curl-ups or sit-ups and place feet beneath support pads, (2) keep knees at constant 110° flexion throughout exercise, (3) place hands at waist, (4) pin chin to chest, (5) curl up in slow, methodical fashion, (6) pause when trunk reaches about 45°, (7) slowly return to starting position, (8) breathe continuously.

Exercise Description Even though the sit-up is the traditional exercise for abdominal development, it's often performed incorrectly. Results obtained from electromyographical (EMG) studies during the 1950s and 1960s indicated that the greatest abdominal muscle activity was during the initial 30°–45°. During the rest of a sit-up, the hip flexors are heavily activated. Hip flexor activity increases when the knees are straightened. This places greater stress on the lower back and less stress on the abdominal muscles. The best way to do sit-ups is with the feet unanchored and the knees at a constant angle of 110°.

Do sit-ups by curling up or gradually flexing your spine rather than by arching or flattening your lower back. If your back is flat or arched, hip flexors provide the major thrust during the movement. Lie on the floor with your hands at your waist, your feet planted but unanchored, and your knees at 110° (fig. 6.22a). Put your chin on your chest and slowly curl up until your trunk reaches a 30°–45° angle above the floor (fig. 6.22b). Your trunk will reach this angle just after your scapulae (shoulder blades) leave the floor. If you flex your trunk beyond 30°–45°, you'll heavily recruit the iliopsoas muscles (fig. 6.22c). Pause deliberately, then slowly return to the starting position (fig. 6.22a).

Important Areas to Warm Up It's nice to include low back and abdominal exercises in your general warm-up routine (see appendix C, exercises 6 and 7). This helps to prewarm your midsection before you move on to more taxing movements. Do controlled side-bends or twisting-type exercises to help loosen stubborn external and internal obliques (see appendix C, stretch 8). When you do twisting movements, be sure to keep your knees slightly flexed to reduce the stress on your

A

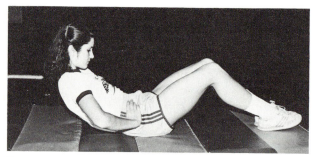

B

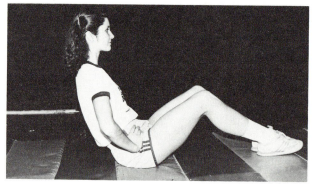

C

Figure 6.22

Even though the sit-up is the standard exercise for abdominal development, it is often performed incorrectly. *A.* The best way to strengthen your abdominals is by keeping your feet unanchored in the starting position. You may place your hands at your waist or by your side to further decrease upper body resistance. *B.* Your abdominal muscles work only up to the point where your trunk reaches about 30°–45°. *C.* Beyond this point the hip flexors are largely activated.

lower back. If you plan to use resistance to work the abdominals, warm up specifically by doing one to two sets of high-repetition curl-ups or other light abdominal exercises.

Spotting You can do sit-ups safely without a spotter. However, if you have limited abdominal strength, you can spot yourself by pulling with your hands on the back of your thighs during the hard part of the exercise. Try to develop abdominal strength by doing pelvic tilts before moving on to abdominal curl-ups (see appendix C, exercises 6a and b).

Contraindications If you've had a low back injury, hernia, or recent abdominal surgery, you should avoid sit-ups or curl ups until you are cleared by a sports medicine physician. Unlike pelvic tilts, sit-ups aggravate minor neck muscle pulls. When in doubt, check with a sports medicine specialist before doing abdominal work.

Coaches' Corner Sit-ups with straight knees place the iliopsoas, rectus femoris, and sartorius muscles on stretch, causing them to be more active than when the knees are bent and maintained at a constant angle of 110°. Thus, if you do straight-knee sit-ups, the iliopsoas muscles tug on your spinal column and place more stress on your lower back and less on your abdominals (see chapter 2, fig. 2.6).

When you anchor your feet, your legs and thighs are more stable and the hip flexors rather than the abdominals initiate the movement. When your feet aren't anchored, the hip extensors fire to keep your lower body stabilized on the floor. The contraction of the hip extensors causes reciprocal inhibition of the hip flexors (iliopsoas, rectus femoris, and sartorius), which maximizes the work done by the abdominals (see chapter 4, Reciprocal Innervation, and fig. 4.8). The lower rectus abdominis muscles are more active when your feet are anchored; the upper rectus muscles are more active when your feet aren't anchored.

Even though your feet may be unanchored and your knees bent (110°), it's difficult (if not impossible) to perform a full-range sit-up without using the iliopsoas. These muscles are very active during the midrange and at both ends of the exercise. Abdominal muscles are most active during the first 45° of the movement (Flint & Gudgell 1965; LaBan, Raptou & Johnson 1965). Thus, curl-ups or partial sit-ups are all that you really need to do to strengthen your abdominals.

To isolate the external and internal obliques and other important rotational muscles, you can do a variety of twisting and side-bend exercises (fig. 6.23 and appendix C, exercise 8). Make sure that your hips are stable and that you move slowly.

As we mentioned previously, most weight training exercises work in a single plane. By doing rotary-type sit-ups and back extensions, you'll develop strength needed to reduce the risk of back injury. These exercises are especially important if you are involved in sports.

What has research told us about the most effective way to perform sit-ups? Why is it undesirable to anchor your feet?

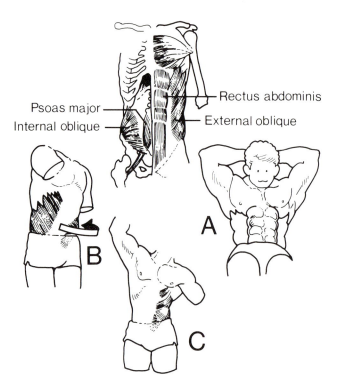

Figure 6.23

A. By doing sit-ups or curl-ups, you primarily work the rectus abdominis muscles. You also work the external and internal obliques. Flexion is accomplished when your paired muscles contract together or bilaterally. To more fully isolate the external and internal obliques, do slow, controlled twisting movements (*B*) or side bends (*C*). *B.* Trunk rotation from right to left is made possible by contracting parallel fibers of your right external and left internal oblique. Muscles on opposite sides of the body are said to be contralateral. *C.* When you do side bends, you flex your trunk laterally. To do this, the obliques, psoas major, and other muscles on the same side must contract together. Muscles on the same side are termed ipsilateral.

Summary

Sound weight training programs are based on partitioning the body into the following symmetrical regions: (1) lower extremity (hip, thigh, and leg), (2) chest, (3) shoulder, (4) back (upper and lower), (5) arm, (6) forearm, (7) neck, and (8) abdominal. The Basic Dozen are twelve groups of complementary exercises that work each of these areas. Beginning, intermediate, and advanced programs are derived from these twelve groups of fundamental movements. A program designed to achieve balanced development includes at least one exercise from each category of the Basic Dozen.

Persons with current or previous injuries should consult sports medicine specialists before they engage in weight training. Generally, fully cleared beginners should do three sets of 8–12 repetitions from each category of the Basic Dozen. Relatively light weights should be used during an initial two- to three-week accommodation period. Exercises should be done in a slow, methodical fashion through the full range of motion to maximize intramuscular tension as well as safety. Bouncing, jerking, and other extraneous movements should be avoided. A spotter should be present to help those who perform free-weight movements.

The squat is the primary exercise for developing the lower body. It works the hips, thighs, and lower back. Alternatives to the squat include the front squat and leg press. Following medical clearance, those with previous low back injuries may be able to tolerate leg presses because of added back support.

The leg extension, leg curl, and lunge are polish or refinement exercises for the lower body. The leg extension develops the anterior thigh whereas the leg curl works on the posterior thigh. The lunge develops the hips, thighs, and legs. The lunge is a good alternative exercise for both the leg extension and leg curl. It is especially valuable when leg extension–leg curl machines are heavily used or unavailable.

The straight-knee calf raise works the gastrocnemius, which crosses the knee joint. In contrast, the bent-knee calf raise engages the soleus, which doesn't cross the knee joint and lies deep to the gastrocnemius.

The bench press is the pillar of strength multi-joint exercise for the upper body. It develops the chest, anterior shoulder, and posterior arm. The chest can be taxed more fully by using a wide grip and keeping the elbows directly beneath the bar. The chest fly uses chest and anterior shoulder muscles and is a good alternative or supplement to the bench press.

The upright row and parallel dip are excellent multi-joint movements. The upright row works shoulder, anterior arm, and neck muscles, whereas the dip works shoulder, posterior arm, and chest muscles. Clinically obese trainees or those with limited upper body strength are encouraged to perform the upright row. Negative resistance dip movements, triceps extensions, and bench presses may be used to increase strength for dipping.

Military and behind-the-neck presses are used to develop shoulder, neck, and posterior arm muscles. These may be performed from a seated or standing position. Lifters should use the hips, thighs, and legs rather than the lower back in cleaning a weight from the floor. During all standing exercises (1) the feet should be placed slightly wider than the shoulders, (2) the eyes are focused on a point straight ahead to maintain balance, and (3) the abdominals are contracted, the back is flattened, and knees are flexed at a constant angle to protect the lower back.

The lat pull, bent-over row, and pull-up are used for upper back and shoulder development. The lat pull is the exercise of choice for obese beginners or those who've had low back problems. The bent-over row is best for developing rear shoulder muscles and other muscles that complement those worked by the bench press. The pull-up is an excellent body-resistive exercise but is difficult for beginners. A shoulder-width grip is ideal for developing latissimus dorsi and teres major muscles.

The triceps extension may be done from a standing position by using a lat station or from a supine position by using a free-weight, dumbbell, or appropriate cable device. Conditionally cleared persons with elbow problems can often tolerate the standing but not the supine version of this movement. Like the standing triceps extension, the biceps curl should be done with the elbows pinned to the front of the abdominals.

The back extension and sit-up are complementary exercises that can be incorporated into warm-up. Beginners or conditionally cleared persons should first do back exercises from the floor. The best way to develop abdominal strength is by curling up to 45° with the feet unanchored and the knees flexed at about 110°.

Most weight training exercises work muscles in a single plane. The risk of low back injury may be reduced by doing multiplanar exercises that emphasize strength and flexibility of rotational muscles in the lower back and abdomen.

Medical Screening   Appendix A

Last Name First Middle	Address

Date of birth	Social security number	Home telephone	Business telephone

Current job title	Date	Signature

I. Family history
  A. Please indicate if any of your blood relatives have had the following:
    1. Heart disease (heart attack, angina, rhythm disorder, heart surgery)   Yes   No
    2. Hypertension (high blood pressure)   Yes   No
    3. Stroke   Yes   No
    4. Diabetes   Yes   No
    5. Arthritis/gout   Yes   No
    6. Epilepsy/seizure disorder   Yes   No
    7. Neuromuscular disorder   Yes   No
II. Past medical history
  A. List all serious **illnesses** you have had in your life:

  B. List all serious **injuries** you have had in your life:

  C. List all **hospitalizations** you have had in your life:

  D. Please indicate if you have ever had any of the following:
    1. Back injury or strain lasting more than a day or two   Yes   No
    2. Concussion or other serious head injury   Yes   No
    3. Broken bones   Yes   No
    4. Severe sprains of neck, shoulder, elbow, wrist, hip, knee, or ankle   Yes   No
    5. Arthritis/gout   Yes   No
    6. Any other serious diseases of the bones, muscles, or joints   Yes   No
    7. Hernia   Yes   No
    8. Heart disease/rheumatic fever   Yes   No
    9. Hypertension (high blood pressure)   Yes   No
    10. Diabetes   Yes   No
    11. Thyroid or other hormonal or metabolic problems   Yes   No
    12. Liver disease/disorder   Yes   No
    13. Kidney disease/disorder   Yes   No
    14. Allergies/asthma   Yes   No
    15. Collapsed lung   Yes   No
    16. Any other unusual lung or chest disorder   Yes   No
    17. Any unusual disease of the nervous system   Yes   No

E. Have you had any recent illnesses? If yes, please explain. Yes No

F. Are you taking any medications, vitamins, tonics, etc? If yes, please explain. Yes No

G. Have you ever smoked cigarettes? Yes No
Do you smoke now? Yes No
If yes, how many cigarettes per day?
If you have quit, when did you stop?
How many years did you smoke over a pack a day?

H. Are you a regular exerciser? Yes No
If yes, how many days do you exercise per week?
Briefly describe your exercise program.

I. Do you drink coffee? Yes No
If yes, how many cups per day?

III. Current history
A. Please indicate if you now have any of the following:
1. Frequent headaches Yes No
2. Migraine attacks Yes No
3. Dizziness (light-headedness) Yes No
4. Chronic or smoker's cough Yes No
5. Frequent heavy chest colds Yes No
6. Chest pain when breathing Yes No
7. Wheezing/asthma Yes No
8. Coughing up blood Yes No
9. Raising of sputum or phlegm daily Yes No
10. Pneumonia, pleurisy, or tuberculosis Yes No
11. Recent close association with a case of active tuberculosis Yes No
12. More shortness of breath than others your age on exertion/ activity Yes No
13. Hypertension (high blood pressure) Yes No
14. Heart trouble/heart murmur Yes No
15. Tightness, pain, heaviness, squeezing, or pressure around chest Yes No
16. Fast, racing, or irregular pulse Yes No
17. Palpitations, skipped heart beats, fluttering, or pounding in chest Yes No
18. Swelling of feet, ankles, or legs Yes No
19. Trouble breathing when lying flat Yes No
20. Fainting spells or unconsciousness Yes No
21. Convulsions or treatment for epilepsy Yes No
22. Paralysis or weakness of muscles Yes No
23. Numbness, tingling, or "pins and needles" of hands, feet, arms, or legs Yes No
24. Shaking, tremors, or trembling of hands Yes No
25. Difficulty in walking or keeping your balance Yes No

IV. Physician's section
   A. Patient's status (check one)
      1. Not cleared for participation in weight training
      2. Conditionally cleared for participation in weight training
      3. Fully cleared for participation in weight training
   B. Contraindications

   C. Additional Comments

_____

(Physician's signature)

Developed by John Thomas Redfield, M.D., Occupational Medicine

Waiver Form   Appendix B

I, the undersigned, hereby agree that I shall indemnify and hold _____ (insert name of university, institution, company, or club) and their agents, officers, and employees, harmless from any and all injuries while participating in _____ (insert name of course, activity, program, or contest). I understand that there are certain physical hazards involved in the above stated _____ (insert course, activity, program, or contest) and I agree to assume the risks thereof. I also agree that I have been informed as to the availability of _____ (insert student, employee, or group) health insurance that may be purchased. I know that if I wish additional accident insurance coverage for said _____ (insert course, activity, program, or contest) that I have the responsibility of procuring it myself.

I hereby waive personally any and all claims of every kind, nature, and description that I might otherwise assert against _____ (insert name of university, institution, company, or club), its officers, employees, and agents, arising out of or in any manner connected with the said _____ (insert course, activity, program, or contest).

Dated this _____ day of _____ , 19 _____ .

_____	_____
Name of Participant	Signature
_____	_____
Address	Phone
_____	_____
Name of Witness	Signature
_____	_____
Address	Phone

Basic Dozen Warm-up/Cool-down Routine

Appendix C

Like the beginning weight training exercises, the Basic Dozen Warm-up/Cool-down routine proceeds from larger to smaller muscle groups (Figure C 1). Larger, lower body muscles are stretched first to help enhance overall blood flow. To reduce low back stress each lower body stretch may be done from the floor (stretches 1–5). Abdominal and low back movements (stretches 6 and 7) provide a smooth transition between lower body stretches done from the floor and upper body stretches done in a standing position just prior to exercise.

Before you stretch, start out by walking, jogging, or cycling lightly for 5–10 minutes. When doing a standing stretch, remember to bend your knees, contract your abdominals, and flatten your back. Most of the standing stretches can also be done from a seated position (stretches 5, 9, 10, 11, and 12). Repeat individual stretches more than once to warm up particularly stubborn muscles. Following moderate to intense exercise, cool down by doing a light aerobic activity for 5–10 minutes, then do the Basic Dozen stretches. This will help minimize pooling of blood and delayed muscle soreness.

Once you've been at it for a while, you can improve your flexibility further by doing stretches in the morning (to help you get going) and in the evening (to help you relax). Remember, as always, consistency is the key!

Lower Body Stretches

Hip and Back Stretch (1)

Common Terminology for Muscles Stretched (1) Hip, (2) outer thigh, (3) lower back, and (4) outer abdominal.

Equivalent Anatomical Terminology (1a) Gluteal group, (1b) tensor fasciae latae, (2) vastus lateralis, (3) erector spinae (sacrospinalis), (4a) external oblique, and (4b) internal oblique.

Mini-Form Check (1) Lie down on floor, (2) place feet shoulder width on floor, (3) keep knees flexed at 110°, (4) contract abdominals, (5) flatten back, (6) keep head down, neck relaxed and eyes above, (7) place right thigh over left, (8) let weight of right thigh slowly carry left thigh toward ground, (9) keep hips and shoulders square, (10) pause for 20–30 seconds, (11) relax and breathe continuously, (12) slowly return to starting position, (13) repeat with opposite side.

Hamstring and Adductor Stretch (2a, b, and c)

Common Terminology for Muscles Stretched (1) Back of thigh, (2) back of leg, (3) inside of thigh, and (4) lower back.

Equivalent Anatomical Terminology (1) Posterior thigh (hamstring group), (2) gastrocnemius, (3) adductor group and (4) erector spinae (sacrospinalis).

Mini-Form Check (1) Seated "V" position on floor, (2) place feet comfortably wide apart, perpendicular to floor and point toes toward face, (3) extend knees without pain, (4) place hands on either side of right thigh, (5) keep head up, (6) drive chest down, (7) slowly move chest toward thigh and slide right hand to ankle and left hand to knee, (8) pause for 20–30 seconds in comfortably stretched position, (9) relax and breathe continuously, (10) gradually return to starting position, (11) repeat with left side, (12) place hands on inside of either thigh, (13) slowly move chest toward floor and slide hands toward ankles, (14) pause for 20–30 seconds in comfortably stretched position, (15) relax and breathe continuously, (16) slowly return to starting position.

Groin (Adductor) Stretch (3)

Common Terminology for Muscles Stretched (1) Inside of thigh and (2) lower back.

Equivalent Anatomical Terminology (1) Adductor group and (2) erector spinae (sacrospinalis).

Mini-Form Check (1) Sit in "V" position on floor, (2) put balls of feet together with heels toward groin, (3) place hands on ankles and elbows on knees, (4) carefully press down on knees with elbows until adductors are comfortably stretched, (5) pause for 20–30 seconds, (6) relax and breathe continuously, (7) slowly return to starting position.

Quadriceps Stretch (4)

Common Terminology for Muscles Stretched (1) Front of thigh.

Equivalent Anatomical Terminology (1a) Anterior thigh (rectus femoris, vastus lateralis, vastus intermedius, and vastus medialis) and (1b) iliopsoas.

Mini-Form Check (1) Sit in "side" position with right hip and right thigh resting on floor and right knee flexed, (2) place right hand on floor for support, (3) flex left knee above right foot, (4) put left hand on left ankle, (5) contract abdominals and flatten back, (6) without arching back, pull left heel toward hip until thigh comfortably stretched, (7) pause for 20–30 seconds, (8) relax and breathe continuously, (9) slowly return to starting position, (10) repeat with opposite side.

Seated Calf Stretch (5a)

Common Terminology for Muscles Stretched (1) Back of leg.

Equivalent Anatomical Terminology (1a) Gastrocnemius, (1b) soleus.

Mini-Form Check (1) Assume seated "L" position on floor, (2a) keep both knees straight to stretch gastrocnemius OR (2b) both knees flexed at constant angle to stretch soleus OR (2c) one knee straight and the other flexed, (3) grasp toes with hands and pull gently until calves are comfortably stretched (4) pause for 20–30 seconds, (5) relax and breathe continuously, (6) gradually return to starting position, (7) repeat with opposite side if nonsymmetrical stretch.

Standing Calf Stretch (5b)

Common Terminology for Muscles Stretched (1) Back of leg.

Equivalent Anatomical Terminology (1a) Gastrocnemius and (1b) soleus.

Mini-Form Check (1) Stand about 3 feet away from a wall or other stable structure, (2) position toes straight ahead and plant heels, (3a) keep both knees straight to stretch gastrocnemius OR (3b) both knees flexed at constant angle to stretch soleus OR (3c) put left foot forward one step toward wall, keep left knee bent to stretch soleus and right knee straight to stretch gastrocnemius, (4) place hands in pronated position on wall about shoulder width apart wall, (5) keep heels planted and slowly lean toward wall by bending elbows and driving knees toward balls of feet, (6) pause for 20–30 seconds in comfortably stretched position, (7) relax and breathe continuously, (8) gradually return to starting position, (9) repeat with opposite side if nonsymmetrical stretch.

Lower Back and Abdominal Calisthenics

Pelvic Tilt (6a)

Common Terminology for Muscles Stretched (1) Abdominal and (2) lower back.

Equivalent Anatomical Terminology (1a) Rectus abdominis, (1b) external oblique, (1c) internal oblique, (1d) transversus abdominis, (1e) pyramidalis, (2a) erector spinae (sacrospinalis), (2b) iliopsoas, and (2c) quadratus lumborum.

Mini-Form Check (1) Lie on floor with feet planted, yet unanchored at about shoulder width, (2) keep knees flexed at 110°, (3) place hands at waist or on floor, (4) move head back, focus eyes above and relax neck, (5) inhale, distend abdominals and carefully arch back, (6) exhale and powerfully contract abdominals and flatten back (pretend you're crushing a large sponge beneath your back), (7) repeat 10–20 times.

Abdominal Curl-Up (6b)

Common Terminology for Muscles Stretched (1) Abdominal, (2) hip flexor and (3) front of neck.

Equivalent Anatomical Terminology (1a) Rectus abdominis, (1b) exernal oblique, (1c) internal oblique, (1d) transversus abdominis, (1e) pyramidalis, (2a) iliopsoas, (2b) rectus femoris, (2c) sartorius, and (3) anterior neck muscles, most notably sternocleidomastoid.

Mini-Form Check (1) Lie on floor with feet planted, yet unanchored at about shoulder width, (2) keep knees flexed at 110°, (3) place hands at waist, on floor or clasp behind head, (4) inhale before start, (5) put chin to chest, (6) exhale and slowly curl up until trunk reaches about 45°, (7) pause, (8) inhale and carefully return to starting position, (9) repeat 10–20 times.

Back and Hip Extension (7)

Common Terminology for Muscles Stretched (1) Low back, (2) hip, (3) back of thigh, (4) upper back, (5) back of shoulder, and (6) back of neck.

Equivalent Anatomical Terminology (1a) Erector spinae (sacrospinalis), (1b) quadratus lumborum, and other deep back muscles, (2) gluteal group, (3) hamstring group, (4a) rhomboid group, (4b) trapezius (middle fibers), (4c) splenius cervicis and other deep back muscles, (5) deltoid (middle and posterior fibers), (6a) trapezius (upper fibers), and (6b) splenius capitis and other deep neck muscles.

Mini-Form Check (1) Lie on floor in prone position with chin planted, (2) extend elbows over head and pronate hands, (3) extend knees, (4) inhale before start, (5) exhale and lift right arm and left thigh toward ceiling, (6) pause, (7) inhale and slowly return to starting position, (8) repeat with left arm and right thigh, (9) repeat 10–20 times, alternating sides as indicated for each repetition.

Upper Body Stretches

Side Bends (8)

Common Terminology for Muscles Stretched (1) Outer abdominal, (2) upper back, (3) chest, (4) back of shoulder, and (5) lower back.

Equivalent Anatomical Terminology (1a) External oblique, (1b) internal oblique, (1c) rectus abdominis, (2a) latissimus dorsi, (2b) teres major, (3a) pectoral group, (3b) serratus anterior, (4) posterior deltoid, (5a) erector spinae, (5b) quadratus lumborum, and other deep back muscles.

Mini-Form Check (1) Stand with feet slightly wider than shoulders, (2) keep knees flexed at constant angle, (3) contract abdominals, (4) flatten back, (5) focus eyes straight ahead, (6) move right hand toward right ankle while dragging left hand up ribcage toward left armpit, (7) move trunk in arclike fashion down toward right ankle, (8) don't arch back or lean forward, keep trunk in a plane perpendicular to the floor, (9) pause in comfortable, stretched position, (10) breathe continuously, (11) without bouncing, slowly return to starting position, (12) repeat with opposite side, (13) repeat 10 times, alternating sides between repetitions, (14) repeat with one hand overhead for further stretching, (15) repeat with opposite side, (16) repeat 10 times, alternating sides for each repetition.

Shoulder Girdle Stretch (9)

Common Terminology for Muscles Stretched (1) Chest, (2) front of shoulder, (3) back of arm, (4) upper back, (5) back of shoulder, and (6) front of arm.

Equivalent Anatomical Terminology (1a) Pectoral group, (1b) serratus anterior, (2) anterior deltoid, (3) triceps brachii, (4a) latissimus dorsi, (4b) teres major, (4c) rhomboid group, (4d) trapezius (middle fibers), (5a) posterior deltoid, (5b) infraspinatus, (6a) biceps brachii, and (6b) brachialis.

Mini-Form Check (1) Stand with feet slightly wider than shoulders, (2) keep knees flexed at constant angle, (3) contract abdominals, (4) flatten back, (5) focus eyes straight ahead, (6) pronate hands, (7) put left arm over right and flex elbows at about 90° high in front of chest, (8) sweep elbows back in arclike fashion, (9) pause in fully stretched position, (10) breathe continuously, (11) slowly return to starting position, (12) pause, (13) repeat with right arm over left, (14) repeat 10–20 times switching arm position between repetitions.

Triceps and Upper Back Stretch (10)

Common Terminology for Muscles Stretched (1) Back of arm, (2) upper back, (3) chest, and (4) back of shoulder.

Equivalent Anatomical Terminology (1) Triceps brachii, (2a) latissimus dorsi, (2b) rhomboid group, (2c) trapezius (upper and middle fibers), (3a) pectoral group, (3b) serratus anterior, (4a) posterior deltoid, and (4b) infraspinatus.

Mini-Form Check (1) Stand with feet slightly wider than shoulders, (2) keep knees flexed at constant angle, (3) contract abdominals, (4) flatten back, (5) focus eyes straight ahead, (6) place right forearm over then behind head, (7) pin right arm to ear, (8) lightly grasp right elbow with left hand, (9) "walk" hand down spine to comfortable, stretched position, (10) pause, relax, and breathe continuously, (11) slowly return to starting position, (12) repeat with opposite side.

Shoulder Shrug (11)

Common Terminology for Muscles Stretched (1) Upper back and (2) neck.

Equivalent Anatomical Terminology (1a) trapezius (middle fibers), (1b) rhomboid group, (2a) trapezius (upper fibers), and (2b) levator scapulae.

Mini-Form Check (1) Stand with feet slightly wider than shoulders, (2) keep knees flexed at constant angle, (3) contract abdominals, (4) flatten back, (5) focus eyes straight ahead, (6) gently raise both shoulders toward ears, (7) pause and breathe continuously, (8) slowly move shoulders back, (9) pause and breathe continuously, (10) move shoulders down to fully stretched position, (11) pause, relax, and breathe continuously, (12) repeat 10 times, (13) repeat 10 times with right shoulder only, moving in counterclockwise fashion, (14) repeat 10 times with left shoulder only, moving in counterclockwise fashion.

Neck Stretch (12)

Common Terminology for Muscles Stretched (1) Front of neck and (2) back of neck.

Equivalent Anatomical Terminology (1) Anterior neck muscles, most notably the sternocleidomastoid, (2a) trapezius (upper and middle fibers), (2b) levator scapulae, and (2c) splenius capitis and other deep posterior neck muscles.

Mini-Form Check (1) Stand with feet slightly wider than shoulders, (2) keep knees flexed at constant angle, (3) contract abdominals, (4) flatten back, (5) focus eyes straight ahead, (6) gently move chin down, then toward right shoulder in arclike fashion, (7) pause, relax, and breathe continuously, (8) slowly return to starting position, (9) gently move chin down, then toward left shoulder in arclike fashion, (10) repeat 10–20 times.

Safe Maximum Testing Appendix D

Medical Clearance

All subjects should be medically cleared before participating in strength, endurance, or flexibility tests. Medical clearance will minimize the risk of injury and may also afford some legal protection to supervising personnel should an injury occur during testing.

The sports medicine physician is the sole authority for medical clearance. Some of the questions the physician will use to determine whether 1-RM testing is safe are listed below.

1. Has the subject ever had heart problems, hypertension, or other cardiovascular diseases or disorders?
2. Has the subject ever had diseases or disorders of the muscles, bones, or joints?
3. Has the subject ever had a concussion or other serious head injury?
4. Has the subject ever experienced convulsions, blackouts, or orthostatic hypotension?
5. Has the subject ever had a chest or lung disorder?
6. Has the subject ever had a serious injury to an internal organ?
7. Has the subject ever had a nervous system disease or disorder?
8. Has the subject ever had glaucoma or other eye diseases or disorders?
9. Is the subject prepubescent, elderly, or pregnant?
10. Does the subject have any recent injury or soreness that may be aggravated by maximum testing?

If the answer to any of the preceding questions is "yes," then the physician may not clear the subject for maximum testing.

Safety Check

Once a subject has been medically cleared by a sports medicine physician, the instructor, fitness consultant, or coach should use the following questions to verify that testing is safe and appropriate.

1. Do the potential risks of injury outweigh the benefits gained from maximum testing? Will testing be beneficial in terms of motivation or provide necessary information that could not be obtained from 1-RM prediction equations or charts?

2. Is first aid equipment available at the testing site? Are there personnel that will be present for testing that are certified in first aid and/or cardiopulmonary resuscitation (CPR)?
3. Have emergency procedures been mapped out and posted near the testing area? Are local ambulance service and hospital phone numbers posted near the testing area?
4. Are the facilities and equipment safe and appropriate for testing?
5. Have the procedures for testing been standardized?
6. Is the supervisor experienced in maximum testing for this particular individual or group of individuals?
7. Are experienced spotters available?
8. Has the subject been given adequate practice time in order to master the skill involved?
9. In the past 24–48 hours has the subject had adequate sleep and a proper diet?
10. Is the subject dressed safely and appropriately for testing?
11. Has the subject completed appropriate and thorough general and specific warm-up?
12. Is the subject well-informed with respect to the testing protocol? Does the subject have a "feel" for appropriate starting weights, rest intervals, and progressions during testing?

If any of the preceding questions are answered "no," then a test should not be administered.

Strength Tests

Static strength can be measured by using a cable tensiometer, dynamometer, or constant velocity ($\neg v = 0°/\text{sec}$) isokinetic machine. Dynamic strength can be assessed on either an isotonic or isokinetic device ($\neg v > 0°/\text{sec}$). The testing device and protocol are selected according to relative expense, ease of administration, and appropriateness for a given individual or population. Tests for athletes should be sports-specific, while those for employees should be job-specific. Generally, tests should assess the strength of major muscle groups and anterior-posterior/superior-inferior balances.

Guidelines for Maximum Testing

Maximum tests may be neither safe nor practical for the general public. In many cases, 1-RM strength tests contribute significantly to soreness, injury, and noncompliance. Higher-repetitions testing together with 1-RM prediction charts or equations often provide an ideal alternative (see appendix E). To minimize the risk of injury, controlled and deliberate movements should be required for isotonic strength testing (see chapter 6).

Techniques for competitive lifts used by athletes are described in appendix G. While isotonic speed-resistance testing may be warranted for selected athletic populations, testing of this type is neither desirable nor appropriate for the general public (especially for those who are prepubescent, elderly, or pregnant).

As a general rule, maximum tests should not be administered more than once every two months. It's unrealistic to expect significant training effects to take place in shorter periods of time. Repeated maximum tests within the same month may induce overtraining, which can act to diminish performance and motivation. In contrast, by extending time between maximum tests, subjects may more readily enhance their test performance as well as their motivation for training.

The testing supervisor should observe trainees closely during specific warm-up and make them aware of deviations in technique. Trainees should be informed that lifts which deviate from proper technique will not be counted and that spotters will be signaled to return the resistance safely to the starting position if the subject assumes a high-risk position. After the subject has performed multiple sets of specific warm-up (up to 85% of 1-RM), the following protocol may be used as a general guide for maximum testing:

Trial 1: 90– 95% of estimated 1-RM
Trial 2: 100–105% of estimated 1-RM
Trial 3: 105–110% of estimated 1-RM
Trial 4: 110–115% of estimated 1-RM

Subjects should avoid overestimating their first attempt and should try to achieve their 1-RM within three to four lifts. Prior to each trial, the testing supervisor should verify and record the resistance. Each attempt should be spotted by a minimum of two spotters and closely observed by the testing supervisor. If the weight attempted by the subject is lifted easily, the resistance should be increased by about 5–10% (increments may be limited by the testing device; actually, the best guide is an experienced trainee). Each successful trial should be recorded.

Rest intervals may vary according to the characteristics of the individual; the mode, intensity, and frequency of the exercise being tested; and the environmental conditions. Generally, a minimum of 3–5 minutes between trials should be given for 1-RM testing. Rest time should allow for adequate physical and psychological recovery. If a battery of tests must be administered on the same day, the testing order should be standardized. Strength tests should always precede muscular endurance tests.

Predicting Maximum Lifts   Appendix E

Although they are by no means perfect, prediction coefficients, equations, and charts may help you estimate your one-repetition maximum (1-RM) for most resistive exercises. You can then use these estimates to devise a periodization plan or to map out the sets you'll do in a particular workout. Since the coefficients, equation, and chart in this appendix were developed by observing intermediate to advanced trainees, they may be more appropriate for you once you've refined your technique. As with other predictions, the closer you are to your true maximum, the better the prediction.

Let's say that you're fresh from a warm-up and you use 55 lb for bench pressing. Much to your surprise, you complete an exhaustive set of eight repetitions. Then according to the chart (table E.1), your predicted 1-RM is 70 lb. If the exact weight you handled is not on the chart, find the column that corresponds to the number of repetitions you did. Then move down the column until the weight you used is within a particular range. For example, if you did six repetitions with 35 lb, track the 6-RM column until you reach the range 33.4 lb–37.6 lb. By moving over to the 100% (1-RM) column, you'll find that your predicted 1-RM is between 40 lb and 45 lb. You can also estimate your 1-RM for weights not on the chart by using the prediction coefficients or exponential equation. Choose one of the below coefficients according to the number of strict repetitions you've completed. Then, simply multiply that coefficient by the weight you've handled to estimate your 1-RM. Using the previous example, if you complete six repetitions with 35 lb, your estimated 1-RM is 1.20 × 35.0 = 42.0 lb, which falls within the range obtained from the chart (40–45 lb). The coefficients and equation make the best 1-RM predictions for weights lifted between one and six times.

Repetitions	Coefficient	Repetitions	Coefficient
1	1.00	6	1.20
2	1.07	7	1.23
3	1.10	8	1.27
4	1.13	9	1.32
5	1.16	10	1.36

$$E = (R^{0.1})W$$

where R = the number of repetitions,

W = the weight in lb that you lifted, and

E = your estimated one-repetition maximum.

Table E.1   Chart for Estimating One-Repetition Maximum

% of 1-RM	100.0%	93.5%	91.0%	88.5%	86.0%	83.5%	81.0%	78.5%	76.0%	73.5%
Repetitions	1	2	3	4	5	6	7	8	9	10
	0.0	0.0	0.0	0.0	0.0	0.0	0.0	0.0	0.0	0.0
	5.0	4.7	4.5	4.4	4.3	4.2	4.1	3.9	3.8	3.7
	10.0	9.4	9.1	8.9	8.6	8.4	8.2	7.9	7.6	7.4
	15.0	14.0	13.7	13.3	12.9	12.5	12.2	11.8	11.4	11.0
	20.0	18.7	18.2	17.7	17.2	16.7	16.2	15.7	15.2	14.7
	25.0	23.4	22.8	22.1	21.5	20.9	20.2	19.6	19.0	18.4
	30.0	28.1	27.3	26.6	25.8	25.1	24.3	23.6	22.8	22.1
	35.0	32.7	31.9	31.0	30.1	29.2	28.4	27.5	26.6	25.7
	40.0	37.4	36.4	35.4	34.4	33.4	32.4	31.4	30.4	29.4
	45.0	42.1	41.0	39.8	38.7	37.6	36.5	35.3	34.2	33.1
	50.0	46.8	45.5	44.3	43.0	41.8	40.5	39.3	38.0	36.8
	55.0	51.4	50.1	48.7	47.3	45.9	44.6	43.2	41.8	40.4
	60.0	56.1	54.6	53.1	51.6	50.1	48.6	47.1	45.6	44.1
	65.0	60.8	59.2	57.5	55.9	54.3	52.7	51.0	49.4	47.8
	70.0	65.5	63.7	62.0	60.2	58.5	56.7	55.0	53.2	51.5
	75.0	70.1	68.3	66.4	64.5	62.6	60.8	58.9	57.0	55.1
	80.0	74.8	72.8	70.8	68.8	66.8	64.8	62.8	60.8	58.8
	85.0	79.5	77.4	75.2	73.1	71.0	68.9	66.7	64.6	62.5
	90.0	84.2	81.9	79.7	77.4	75.2	72.9	70.7	68.4	66.2
	95.0	88.8	86.5	84.1	81.7	79.3	77.0	74.6	72.2	69.8
	100.0	93.5	91.0	88.5	86.0	83.5	81.0	78.5	76.0	73.5
	105.0	98.2	95.6	92.9	90.3	87.7	85.1	82.4	79.8	77.2
	110.0	102.9	100.1	97.4	94.6	91.9	89.1	86.4	83.6	80.9
	115.0	107.5	104.7	101.8	98.9	96.0	93.2	90.3	87.4	84.5
	120.0	112.2	109.2	106.2	103.2	100.2	97.2	94.2	91.2	88.2
	125.0	116.9	113.8	110.6	107.5	104.4	101.3	98.1	95.0	91.9
	130.0	121.6	118.3	115.1	111.8	108.6	105.3	102.1	98.8	95.6
	135.0	126.2	122.9	119.5	116.1	112.7	109.4	106.0	102.6	99.2
	140.0	130.9	127.4	123.9	120.4	116.9	113.4	109.9	106.4	102.9
	145.0	135.6	132.0	128.3	124.7	121.1	117.5	113.8	110.2	106.6
	150.0	140.3	136.5	132.8	129.0	125.3	121.5	117.8	114.0	110.3
	155.0	144.9	141.1	137.2	133.3	129.4	125.6	121.7	117.8	113.9
	160.0	149.6	145.6	141.6	137.6	133.6	129.6	125.6	121.6	117.6
	165.0	154.3	150.2	146.0	141.9	137.8	133.7	129.5	125.4	121.3
	170.0	159.0	154.7	150.5	146.2	142.0	137.7	133.5	129.2	125.0
	175.0	163.6	159.3	154.9	150.5	146.1	141.8	137.4	133.0	128.6
	180.0	168.3	163.8	159.3	154.8	150.3	145.8	141.3	136.8	132.3
	185.0	173.0	168.4	163.7	159.1	154.5	149.9	145.2	140.6	136.0
	190.0	177.7	172.9	168.2	163.4	158.7	153.9	149.2	144.4	139.7
	195.0	182.3	177.5	172.6	167.7	162.8	158.0	153.1	148.2	143.3
	200.0	187.0	182.0	177.0	172.0	167.0	162.0	157.0	152.0	147.0
	205.0	191.7	186.6	181.4	176.3	171.2	166.1	160.9	155.8	150.7
	210.0	196.4	191.1	185.9	180.6	175.4	170.1	164.9	159.6	154.4
	215.0	201.0	195.7	190.3	184.9	179.5	174.2	168.8	163.4	158.0
	220.0	205.7	200.2	194.7	189.2	183.7	178.2	172.7	167.2	161.7
	225.0	210.4	204.8	199.1	193.5	187.9	182.3	176.6	171.0	165.4

Table E.1 *Continued*

% of 1-RM	100.0%	93.5%	91.0%	88.5%	86.0%	83.5%	81.0%	78.5%	76.0%	73.5%
Repetitions	1	2	3	4	5	6	7	8	9	10
	230.0	215.1	209.3	203.6	197.8	192.1	186.3	180.6	174.8	169.1
	235.0	219.7	213.9	208.0	202.1	196.2	190.4	184.5	178.6	172.7
	240.0	224.4	218.4	212.4	206.4	200.4	194.4	188.4	182.4	176.4
	245.0	229.1	223.0	216.8	210.7	204.6	198.5	192.3	186.2	180.1
	250.0	233.8	227.5	221.3	215.0	208.8	202.5	196.3	190.0	183.8
	255.0	238.4	232.1	225.7	219.3	212.9	206.6	200.2	193.8	187.4
	260.0	243.1	236.6	230.1	223.6	217.1	210.6	204.1	197.6	191.2
	265.0	247.8	241.2	234.5	227.9	221.3	214.7	208.1	201.4	194.8
	270.0	252.5	245.7	239.0	232.2	225.5	218.7	212.0	205.2	198.5
	275.0	257.1	250.3	243.4	236.5	229.6	222.8	215.9	209.0	202.1
	280.0	261.8	254.8	247.8	240.8	233.8	226.8	219.8	212.8	205.8
	285.0	266.5	259.4	252.2	245.1	238.0	230.9	223.7	216.6	209.5
	290.0	271.2	263.9	256.7	249.4	242.5	234.9	227.7	220.4	213.2
	295.0	275.9	268.5	261.1	253.7	246.3	239.0	231.6	224.2	216.8
	300.0	280.5	273.0	265.5	258.0	250.5	243.0	235.5	228.0	220.5
	305.0	285.2	277.6	269.9	262.3	254.7	247.1	239.4	231.8	224.2
	310.0	289.9	282.1	274.4	266.6	258.9	251.1	243.4	235.6	227.9
	315.0	294.5	286.7	278.8	270.9	263.0	255.2	247.3	239.4	231.5
	320.0	299.2	291.2	283.2	275.2	267.2	259.2	251.2	243.2	235.2
	325.0	303.9	295.8	287.6	279.5	271.4	263.3	255.1	247.0	238.9
	330.0	308.6	300.3	292.1	283.8	275.9	267.3	259.1	250.8	242.6
	335.0	313.2	304.9	296.5	288.1	279.7	271.4	263.0	254.6	246.2
	340.0	317.9	309.4	300.9	292.4	283.9	275.4	266.9	258.4	249.9
	345.0	322.6	314.0	305.3	296.7	288.1	279.5	270.8	262.2	253.6
	350.0	327.3	318.5	309.8	301.0	292.3	283.5	274.8	266.0	257.3
	355.0	331.9	323.1	314.2	305.3	296.4	287.6	278.7	269.8	260.9
	360.0	336.6	327.6	318.6	309.6	300.6	291.6	282.6	273.6	264.6
	365.0	341.3	332.2	323.0	313.9	304.8	295.7	286.5	277.4	268.3
	370.0	346.0	336.7	327.5	318.2	309.0	299.7	290.5	281.2	272.0
	375.0	350.6	341.3	331.9	322.5	313.1	303.8	294.4	285.0	275.6
	380.0	355.3	345.8	336.3	326.8	317.3	307.8	298.3	288.8	279.3
	385.0	360.0	350.4	340.7	331.1	321.5	311.9	302.2	292.6	283.0
	390.0	364.7	354.9	345.2	335.4	325.7	315.9	306.2	296.4	286.7
	395.0	369.3	359.5	349.6	339.7	329.8	320.0	310.1	300.2	290.3
	400.0	374.0	364.0	354.0	344.0	334.0	324.0	314.0	304.0	294.0
	405.0	378.7	368.6	358.4	348.3	338.2	328.1	317.9	307.8	297.7
	410.0	383.4	373.1	362.9	352.6	342.4	332.1	321.9	311.6	301.4
	415.0	388.0	377.7	367.3	356.9	346.5	336.2	325.8	315.4	305.0
	420.0	392.7	382.2	371.7	361.2	350.7	340.2	329.7	319.2	308.7
	425.0	397.4	386.8	376.1	365.5	354.9	344.3	333.6	323.0	312.4
	430.0	402.1	391.3	380.6	369.8	359.1	348.3	337.6	326.8	316.1
	435.0	406.7	395.9	385.0	374.1	363.2	352.4	341.5	330.6	319.7
	440.0	411.4	400.4	389.4	378.4	367.4	356.4	345.4	334.4	323.4
	445.0	416.1	405.0	393.8	382.7	371.6	360.5	349.3	338.2	327.1
	450.0	420.8	409.5	398.3	387.0	375.8	364.5	353.3	342.0	330.8
	455.0	425.4	414.1	402.7	391.3	379.9	368.6	357.2	345.8	334.4

Table E.1 *Continued*

% of 1-RM	100.0%	93.5%	91.0%	88.5%	86.0%	83.5%	81.0%	78.5%	76.0%	73.5%
Repetitions	*1*	*2*	*3*	*4*	*5*	*6*	*7*	*8*	*9*	*10*
	460.0	430.1	418.6	407.1	395.6	384.1	372.6	361.1	349.6	338.1
	465.0	434.8	423.2	411.5	399.9	388.3	376.7	365.0	353.4	341.8
	470.0	439.5	427.7	416.0	404.2	392.5	380.7	369.0	357.2	345.5
	475.0	444.1	432.3	420.4	408.5	396.6	384.8	372.9	361.0	349.1
	480.0	448.8	436.8	424.8	412.8	400.8	388.8	376.8	364.8	352.8
	485.0	453.5	441.4	429.2	417.1	405.0	392.9	380.7	368.6	356.5
	490.0	458.2	445.9	433.7	421.4	409.2	396.9	384.7	372.4	360.2
	495.0	462.8	450.5	438.1	425.7	413.3	401.0	388.6	376.2	363.8
	500.0	467.5	455.0	442.5	430.0	417.5	405.0	392.5	380.0	367.5

Muscles Worked by Intermediate and Advanced Exercises

Appendix F

As we mentioned in chapter 6, the Basic Dozen beginning weight training exercises act as the foundation for all intermediate and advanced programs. What do we mean by intermediate and advanced exercises? Although some are a bit more difficult to perform than beginning movements, most intermediate and advanced exercises merely require different equipment and/or subtle changes in body position to work muscles from a slightly different angle. It may be best to call them specialty exercises since they are used to specialize or further isolate specific muscles or even parts of muscles.

A good example of a specialty exercise is the inclined bench press. For this movement you keep your trunk at an angle of 40°–55° so you can highlight the upper part of your chest. You may also do a declined bench press to focus on working the lower part of your pectorals. Instead of using a standard barbell you may use dumbbells, short bars with identical solid spheres or adjustable plates attached to each end. These devices, most often used in pairs, require more balance and can enhance your range of motion. Finally, for many upper body specialty exercises, you can choose to move dumbbells or other equipment (e.g., cables) concentrically or eccentrically as well as simultaneously, independently, or alternately. It's easy to see that there are literally thousands of combinations of specialty exercises for working skeletal muscles.

As in chapter 6, you'll notice that the specialty movements in table F.1 are divided according to the eight major regions of the body. You'll find sample intermediate and advanced programs that incorporate these exercises in appendix H.

Just like a potter uses his or her hands to mold a piece of clay into a rough form, you can use the Basic Dozen weight training exercises to change the overall shape of your muscles. When you've reached the point where you want to further refine and delineate your muscles, use specialty exercises, just as a potter employs unique tools to put the finishing touches on a work of art.

Table F.1 Body Regions and Specific Muscles Worked by Selected Intermediate and Advanced Weight Training Exercises

Exercise	Body Regions[a]	Specific Muscles[b]
1. Front/hack/Russian squat	Lower extremity	Hip, thigh, and lower back
2. Thigh abduction	Hip and thigh	Outside of hip and thigh
3. Thigh adduction	Thigh	Inside of thigh
4. a. Bench press (close-grip supine)	Chest, shoulder, and arm	Chest, front of shoulder, and back of arm
b. Inclined chest fly (dumbbell)		Upper chest and front of shoulder
c. Bench press (inclined barbell)		Upper chest, front of shoulder, and back of arm
d. Bench press (declined barbell)		Lower chest, front of shoulder, and back of arm
5. a. Deltoid fly (anterior and middle)	Shoulder, neck, and back	Front and middle of shoulder, and neck
b. Deltoid fly (posterior)	Shoulder and back	Back of shoulder and upper back
6. a. Lat cable row (seated)	Back, shoulder, arm, and forearm	Upper and lateral back, back of shoulder, front of arm, and forearm
b. Pull-over		Lateral and upper back, back of shoulder, and back of arm
7. a. Triceps extension (dumbbell 2-arm)	Arm and forearm	Back of arm and front of forearm
b. Triceps extension (dumbbell 1-arm)		Back of arm and front of forearm
8. a. Biceps curl (dumbbell unisymm.)	Arm and forearm	Front of arm and forearm
b. Biceps curl (dumbbell duosymm.)		Front of arm and forearm
c. Biceps curl (Scott/inclined E-Z)		Front of arm and forearm
9. Abdominal movements (alternatives)	Abdomen	Upper and lower abdominal
10. Dead lift	Back, lower extremity, and neck	Lower and upper back, hip, thigh, and neck
11. Clean and jerk	Lower extremity, back, neck, shoulder, arm, and forearm	Hip, thigh, calf, upper and lower back, neck, shoulder, arm, and forearm
12. Snatch	Lower extremity, back, neck, shoulder, arm, and forearm	Hip, thigh, calf, upper and lower back, neck, shoulder, arm, and forearm
13. a. Wrist flexion	Forearm	Front of forearm
b. Wrist extension		Back of forearm
14. Shoulder shrug	Neck	Front and back of neck
15. 4-way neck	Neck	Front and back of neck
16. a. Foot inversion	Leg	Inside of leg (invertors)
b. Foot eversion		Outside of leg (evertors)

[a]Body regions that are affected by the entire group of exercises listed under the same number in column 1.
[b]Lay terminology for specific muscles that are worked by each of the exercises listed in column 1.

Selected Competitive Lifts

Appendix G

Dead Lift (11)

Common Terminology for Muscles Exercised (1) Hip, (2) front of thigh, (3) back of thigh, (4) lower back, (5) upper back, (6) neck, (7) back of forearm, and (8) front of forearm.

Equivalent Anatomical Terminology (1) Gluteal group, (2) quadriceps group, (3) hamstring group, (4) erector spinae, (4b) quadratus lumborum and other deep back muscles, (5a) trapezius (lower and middle fibers), (5b) rhomboids, (6a) trapezius (upper fibers), (6b) levator scapulae, (6c) splenius capitis, splenius cervicis, and other deep posterior neck muscles (upper branches of the erector spinae), (7) brachioradialis and other posterior forearm muscles, and (8) flexor digitorum profundus and other anterior forearm muscles.

Mini-Form Check (1a) Stand with feet about 10–12 inches apart and slightly toed-out beneath bar (standard stance) *or* (1b) stand with feet wider than shoulders and toed-out beneath bar (sumo-style stance), (2) move shins as close as possible to bar, (3) use alternate grip with hands shoulder-width apart, (4) position thighs near parallel to floor, (5) contract abdominals, (6a) flatten back and maintain 30°–40° above parallel to floor (standard stance) *or* (6b) flatten back and maintain near 45°–50° above parallel to floor (sumo-style stance), (7) extend elbows, (8) use hips and thighs to lift bar from floor in a powerful yet smooth fashion, (9) when bar passes lower portion of quadriceps, forcefully extend trunk at hips to bring hips in line with shoulders, (10) elevate and retract shoulders by powerfully contracting trapezius, (11) pause, (12) breathe continuously.

Clean and Jerk (12)

Common Terminology for Muscles Exercised (1) Hip, (2) front of thigh, (3) back of thigh, (4) calf, (5) lower back, (6) upper back, (7) neck, (8) shoulder, (9) front of arm, (10) back of arm, (11) back of forearm, and (12) front of forearm.

Equivalent Anatomical Terminology (1) Gluteal group, (2) quadriceps group, (3) hamstring group, (4a) soelus, (4b) gastrocnemius, (5a) erector spinae, (5b) quadratus lumborum and other deep back muscles, (6a) trapezius (lower and middle fibers), (6b) rhomboids, (7a) trapezius (upper fibers), (7b) levator scapulae, (7c) splenius capitis, splenius cervicis, and other deep posterior neck muscles, (8) deltoid, (9a) biceps brachii, (9b) brachialis, (10) triceps brachii, (11) brachioradialis and other posterior forearm muscles, and (12) flexor carpi radialis, flexor digitorum profundus, and other anterior forearm muscles.

Mini-Form Check (1) Place feet in position comfortable for jumping, at about hip-width, with toes straight ahead, (2) move shins close to bar, (3) grasp bar with pronated grip, slightly wider than shoulders, (4) move head and shoulders just in front of bar, (5) extend elbows, (6) flatten back and position about 20° above parallel (thighs should be above parallel to floor), (7) contract abdominals, (8) keep bar close to body throughout movement, (9) during initial pull use hips and thighs to slowly yet powerfully lift bar from floor (don't jerk), (10) when bar reaches mid-thigh level, thrust hips forward and upward and head backward, (11) accelerate bar by powerfully extending back, shrugging shoulders, and rising up on toes, (12) raise elbows high and outside but still keep bar close to body, (13) jump (feet should leave floor at top of pull when bar is near chest level), (14) pivot body around and beneath bar by quickly bending knees and dipping elbows, (15) feet should land wider with slight toe-out and a bit forward compared to starting position, (16) after the catch, pause to control bar on deltoid platform with elbows up, (17) powerfully squat bar up to assume standing position, (18) partially flex hips and knees preceding jerk, (19) thrust bar overhead by using hips, thighs, shoulders, then triceps, (20) pause to control at full extension, (21) carefully return bar to the floor, (22) breathe continuously.

Snatch (13)

Common Terminology for Muscles Exercised (1) Hip, (2) front of thigh, (3) back of thigh, (4) calf, (5) lower back, (6) upper back, (7) neck, (8) shoulder, (9) front of arm, (10) back of arm, (11) back of forearm, and (12) front of forearm.

Equivalent Anatomical Terminology (1) Gluteal group, (2) quadriceps group, (3) hamstring group, (4a) soleus, (4b) gastrocnemius, (5a) erector spinae, (5b) quadratus lumborum and other deep back muscles, (6a) trapezius (lower and middle fibers), (6b) rhomboids, (7a) trapezius (upper fibers), (7b) levator scapulae, (7c) splenius capitis, splenius cervicis, and other deep posterior neck muscles, (8) deltoid, (9a) biceps brachii, (9b) brachialis, (10) triceps brachii, (11) brachioradialis and other posterior forearm muscles, and (12) flexor carpi radialis, flexor digitorum profundus, and other anterior forearm muscles.

Mini-Form Check (1) Place feet in position comfortable for jumping, at about hip-width, with toes straight ahead, (2) move shins close to bar, (3) use a wide pronated grip to grasp bar a few inches inside of inner collars or plates, (4) move head and shoulders just in front of bar, (5) extend elbows, (6) flatten back and position about 20° above parallel (thighs should be above parallel to floor), (7) contract abdominals, (8) keep bar close to body throughout movement, (9) during initial pull use hips and thighs to slowly yet powerfully lift bar from floor (don't jerk), (10) when bar reaches mid-thigh level, thrust hips forward and upward and head backward, (11) accelerate bar by powerfully extending back, shrugging shoulders, and rising up on toes, (12) raise elbows high and outside, but still keep bar close to body, (13) jump (feet should leave floor at top of pull when bar is near chest level), (14) pivot body around bar by quickly squatting beneath it, while driving elbows to a locked position overhead, (15) feet should land wider than shoulder width with slight toe-out, (16) after the catch, pause to control bar overhead and forcefully contract deltoids and triceps to maintain locked shoulders and elbows, (17) powerfully squat bar up to assume standing position, (18) pause to control bar, (19) carefully return bar to floor, (20) breathe continuously.

Intermediate and Advanced Program Designs

As a beginner you'll probably work out three times per week and do three sets of 8–12 repetitions of the Basic Dozen during each of your workouts (see chapter 6). This is much like moving through an automated car wash—you'll highlight all major body parts during a single session.

If you move on to an intermediate or advanced program you'll include accessory exercises above and beyond the Basic Dozen. This makes it necessary to use split routines, which may increase your workout frequency to four to six days per week. With a split routine, body parts are partitioned into balanced regions which are assigned to specific workout days. You don't work your entire body in a single session, but instead train unique body parts on separate days.

Despite the fact that intermediate and advanced weight trainers generally work out four to six days per week (sometimes twice a day), they avoid working the same major muscles more than twice a week. Workouts are staggered with a minimum of two-days' rest between sessions involving similar muscles. This special workout staggering should provide for (1) adequate time for physiological and psychological recovery between sessions, (2) variety to minimize boredom, (3) controlled workout volume to reduce the tendency to overtrain, and (4) enhanced potential for strength gain.

Common ways of partitioning muscles to devise intermediate and advanced programs include (1) major-minor (large-small), (2) agonistic-antagonistic (push-pull), and (3) superior-inferior (upper-lower body) groups (table H.1).

To develop push-pull-squat routines, Olympic lifters and other power-event athletes partition exercises into one of four categories:

1. push exercises including the bench press, inclined bench press, behind-the-neck press, military press, and jerk;
2. pull movements including the power clean, power snatch, and high pulls (from the floor, from blocks, or from the hang position);
3. squat exercises including regular (back) squats, front squats, hack squats, and leg presses; or
4. accessory exercises for back (upper and lower), abdominal, chest, shoulder, and arm muscles.

Table H.1 Sample Exercises for Major-Minor, Agonistic-Antagonistic, and Superior-Inferior Programs

Program Type	Muscular Regions	Sample Exercises
Major-Minor (M-M)[a]	Chest and lower extremity	Bench press and accessory chest; squat and accessory thigh and leg exercises.
	Back, shoulder, and arm	Lat pull, military press, biceps curl, triceps extension, and accessory SJA exercises[d]
Agonistic-Antagonistic (A-A)[b]	Chest, shoulder, and triceps	Bench press and accessory chest; military press, triceps extension, and accessory SJA exercises
	Lower extremity, back, and biceps	Squat and accessory thigh and leg exercises; lat pull and accessory back exercises
Superior-Inferior (S-I)[c]	Chest, shoulder, back, and arm	Bench press and accessory chest; military press, lat pull, biceps curl, triceps extension, and accessory SJA exercises
	Lower extremity	Squat and accessory thigh and leg exercises

Note: The list of sample exercises associated with a particular muscular region is not meant to be all-inclusive.

[a]Major-minor muscle grouping may be used to devise either four-day or six-day routines. For a four-day routine, chest and lower extremity muscles are worked on MH; back, shoulder, and arm on UF. Abdominal and low back work may be included with warm-up and highlighted on chest and lower extremity days. For a six-day routine, chest and low extremity muscles are exercised on MH; back and shoulder on UF; arm, abdominal, and lower back on WS. Six-day split routines cover the first muscular group in the morning and second in the afternoon or evening.

[b]Agonistic-antagonistic four-day designs usually group chest, shoulder, and triceps on MH; lower extremity, back, and biceps on UF. For six-day designs: chest and triceps on MH; back and biceps on UF; lower extremity and shoulder work on WS.

[c]Superior-inferior four-day designs have chest, shoulder, back, and arm exercises on MH; lower extremity, abdominal, and lower back on UF. For six-day programs: chest, back, and shoulders on MH; lower extremity, abdominals, and lower back on UF; arm and other specialty work on WS.

[d]Emphasis on single-joint-action (SJA) accessory exercises.

For a workout, athletes are urged to select one exercise from each category. Major push, pull, and squat exercises may be done three times per week during a load phase, but are usually performed only once or twice per week during a peak or taper phase close to competition. Periodization is used extensively, as workouts alternate between light, medium, and heavy intensities. High-intensity workouts are never done in high volume (see chapter 5, Periodization or Cyclic Training).

Table H.2   Sample Major-Minor Program

Body Parts	Days	Selected Exercises	Sets and Repetitions
Chest and lower extremity[a]	MH	Bench press[c]	3–4 × 6–10
		Inclined chest fly	2–3 × 8–10
		or Inclined bench press	
		or Supine chest fly	
		or Declined bench press	
		Squat	3–4 × 6–10
		or Front squat	
		or Hack squat	
		or Leg press	
		Lunge	2–3 × 8–10
		or Leg extension	
		Leg curl	3–4 × 8–10
		Calf raise (straight knee)	4–5 × 10–12
		or Calf raise (bent knee)	
Back, shoulder, and arm[b]	UF	Lat pull (wide grip)	3–4 × 6–10
		or Lat pull (close grip)	
		Pull-Up	2–3 × 8–12
		or Pull-over	
		or Bent-over row	
		or Seated cable row	
		Behind-the-neck press	3–4 × 6–10
		or Military press	
		or Upright row	
		or Dumbbell (DB) press	
		Posterior deltoid DB-raise	2–3 × 8–10
		or Posterior deltoid cable raise	
		Biceps curl (barbell)	3–4 × 6–10
		or Inclined E-Z curl	
		DB concentration curl	2–3 × 8–12
		or Alternate DB work	
		Triceps extension (supine E-Z bar)	3–4 × 6–10
		or Standing at lat station	
		or Standing French press	
		or Parallel dip	
		DB triceps extension (single arm)	2–3 × 8–10

Note: A sample intermediate weight training program with exercises divided according to the M-M design. The number of sets indicated does not include specific warm-up sets. Repetition schedules may vary according to cyclic training and microcycles.

[a]Do lower back and abdominal exercises each day with warm-up and/or with lower body and chest workouts.

[b]Neck and forearm exercises may be the perfect complement for shoulder and arm work. Start by doing 2–3 sets of neck and wrist flexions and extensions.

[c]Vary the exercise sequence according to your primary emphasis. For example, when inferior muscles lag behind superior muscles, do lower body exercises before chest work.

Aerobics for Intermediate to Advanced Trainees

When time devoted toward weight training is increased, there's a general tendency to de-emphasize aerobic exercise. Remember that you'll definitely increase your strength by using conventional weight training, but it's highly unlikely that you'll improve your aerobic capacity (Nagle & Irwin 1960; Fahey & Brown 1973; Allen, Byrd & Smith 1976; Hickson 1980; Hickson, Rosenkoetter & Brown 1980; Hickson et al. 1988). To ensure that you'll maintain optimal levels of cardiovascular fitness and percentage body fat, be sure to include aerobic exercise in your total fitness plan (American College of Sports Medicine 1978; Pollock, Wilmore & Fox 1984).

Studies comparing combined endurance and strength training with either type of training alone are difficult to interpret. When subjects participate in two intense programs at the same time and in weekly 1-RM tests, they're bound to overtrain. The velocity at which endurance training takes place may influence performance on isokinetic strength tests. Data obtained from isokinetic devices at high speeds may be invalid, since at progressively higher speeds, less and less of a movement is truly isokinetic. The mode, frequency, intensity, duration, and distribution of training sessions must all be considered (Sale et al. 1988).

Your own combined strength- and endurance-training program may have variable effects based on (1) your physical condition, (2) the mode, intensity, frequency, and duration of both your aerobic and strength programs, and (3) the distribution of your training sessions. There's no question that by simultaneously training for endurance and strength, you can increase both your aerobic capacity and muscular strength (Dudley & Fleck 1987; Dudley & Djamil 1985; Hickson 1980). However, by combining high-intensity interval cycling with isotonic strength training, you may hinder your lower body strength gains after eight weeks of training (Hickson 1980). By combining isokinetic strength training and cycling at a slow pedal frequency (60 rpm), you may inhibit strength gains at fast, but not slow velocities of contraction (Dudley & Djamil 1985). If you're untrained and you combine strength training at a moderate intensity (75% of 1-RM) with endurance running, you may not inhibit your strength gains (Volpe et al. 1988). If you're an elite power lifter, you may be able to increase your aerobic capacity merely by avoiding heavy strength training for a seven-month period (Staron, Hagerman & Hikida 1981). Of course, this wouldn't help your maximum lifting. If you're planning to peak for an upcoming weight lifting contest, it may be to your advantage to limit the volume and intensity of your aerobic exercise.

As a weight trainer you should seek to develop total fitness as a lifetime goal. To maximize your increases in strength with a moderate volume and frequency program, it's best to do your strength and endurance training on separate days (Sale et al. 1988). Run, swim, or cycle on your "off" weight training days. Even if you're on an advanced six-day program, you can exercise aerobically on days that you don't do lower extremity work (this should leave a total of four days open for aerobic exercise).

Circuit Weight Training   Appendix I

In 1968, J. P. O'Shea introduced circuit weight training (CWT) by applying the concepts of circuit and interval training to conventional weight training. CWT is exercising through a special sequence of weight training stations while limiting the rest between sets. It can be used in a variety of settings (e.g., corporate, industrial, athletic, and rehabilitative) to enhance physical fitness, performance, and morale. Since spotting may not be required and changing the resistance is quick and easy for most CWT machines, large groups can complete extensive circuits in a relatively short time. During a single CWT session, an instructor can observe and modify the technique of many trainees in just a few minutes. This makes CWT ideal for minimizing the risk of injury and maximizing client adherence to a program. Persons exposed to CWT are provided with a practical, safe, and efficient way to weight train for the rest of their lives. Two sample CWT programs are illustrated in this appendix.

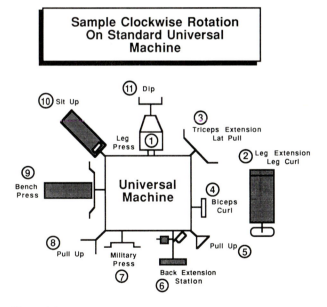

Figure I.1
Stationary multicircuit machines limit the ability to change exercise sequence but minimize spotting and difficulty in changing weights. The sample clockwise rotation pictured above is ideal for working a large number of athletes or employees in a short period of time. The leg extension/leg curl station is the only compound station in the sequence.

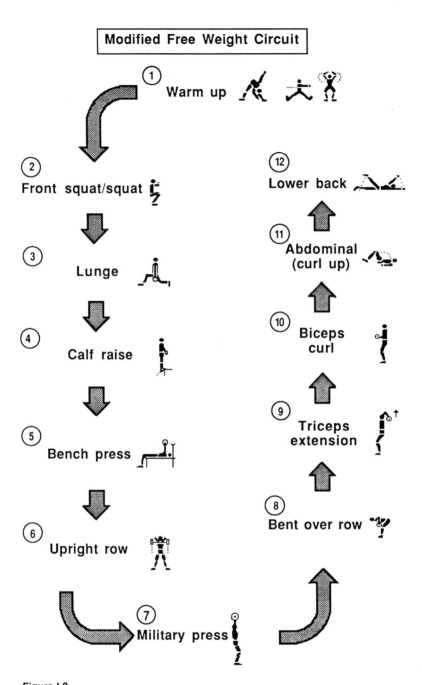

Modified Free Weight Circuit

1. Warm up
2. Front squat/squat
3. Lunge
4. Calf raise
5. Bench press
6. Upright row
7. Military press
8. Bent over row
9. Triceps extension
10. Biceps curl
11. Abdominal (curl up)
12. Lower back

Figure I.2
Free-weight circuit weight training programs offer ease of portability but require additional spotting and time to change weights. The design pictured above is based on the Basic Dozen.

Androgenic-Anabolic Steroids Appendix J

Steroids are hormones that are chemically similar to cholesterol. They are manufactured and released by the gonads (the testes and ovaries) and the adrenal cortices (the outer shells of the two paired organs above the kidneys). Testosterone is the major male sex steroid. It's responsible for androgenic or man-producing effects including enlargement of the testes; growth of genital, facial, and axillary hair; and deepening of the voice. Testosterone also has anabolic properties, which means that it promotes protein synthesis and tissue building.

Androgenic-anabolic steroids, often simply called steroids by athletes, are hormones that are chemically similar to testosterone. Clinically, they're used to treat patients with protein deficiencies, osteoporosis (bone thinning), severe burns, muscular dystrophy, and anemia (Govoni & Hayes 1978; Harvard Medical School 1983). Although it is the anabolic characteristics of steroids that athletes are most interested in, it's difficult (if not impossible) to separate these effects from the androgenic effects. This is because androgenic effects are actually anabolic effects in sex-linked tissues (Brooks & Fahey 1984; Haupt & Rovere 1984a, b).

Steroids have been used since World War II. They were first introduced to the sports scene in 1954 when Russian weight lifters reportedly used them to prepare for the world championships in Vienna, Austria (Wade 1972). Today the use of steroids is quite common. Wright surveyed 79 athletes and found that steroid use was high among power lifters (94.7%), body builders (92.9%), football players (77.8%), and track and field athletes (71.4%). Some used steroids for continuous periods as long as six months (Wright cited in Barnes 1983). Steroids have become increasingly popular with endurance athletes, who've been enticed by the drugs' potential to increase their blood's oxygen-carrying capacity. Even nonathletic adolescents and children have used muscle-building drugs to improve physical appearance (Murphy 1986).

Steroids are taken either orally (PO, Latin for *per os* [by mouth]) or parenterally (not by mouth). Parenteral routes include injections that are intramuscular (IM, within a muscle), subcutaneous (SQ, beneath the skin), or intravenous (IV, within a vein). If pure testosterone, a white, crystalline powder, is taken orally, a large percentage of its activity is diminished by digestive enzymes. Consequently, when used therapeutically, testosterone is mixed with sterile sesame oil and given by intramuscular injection (Wynn 1975). Research chemists manipulated the structure of testosterone to develop drugs that were protected from digestive enzymes. Although orally active drugs were produced, chemical modifications also created additional side effects. Compared to orally active forms (C-17 methylated), injectable (19-nortestosterone) steroids are associated with fewer side effects (Wynn 1975; Shepard, Killinger & Fried 1977; Haupt & Rovere 1984a, b).

While therapeutic dosages of steroids are about 5 mg/day (only 15 mg per day are needed for complete androgen substitution), some athletes have reported taking from 4 to 100 times the recommended amount (Burkett & Falduto 1984; Alen 1985; Pope & Katz 1988). Most athletes obtain steroids without prescriptions and use stacking, which means they take oral and injectable preparations together (Burkett & Falduto 1984).

Do steroids work to increase lean body mass and strength? Yes, but only when the following conditions are satisfied.

1. Trained athletes engage in heavy resistance training just prior to steroid use. Subjects who don't train or do only aerobic exercise while taking steroids will not increase their strength.
2. Athletes continue heavy resistance training throughout the steroid cycle.
3. Athletes maintain a high dietary intake of protein throughout the steroid cycle (Haupt & Rovere 1984a, b). Extra protein should not be obtained from expensive, concentrated pill or powder sources, which are frequently loaded with sugar and other filler by-products. In fact, ten protein pills will provide no more protein than a single, 8-oz. glass of milk (Parr, Porter & Hodgson 1984).

There are multiple side effects associated with the use of steroids. The most common short-term effects include salt and water retention, increased blood pressure, acne, testicular atrophy, gynecomastia, sore nipples, decreased sperm count, prostatic enlargement, and increased aggression (Fahey & Brown 1973; Harkness, Kilshaw & Hobson 1975; Freed et al. 1975; Wynn 1975; Tahmindjis 1976; Strauss et al. 1983; Alen & Suominen 1984). Other reported side effects include hair loss, fever, nausea, diarrhea, nosebleeds, lymph node swelling, increased appetite, burning sensation upon urination, and ulcers (Strauss et al. 1983; Haupt & Rovere 1984a, b). A recent study of body builders and football players indicated that major psychiatric symptoms including paranoia, grandiose delusions, and auditory hallucinations may be common side effects associated with steroid use. Some athletes may develop major depression during the steroid withdrawal period (Pope & Katz 1988).

When males stop taking steroids after short-term use, most of the annoying side effects disappear. However, females who take steroids may have permanent deepening of the voice, facial hair, baldness, and clitoral enlargement. Steroid use by children can induce premature closure of growth plates (Goodman & Gilman 1975; Govoni & Hayes 1978; Arblaster & Blackman 1981; Haupt & Rovere 1984a, b).

Steroids do increase the risk of developing cancer. The only known way to induce prostatic cancer in any species of male animal is by administering testosterone (Noble cited in Puffer 1985). Liver diseases and tumors have been reported in patients taking oral steroids, but not in those using only injectable steroids (Bernstein, Hunter & Yachnin 1971; Ziegenfuss & Carabasi 1973; Bagheri & Boyer 1974; Meadows, Naiman & Valdes-Dapena 1974; Falk et al. 1979). When healthy athletes take oral steroids they can expect transiently elevated liver function tests which indicate some degree of liver degeneration (Shepard, Killinger & Fried 1977; Haupt & Rovere 1984a, b; Alen 1985).

The primary risk factors in the development of coronary artery disease (CAD) are cigarette smoking, high blood cholesterol (hypercholesterolemia), and high blood pressure (hypertension). Steroids can increase total cholesterol and LDL-C (the "bad" form of cholesterol) and decrease HDL-C (the "good" form of cholesterol) (Strauss et al. 1983; Costill, Pearson & Fink 1984; Peterson & Fahey 1984; Alen & Rahkila 1984; Cohen, Noakes & Benade 1988). Since they also promote salt and water retention, which increases blood pressure, steroids can adversely affect two of the three primary CAD risk factors. Further studies are needed to quantify the effects of long-term steroid use on the incidence of CAD.

It's clear that scare tactics will not curb the overwhelming use of steroids. If you're an athlete interested in learning more about steroids, seek reliable resource materials together with the guidance of a qualified sports medicine physician. Teachers and coaches can favorably influence athletes by demonstrating a genuine concern for them, by directing them to knowledgeable sports medicine professionals, and by presenting facts about steroids in a candid, yet nonjudgmental way. Our most powerful tool is education together with the honest portrayal of our own respect and awe for the intricacies of the human body.

Association and Equipment Company Directory

Fitness and Sports Medicine

Amateur Athletic Union
3400 West 86th Street
Indianapolis, Indiana 46268
317–872–2900

American Alliance for Health, Physical
    Education, Recreation & Dance
1900 Association Drive
Reston, Virginia 22091
703–476–3400

American College of Sports Medicine
401 West Michigan Street
Indianapolis, Indiana 46202-3233
317–637–9200

American Orthopaedic Society for Sports
    Medicine
70 West Hubbard, Suite 202
Chicago, Illinois 60610
312–644–2623

American Running and Fitness Association
9310 Old Georgetown Road
Bethesda, Maryland 20814
301–897–0197

Canadian Association of Sports Sciences
333 River Road
Ottawa, Ontario K1L 8H9
613–748–5671

International Federation of Bodybuilders
2875 Bates Road
Montreal, PQ, Canada H3S 1B7
514–731–3783

National Athletic Health Institute
575 East Hardy Street
Inglewood, California 90301
213–674–1600

National Athletic Training Association
1001 East Fourth Street
Greenville, North Carolina 27858
919–752–1725

National Strength & Conditioning
    Association
300 Old City Hall Landmark
916 O Street
Lincoln, Nebraska 68508
402–472–3000

President's Council on Physical Fitness
    and Sports
450 Fifth Street N.W., Suite 7103
Washington, D.C. 20001
202–272–3421

United States Weightlifting Federation
1750 East Boulder Street
Colorado Springs, Colorado 80909–5764
719–578–4508

Weight Training Equipment

AAI-American
200 American Avenue
Jefferson, Iowa 50129
800–247–3978 (U.S.)
910–520–1031 (IA)

Body Masters
700 East Texas Street
P.O. Box 259
Rayne, Louisiana 70578
800–325–8964 (U.S.)
318–334–9611 (LA)

Chattecx Corporation
101 Memorial Drive
P.O. Box 4287
Chattanooga, Tennessee 37405
800–322–7343 (U.S.)
615–870–2281 (TN)

Cybex Division of Lumex Inc.
2100 Smithtown Avenue
P.O. Box 9003
Ronkonkoma, New York 11779–0903
800–645–5392 (U.S.)
516–585–9000 (NY)

Diversified Products
309 Williamson Avenue
Opelika, Alabama 36801
800–633–5730 (U.S.)
205–749–9001 (AL)

Flex Equipment, Inc.
1525 West Orange Grove Street
Orange, California 92668
714–633–6340

Hydra-Fitness Industries
2121 Industrial Boulevard
P.O. Box 599
Belton, Texas 76513-0599
800–433–3111 (U.S.)
800–792–3013 (TX)
817–939–1831

Keiser Sports Health Equipment
411 South West Avenue
Fresno, California 93706
800–922–4409 (U.S.)
800–922–9290 (CA)
209–266–2715

Lapko Enterprises, Inc.
2800 South River Road
Des Plaines, Illinois 60018
800–848–8884 (U.S.)
312–803–0200 (IL)

Loredan Biomedical, Inc.
1632 Da Vinci Court
P.O. Box 1154
Davis, California 95617
916–758–3622

Nautilus Sports/Medical Industries, Inc.
P.O. Box 1783
DeLand, Florida 32721–1783
800–874–8941 (U.S.)
904–228–2884 (FL)

Samson Equipment
741 West May
Las Cruces, New Mexico 88005
505–523–1238

Soloflex, Inc.
Hawthorn Farm Industrial Park
570 N.E. 53rd
Hillsboro, Oregon 97124–6494
800–547–8802 (U.S.)
503–640–8891 (OR)

Universal Gym Equipment, Inc.
930 27th Avenue, S.W.
Cedar Rapids, Iowa 52406
800–553–7901
319–365–7561 (IA)

Weider Health & Fitness
2677 El Presidio Street
Carson, California 90810
800–423–5713 (U.S.)
800–382–3399 (CA)

York Barbell Company, Inc.
Box 1707
York, Pennsylvania 17405
800–358–YORK (U.S.)
717–764–0044 (PA)

Ergometers, Treadmills, & Accessories

Life Fitness
9601 Jeronimo Road
Irvine, California 92718–2098
800–634–8637 (U.S.)
714–859–1011 (CA)

Monark Exercise of Sweden
Universal Fitness Products
50 Commercial Street
Plainview, L.I., New York 11803
800–645–7554 (U.S.)
516–349–8600 (NY)

Nordictrack
141 Jonathan Boulevard North
Chaska, Minnesota 55318
612–448–6987

Pacer Industries, Inc.
1121 Crowley Drive
Carrollton, Texas 75006
800 873–9090 (U.S.)
214–446–3535 (FL)

Patex, International, Inc.
Trackmaster Treadmills
P.O. Box 12445
Pensacola, Florida 32501
800–225–2655 (U.S.)
904–438–2655 (FL)

Quinton Instrument Company
2121 Terry Avenue
Seattle, Washington 98121–9967
800–426–0347 (U.S.)
206–223–7373 (WA)

Schwinn Bicycle Company
217 North Jefferson Street
Chicago, Illinois 60606–1111
800–228–3555 (U.S.)
312–454–7532 (IL)

Stairmaster Sports/Medical Products
259 Route 17K
Newburgh, New York 12550
800–772–0089 (U.S.)
914–564–6011 (NY)

The CV Center by Bodyguard
220 Division Street
Northfield, Minnesota 55057
507–663–0486

Trotter, Inc.
1073 Main Street
Millis, Massachusetts 02054
800–227–1632 (U.S.)
617–376–4500 (MA)

References

Abraham, W. M. 1977. Factors in delayed muscle soreness. *Medicine and Science in Sports* 9:11–20.

Alen, M. 1985. Androgenic steroid effects on liver and red cells. *British Journal of Sports Medicine* 19(1):15–20.

Alen, M., and P. Rahkila. 1984. Reduced high-density lipoprotein-cholesterol in power athletes: Use of male sex hormone derivatives, an atherogenic factor. *International Journal of Sports Medicine* 5:341–42.

Alen, M., and J. Suominen. 1984. Effect of androgenic and anabolic steroids on spermatogenesis in power athletes. *International Journal of Sports Medicine* 5:189–92 supplement.

Alexander, M. J. L. 1985. Biomechanical aspects of lumbar spine injuries in athletes: A review. *Canadian Journal of Applied Sport Sciences* 10(1):1–20.

Allen, T. E., R. J. Byrd, and D. P. Smith. 1976. Hemodynamic consequences of circuit weight training. *Research Quarterly* 47:299–306.

Allman, F. L. 1976. Prevention of sports injuries. *Athletic Journal* 56(7):74.

Allman, F. L. 1982. Commentary. In T. A. Brady, B. R. Cahill, and L. M. Bodnar, Weight training-related injuries in the high school athlete. *American Journal of Sports Medicine* 10(1):4–5.

American Academy of Pediatrics. 1983. Weight training and weight lifting: Information for the pediatrician. *The Physician and Sports Medicine* 11(3):157–61.

American College of Sports Medicine. 1978. Position statement on the recommended quantity and quality of exercise for developing and maintaining fitness in healthy adults. *Medicine and Science in Sports* 10:vii–x.

American College of Sports Medicine. 1984. *Position stand on weight-loss programs.* Indianapolis: ACSM.

American College of Sports Medicine. 1986. *Guidelines for exercise testing and prescription.* 3d ed. Philadelphia: Lea & Febiger.

Arblaster, C. I., and G. L. Blackman. 1981. Drugs in sport: The extent of the problem, toxic effects, and control. *Australian Family Physician* 10:145–48.

Armstrong, R. B., R. W. Ogilvie, and J. A. Schwane. 1983. Eccentric exercise-induced injury to rat skeletal muscle. *Jounal of Applied Physiology: Respiratory, Environmental and Exercise Physiology* 54(1):80–93.

Asmussen, E. 1953. Positive and negative muscular work. *Acta Physiologica Scandinavica* 28:364–82.

Bagheri, S. A., and J. L. Boyer. 1974. Peliosis hepatis associated with androgenic-anabolic steroid therapy. A severe form of hepatic injury. *Annals of Internal Medicine* 81:610–18.

Barnes, L. 1983. Steroid use pandemic, strength coaches told. *The Physician and Sports Medicine* 11(9):25, 29.

Bender, J. A., and H. M. Kaplan. 1963. The multiple angle testing method for the evaluation of muscle strength. *Journal of Bone and Joint Surgery* 45-A:135–40.

Benninghoff, C. F. 1938. Weight lifting. *Journal of Physical Education* 35(6):96.

Berger, R. A. 1962a. Comparison of static and dynamic strength increases. *Research Quarterly* 33(3):329–33.

Berger, R. A. 1962b. Effects of varied weight training programs on strength. *Research Quarterly* 33(2):168–81.

Berger, R. A. 1962c. Optimum repetitions for the development of strength. *Research Quarterly* 33(3):334–38.

Berger, R. A. 1984. *Introduction to weight training.* Englewood Cliffs, NJ: Prentice-Hall, Inc.

Bernstein, M. S., R. L. Hunter, and S. Yachnin. 1971. Hepatoma and peliosis hepatis developing in a patient with Fanconi's anemia. *New England Journal of Medicine* 284:1135–36.

Bigland, B., and O. C. J. Lippold. 1954. The relation between force, velocity, and integrated electrical activity in human muscles. *Journal of Physiology* 123:214.

Brady, T. A., B. R. Cahill, and L. M. Bodnar. 1982. Weight training-related injuries in the high school athlete. *American Journal of Sports Medicine* 10(1):1–5.

Brooks, G. A., and T. D. Fahey. 1984. *Exercise physiology: Human bioenergetics and its applications.* New York: John Wiley & Sons.

Brown, A. B., N. McCartney, D. Moroz, D. G. Sale, S. A. Garner, and J. D. MacDougall. 1988. Strength training effects in aging (abstract). *Medicine and Science in Sports and Exercise* 20(2):S80.

Brown, C. H., and J. H. Wilmore. 1974. The effects of maximal resistance training on the strength and body composition of women athletes. *Medicine and Science in Sports* 6(3):174–77.

Burkett, L. N. 1970. Causative factors in hamstring strains. *Medicine and Science in Sports* 2:39–42.

Burkett, L. N., and M. T. Falduto. 1984. Steroid use by athletes in a metropolitan area. *The Physician and Sports Medicine* 12(8):69–74.

Caiozzo, V. J., J. J. Perrine, and V. R. Edgerton. 1981. Training-induced alterations of the in vivo force-velocity relationship of human muscle. *Journal of Applied Physiology: Respiratory, Environmental and Exercise Physiology* 51(3):750–54.

Cantu, R. C. 1980. Lumbar spine injuries. In *The exercising adult,* ed. R. C. Cantu. Lexington, MA: Collamore Press.

Capen, E. K., J. A. Bright, and P. A. Line. 1961. The effects of weight training on strength, power, muscular endurance and anthropometric measurements on a select group of college women. *Journal of the Association for Physical and Mental Rehabilitation* 15:169–73, 180.

Carswell, H. 1984. Headaches: A weighty problem for lifters? *The Physician and Sports Medicine* 12(7):23.

Ciullo, J. V., and D. W. Jackson. 1985. Track and field. In *Sports Injuries Mechanisms, Prevention, and Treatment,* ed. R. C. Schneider, J. C. Kennedy, and M. L. Plant. Baltimore: Williams & Wilkins.

Cohen, J. C., T. D. Noakes, and A. J. S. Benade. 1988. Hypercholesterolemia in male power lifters using anabolic-androgenic steroids. *The Physician and Sports Medicine* 16(8):49–56.

Compton, D., P. M. Hill, and J. D. Sinclair. 1973. Weight-lifters' blackout. *Lancet* II(7840):1234–37.

Costill, D. L., E. F. Coyle, W. F. Fink, G. R. Lesmes, and F. A. Witzmann. 1979. Adaptations in skeletal muscle following strength training. *Journal of Applied Physiology: Respiratory, Environmental and Exercise Physiology* 46(1):96–99.

Costill, D. L., D. R. Pearson, and W. J. Fink. 1984. Anabolic steroid use among athletes: Changes in HDL-C levels. *The Physician and Sports Medicine* 12(6):113–17.

Coyle, E. F., D. C. Feiring, T. C. Rotkis, R. W. Cote, F. B. Roby, W. Lee, and J. H. Wilmore. 1981. Specificity of power improvements through slow and fast isokinetic training. *Journal of Applied Physiology: Respiratory, Environmental and Exercise Physiology* 51(6):1437–42.

Craddock, D. 1978. *Obesity and its management.* 3d ed. New York: Churchill Livingston.

Cureton, K. J., M. A. Collins, D. W. Hill, and F. M. McElhannon. 1988. Muscle hypertrophy in men and women. *Medicine and Science in Sports and Exercise* 20(4):338–44.

Dalen, N., and K. E. Olsson. 1974. Bone mineral content and physical activity. *Acta Orthopaedica Scandinavica* 43:170–74.

DeLorme, T. L. 1945. Restoration of muscle power by heavy-resistance exercise. *Journal of Bone and Joint Surgery* XXVII(4):645–67.

De Pauw, D., and J. Vrijens. 1972. Physique, muscle strength and cardiovascular fitness of weight lifters. *Journal of Sports Medicine and Physical Fitness* 12(3):193–200.

deVries, H. A. 1966. Quantitative electromyographical investigation of the spasm theory of muscle pain. *American Journal of Physical Medicine* 45:119–34.

deVries, H. A. 1986. *Physiology of exercise for physical education and athletics.* 4th ed. Dubuque: Wm. C. Brown Publishers.

Donaldson, C. L., S. B. Hulley, J. M. Vogel, R. S. Hattner, J. H. Bayers, and D. E. McMillan. 1970. Effect of prolonged bedrest on bone mineral. *Metabolism* 19(12):1071–84.

Dubowitz, V., and M. H. Brooke. 1973. *Muscle biopsy: A modern approach.* Philadelphia: W. B. Saunders Company.

Duchateau, J., and K. Hainaut. 1984. Isometric or dynamic training. Differential effects on mechanical properties of a human muscle. *Journal of Applied Physiology: Respiratory, Environmental and Exercise Physiology* 56(2):296–301.

Duda, M. 1986. Prepubescent strength training gains support. *The Physician and Sports Medicine* 14(2):157–61.

Dudley, G. A., and R. Djamil. 1985. Incompatibility of endurance- and strength-training modes of exercise. *Journal of Applied Physiology: Respiratory, Environmental and Exercise Physiology* 59(5):1446–51.

Dudley, G. A., and S. J. Fleck. 1987. Strength and endurance training: Are they mutually exclusive? *Sports Medicine* 4:79–85.

Edgerton, V. R. 1978. Mammalian muscle fiber types and their adaptability. *American Zoology* 18:113–25.

Edington, D. W., and V. R. Edgerton. 1976. *The biology of physical activity.* Boston: Houghton Mifflin Company.

Elder, G. C. B., K. Bradbury, and R. Roberts. 1982. Variability of fiber type distributions within human muscles. *Journal of Applied Physiology: Respiratory, Environmental and Exercise Physiology* 53:1473–80.

Evonuk, E. 1980. Water balance and homeostasis. Lecture in applied physiology at University of Oregon, October 3, Eugene.

Fahey, T. D., L. Akka, and R. Rolph. 1975. Body composition and VO₂ max of exceptional weight-trained athletes. *Journal of Applied Physiology* 39:559–61.

Fahey, T. D., and C. H. Brown. 1973. The effects of an anabolic steroid on the strength, body composition and endurance of college males when accompanied by a weight training program. *Medicine and Science in Sports* 5:272–76.

Fahey, T. D., R. Rolph, P. Moungmee, J. Nagel, and S. Mortara. 1976. Serum testosterone, body composition, and strength of young adults. *Medicine and Science in Sports* 8(1): 31–34.

Falk, H., H. Popper, L. B. Thomas, and K. G. Ishak. 1979. Hepatic angiosarcoma associated with androgenic-anabolic steroids. *Lancet* II(8152):1120–22.

Fenn, W. O., H. Brody, and A. Petrilli. 1931. The tension developed by human muscles at different velocities of shortening. *American Journal of Physiology* 97(1):1–14.

Flint, M. M., and J. Gudgell. 1965. Electromyographic study of abdominal muscular activity during exercise. *Research Quarterly* 36:29–37.

Fox, E. L. 1979. *Sports physiology.* Philadelphia: W. B. Saunders Company.

Fox, E. L., and D. K. Mathews. 1981. *The physiological basis of physical education and athletics.* San Francisco: Saunders College Publishing.

Fox, S. I. 1987. *Human physiology.* 2d ed. Dubuque: Wm. C. Brown Company Publishers.

Francis, K. T. 1983. Delayed muscle soreness: A review. *The Journal of Orthopaedic and Sports Physical Therapy* 5(1):1–13.

Freed, D. L. J., A. J. Banks, D. Longson, and D. M. Burley. 1975. Anabolic steroids in athletics: Crossover double-blind trial on weight lifters. *British Medical Journal* 2:471–73.

Freedson, P., B. Chang, F. Katch, W. Kroll, J. Rippe, J. Alpert, and W. Byrnes. 1984. Intra-arterial blood pressure during free weight and hydraulic resistive exercise (abstract). *Medicine and Science in Sports and Exercise* 16(2):131.

Freidman, M., and R. H. Rosenman. 1974. *Type A behavior and your heart.* Greenwich: Fawcett Publications.

Friden, J., M. Sjostrom, and B. Ekblom. 1981. A morphological study of delayed muscle soreness. *Experientia* 37:506–7.

Gardner, E. D., D. J. Gray, and R. O'Rahilly. 1975. *Anatomy: A regional study of human structure.* 4th ed. Philadelphia: W. B. Saunders Company.

Gardner, G. W. 1963. Specificity of strength changes of the exercised and nonexercised limb following isometric training. *Research Quarterly* 34:98–101.

Gettman, L. R., J. J. Ayres, M. L. Pollock, J. L. Durstine, and W. Grantham. 1979. Physiologic effects on adult men of circuit strength training and jogging. *Archives of Physical Medicine and Rehabilitation* 60:115–20.

Gettman, L. R., J. J. Ayres, M. L. Pollock, and A. Jackson. 1978. The effect of circuit weight training on strength, cardiorespiratory function, and body composition of adult men. *Medicine and Science in Sports* 10:171–76.

Gettman, L. R., L. A. Culter, and T. A. Strathman. 1980. Physiological changes after 20 weeks of isotonic vs isokinetic circuit training. *Journal of Sports Medicine and Physical Fitness* 20:265–74.

Gettman, L. R., and M. L. Pollock. 1981. Circuit weight training: A critical review of its physiological benefits. *The Physician and Sports Medicine* 9(1):44–60.

Gettman, L. R., P. Ward, and R. D. Hagan. 1982. A comparison of combined running and weight training with circuit weight training. *Medicine and Science in Sports and Exercise* 14:229–34.

Gey, G. O., K. H. Cooper, and R. A. Bottenberg. 1970. Effect of ascorbic acid on endurance performance and athletic injury. *Journal of the American Medical Association* 211(1):105.

Gillesby, G. 1938. The physiologists speak on weight lifting. *Journal of Physical Education* 35:16.

Girandola, R. N., and V. Katch. 1973. Effects of nine weeks of physical training on aerobic capacity and body composition in college men. *Archives of Physical Medicine and Rehabilitation* 54:521–24.

Goldberg, A. L. 1972. Mechanisms of growth and atrophy of skeletal muscle. In *Muscle biology,* ed. R. G. Cassens. New York: Marcel Decker, Inc.

Goldberg, A. L., J. D. Etlinger, D. F. Goldspink, and C. Jablecki. 1975. Mechanism of work-induced hypertrophy of skeletal muscle. *Medicine and Science in Sports* 7:185–98.

Gollhofer, A., P. V. Komi, M. Miyashita, and O. Aura. 1987. Fatigue during stretch-shortening cycle exercises: Changes in mechanical performance of human skeletal muscle. *International Journal of Sports Medicine* 8(2):71–78.

Gollnick, P. D., R. B. Armstrong, C. W. Saubert, K. Piehl, and B. Saltin. 1972. Enzyme activity and fiber composition in skeletal muscle of untrained and trained men. *Journal of Applied Physiology* 33:312–19.

Gonyea, W., G. C. Ericson, and F. Bonde-Peterson. 1977. Skeletal muscle fiber splitting induced by weight-lifting exercise in cats. *Acta Physiologica Scandinavica* 99:105–9.

Gonyea, W. J. 1980. Role of exercise in inducing increases in skeletal muscle fiber number. *Journal of Applied Physiology: Respiratory, Environmental and Exercise Physiology* 48(3):421–26.

Gonyea, W. J., and D. Sale. 1982. Physiology of weight-lifting exercise. *Archives of Physical Medicine and Rehabilitation* 63:235–37.

Goodman, L. S., and A. Gilman. 1975. *The pharmacological basis of therapeutics.* 5th ed. New York: Macmillan Publishing Company.

Govoni, L. E., and J. E. Hayes. 1978. *Drugs and nursing implications.* New York: Appleton-Century-Crofts.

Green, H. J., G. A. Klug, H. Reichmann, U. Seedorf, W. Wiehrer, and D. Pette. 1984. Exercise-induced fiber type transitions with regard to myosin, parvalbumin, and sarcoplasmic reticulum in muscles of rats. *Pflugers Archives* 400:432–38.

Gregor, R. J., V. R. Edgerton, J. J. Perrine, D. S. Campion, and C. DeBus. 1979. Torque-velocity relationships and muscle fiber composition in elite female athletes. *Journal of Applied Physiology: Respiratory, Environmental and Exercise Physiology* 47:388–92.

Greist, J. H., M. H. Klein, R. R. Eischens, and J. T. Faris. 1978. Running out of depression. *The Physician and Sports Medicine* 6:49–56.

Guyton, A. C. 1986. *Textbook of medical physiology.* 7th ed. Philadelphia: W. B. Saunders Company.

Gwinup, G., R. Chelvam, and T. Steinberg. 1971. Thickness of subcutaneous fat and activity of underlying muscles. *Annals of Internal Medicine* 74:408–11.

Halkjaer-Kristensen, J., and T. Ingemann-Hansen. 1981. Variations in single fibre areas and fibre composition in needle biopsies from the human quadriceps muscle. *Scandinavian Journal of Clinical Laboratory Investigation.* 41:391–95.

Hamilton, E. M. N., and E. N. Whitney. 1982. *Nutrition: Concepts and controversies.* 2nd ed. St. Paul: West Publishing Company.

Harkness, R. A., B. H. Kilshaw, and B. M. Hobson. 1975. Effects of large doses of anabolic steroids. *British Journal of Sports Medicine* 9:70–73.

Harvard Medical School, Department of Continuing Education. 1983. Steroids: A primer. *The Harvard Medical School Health Letter* 8(12) (October):1–2.

Haupt, H. A., and G. D. Rovere. 1984a. Anabolic steroids—the facts. *Journal of Medical Technology* 1(7):553–57.

Haupt, H. A., and G. D. Rovere. 1984b. Anabolic steroids: A review of literature. *American Journal of Sports Medicine* 12: 469–84.

Hempel, L. S., and C. L. Wells. 1985. Cardiorespiratory cost of the Nautilus express circuit. *The Physician and Sports Medicine* 13(4):82–97.

Hettinger, T. 1961. *Physiology of strength.* Springfield, IL: Charles C. Thomas.

Hettinger, T., and E. A. Mueller. 1953. Muskelleistung und muskeltraining. *Arbeitsphysiologie* 15:111–26.

Hickson, R. C. 1980. Interference of strength development by simultaneously training for strength and endurance. *European Journal of Applied Physiology and Occupational Physiology* 45:255–63.

Hickson, R. C., B. A. Dvorak, E. M. Gorostiaga, T. T. Kurowski, and C. Foster. 1988. Strength training and performance in endurance-trained subjects (abstract). *Medicine and Science in Sports and Exercise* 20(2) supplement: S86.

Hickson, R. C., M. A. Rosenkoetter, and M. M. Brown. 1980. Strength training effects on aerobic power and short-term endurance. *Medicine and Science in Sports and Exercise* 12:336–39.

Hill, A. V. 1922. The maximum work and mechanical efficiency of human muscles, and their most economical speed. *Journal of Physiology* 56:19–41.

Hislop, H. J., and J. J. Perrine. 1967. The isokinetic concept of exercise. *Physical Therapy* 47(2):114–17.

Ho, K. W., R. R. Roy, C. D. Tweedle, W. W. Heusner, W. D. Van Huss, and R. E. Carrow. 1980. Skeletal muscle fiber splitting with weight-lifting exercise in rats. *The American Journal of Anatomy* 157:433–40.

Holloszy, J. O., and F. W. Booth. 1976. Biochemical adaptations to endurance exercise in muscle. *Annual Review of Physiology* 38:273–91.

Hough, T., 1902. Ergographic studies in muscular soreness. *American Journal of Physiology* 7:76–92.

Hubert, H. A., M. Feinleib, P. M. McNamara, and W. P. Castelli. 1983. Obesity as an independent risk factor for cardiovascular disease. A 26-year follow-up of participants in the Framingham heart study. *Circulation* 67:968–77.

Hurley, B. F., J. M. Hagberg, A. P. Goldberg, D. R. Seals, A. A. Ehsani, R. E. Brennan, and J. O. Holloszy. 1988. Resistive training can reduce coronary risk factors without altering VO_2 max or percent body fat. *Medicine and Science in Sports and Exercise* 20(2):150–54.

Hurley, B. F., J. M. Hagberg, D. R. Seals, A. P. Goldberg, and J. O. Holloszy. 1986. Circuit weight training reduces coronary artery disease risk factors independent of changes in VO_2 max (abstract). *Medicine and Science in Sports and Exercise* 18(2) supplement: S68.

Hurley, B. F., and P. F. Kokkinos. 1987. Effects of weight training on risk factors for coronary artery disease. *Sports Medicine* 4:231–38.

Hurley, B. F., D. R. Seals, A. A. Ehsani, L.-J. Cartier, G. P. Dalsky, J. M. Hagberg, and J. O. Holloszy. 1984a. Effects of high-intensity strength training on cardiovascular function. *Medicine and Science in Sports and Exercise* 16(5):483–88.

Hurley, B. F., D. R. Seals, J. M. Hagberg, A. C. Goldberg, S. M. Ostrove, J. O. Holloszy, W. G. Wiest, and A. P. Goldberg. 1984b. High-density-lipoprotein cholesterol in bodybuilders and power lifters. *Journal of the American Medical Association* 252(4):507–13.

Huxley, A. F. 1975. The origin of force in skeletal muscle. *Ciba Foundation Symposium* 31:271–90.

Huxley, H. E. 1965. The mechanism of muscular contraction. *Scientific American* 213(6):18–27.

Issekutz, B., Jr., J. J. Blizzard, N. C. Birkhead, and K. Rodahl. 1966. Effect of prolonged bed rest on urinary calcium output. *Journal of Applied Physiology* 21:1013–20.

Jesse, J. P. 1977. Olympic lifting movements endanger adolescents. *The Physician and Sports Medicine* 5:60–67.

Jones, H. H., J. D. Priest, W. C. Hayes, M. A. Tichenor, and D. A. Nagel. 1977. Humeral hypertrophy in response to exercise. *Journal of Bone and Joint Surgery* 59A:204–8.

Kamen, G., W. Kroll, and S. T. Zigon. 1981. Exercise effects upon reflex time components in weight lifters and distance runners. *Medicine and Science in Sports and Exercise* 13(3):198–204.

Kanehisa, H., and M. Miyashita. 1983a. Effect of isometric and isokinetic muscle training on static strength and dynamic power. *European Journal of Applied Physiology and Occupational Physiology* 50:365–71.

Kanehisa, H., and M. Miyashita. 1983b. Specificity of velocity in strength training. *European Journal of Applied Physiology and Occupational Physiology* 52:104–6.

Karvonen, M., K. Kentala, and O. Mustala. 1957. The effects of training on heart rate. A longitudinal study. *Annales Medicinal Experimentales Biologial Fennial* (Finland Journal of Experimental Medicine) 35:307–15.

Kato, S., and T. Ishiko. 1964. Obstructed growth of children's bones due to excessive labor in remote corners. In *Proceedings of the International Congress of Sports Sciences,* ed. S. Kato. Tokyo: Japanese Union of Sports Sciences.

Keller, B., W. Kroll, F. Katch, and P. Freedson. 1988. Electrical stimulation effects on muscle and fat (abstract). *Medicine and Science in Sports and Exercise* 20(2) supplement: S22.

Kimura, Y., H. Itow, and S. Yamazaki. 1981. The effects of circuit weight training on VO_2 max and body composition of trained and untrained college men. *Nippon Seirigaku Zasshi* (Journal of the Physiological Society of Japan) 43:593–96.

Klafs, C. E., and D. D. Arnheim. 1981. *The science of sports injury prevention and management: Modern principles of athletic training.* 5th ed. St. Louis: The C. V. Mosby Company.

Knuttgen, H. G., F. B. Petersen, and K. Klausen. 1971. O_2 uptake and heart rate responses performed with concentric and eccentric muscle contractions. *Medicine and Science in Sports* 3(1):1–5.

Korcok, M. 1982. Add exercise to calcium in osteoporosis prevention. *Journal of the American Medical Association* 247(8): 1106, 1112.

Kozar, B., and R. M. Lord. 1983. Overuse injury in the young athlete: Reasons for concern. *The Physician and Sports Medicine* 11(7):116–22.

Krolner, B., and B. Toft. 1983. Vertebral bone loss: An unheeded side effect of therapeutic bed rest. *Clinical Science* 64:537–40.

LaBan, M. M., A. D. Raptou, and E. W. Johnson. 1965. Electromyographic study of function of iliopsoas muscle. *Archives of Physical Medicine and Rehabilitation* 46:676–79.

Lake, D. A., and W. J. Gillespie. 1988. NMES does not decrease body fat (abstract). *Medicine and Science in Sports and Exercise* 20(2) supplement: S22.

Lander, J. E. 1982. Comparisons between selected parameters describing an isotonic and isokinetic bench press. Master's thesis, University of Oregon, Eugene.

Lander, J. E. 1987. The effectiveness of weight-belts during squatting (abstract). *Medicine and Science in Sports and Exercise* 19(2) supplement: S64.

Legwold, G. 1982. Does lifting weights harm a prepubescent athlete? *The Physician and Sports Medicine* 10(7):141–44.

Lesmes, G. R., D. L. Costill, E. F. Coyle, and W. J. Fink. 1978. Muscle strength and power changes during maximal isokinetic training. *Medicine and Science in Sports* 10(4):266–69.

Lettunich, J. L., J. D. Seelbach, and V. P. Lombardi. 1984–87. *Community health improvement program fitness appraisal packet.* University of Oregon, Eugene.

Levine, A., S. Wells, and C. Kopf. 1986. New rules of exercise. *U.S. News & World Report* 101(6) (August 11):52–56.

Lexell, J., K. Hendriksson-Larsen, and M. Sjostrom. 1983. Distribution of different fibre types in human skeletal muscles. A study of cross-sections of whole m. vastus lateralis. *Acta Physiologica Scandinavica* 117:115–22.

Lombardi, V. P., and E. Evonuk. 1985. Lactate dehydrogenase activity and maximum oxygen consumption in endurance versus strength trained athletes (abstract). *Medicine and Science in Sports and Exercise* 17(2):231.

McArdle, W. D., and G. F. Foglia. 1969. Energy cost and cardiorespiratory stress of isometric and weight training exercises. *Journal of Sports Medicine and Physical Fitness* 9:23–30.

MacDougall, J. D., D. G. Sale, G. C. B. Elder, and J. R. Sutton. 1982. Muscle ultrastructural characteristics of elite power lifters and bodybuilders. *European Journal of Applied Physiology* 48:117–26.

MacDougall, J. D., D. G. Sale, J. R. Moroz, and J. R. Sutton. 1980. Effects of strength training and immobilization on human muscle fibers. *European Journal of Applied Physiology and Occupational Physiology* 43:25–34.

MacDougall, J. D., D. Tuxen, D. G. Sale, J. R. Moroz, and J. R. Sutton. 1985. Arterial blood pressure response to heavy resistance exercise. *Journal of Applied Physiology* 58(3):785–790.

Massey, B. H., and N. L. Chaudet. 1956. Effects of systematic heavy resistance exercise on range of motion joint movement in young male adults. *Research Quarterly* 27:41–45.

Mayhew, J. L., and P. M. Gross. 1974. Body composition changes in young women with high resistance weight training. *Research Quarterly* 45:433–40.

Meadows, A. T., J. L. Naiman, and M. Valdes-Dapena. 1974. Hepatoma associated with androgen therapy for aplastic anemia. *Journal of Pediatrics* 84:109–10.

Messier, S. P., and M. E. Dill. 1985. Alterations in strength and maximal oxygen uptake consequent to Nautilus circuit weight training. *Research Quarterly for Exercise and Sport* 56(4):345–51.

Micheli, L. 1983. Strength gains in preadolescents. *The Physician and Sports Medicine* 11:25.

Misner, J. S., R. A. Boileau, B. H. Massey, and J. L. Mayhew. 1974. Alterations in the body composition of adult men during selected physical training programs. *Journal of the American Geriatric Society* 22:33–38.

Moffroid, M. T., and R. H. Whipple. 1970. Specificity of speed of exercise. *Physical Therapy* 50(12):1692–1700.

Morganroth, J., B. J. Maron, W. L. Henry, and S. E. Epstein. 1975. Comparative left ventricular dimensions in trained athletes. *Annals of Internal Medicine* 82(4):521–24.

Morris, A., L. Lussier, G. Bell, and J. Dooley. 1983. Hamstring/quadriceps strength ratios in collegiate middle-distance and distance runners. *The Physician and Sports Medicine* 11(10):71–77.

Morris, J. M. 1973. Biomechanics of the spine. *Archives of Surgery* 107:418–23.

Morris, J. M., D. B. Lucas, and B. Bressler. 1961. Role of the trunk in stability of the spine. *The Journal of Bone and Joint Surgery* 43-A(3):327–51.

Murphy, P. 1986. Steroids: Not just for athletes anymore. *The Physician and Sports Medicine* 14(6):48.

Nagle, F. J., and L. W. Irwin. 1960. Effects of two systems of weight training on circulorespiratory endurance and related physiological factors. *Research Quarterly* 31(4):607–15.

National Research Council, Committee on Diet, Nutrition, and Cancer, Assembly of Life Sciences. 1982. *Diet, nutrition, and cancer.* Washington, D.C.: National Academy Press.

National Strength and Conditioning Association. 1986. Roundtable: Practical considerations for utilizing plyometrics (part 1). *National Strength and Conditioning Association Journal* 8(3):14–22.

National Strength and Conditioning Association. 1987a. Roundtable: Breathing during weight training. *National Strength and Conditioning Association Journal* 9(5):17–25.

National Strength and Conditioning Association. 1987b. Roundtable: Cardiovascular effects of weight training (part 1). *National Strength and Conditioning Association Journal* 9(2):10–21.

Nilsson, B. E. R., and N. E. Westlin. 1971. Bone density in athletes. *Clinical Orthopedics* 77:179–82.

Ohtsuki, T. 1983. Decrease in human voluntary isometric arm strength induced by simultaneous bilateral exertion. *Behavioural Brain Research* 7:165–78.

O'Shea, J. P. 1976. *Scientific principles and methods of strength fitness*. Menlo Park: Addison-Wesley Publishing Company.

Pappas, A. M. 1983. Epiphyseal injuries in sports. *The Physician and Sports Medicine* 11(6):140–46.

Parr, R. B., M. A. Porter, and S. C. Hodgson. 1984. Nutrition knowledge and practice of coaches, trainers, and athletes. *The Physician and Sports Medicine* 12(3):127–38.

Perrine, J. J., and V. R. Edgerton. 1978. Muscle force–velocity relationships under isokinetic loading. *Medicine and Science in Sports* 10:159–66.

Petajan, J. H., and C. J. Eagan. 1968. Effect of temperature and physical fitness on the triceps surae reflex. *Journal of Applied Physiology* 25:16–20.

Peter, J., R. Barnard, V. Edgerton, C. Gillespie, and K. Stempel. 1972. Metabolic profiles of three fiber types of skeletal muscle in guinea pigs and rabbits. *Biochemistry* 11:2627–33.

Peterson, C. A., and H. A. Peterson. 1972. Analysis of the incidence of injuries to the epiphyseal growth plate. *Journal of Trauma* 12:275–81.

Peterson, G. E., and T. D. Fahey. 1984. HDL-C in five elite athletes using anabolic-androgenic steroids. *The Physician and Sports Medicine* 12(6):120–30.

Peterson, J. A. 1975. Total conditioning: A case study. *Athletic Journal* 56:40–55.

Peterson, J. A. 1976. The effect of high intensity weight training on cardiovascular function. Paper presented to the Pre-Montreal Olympic Conference of the International Congress of Physical Activity Sciences, July 15, Quebec City, Canada.

Pfeiffer, R. D., and R. S. Francis. 1986. Effects of strength training on muscle development in prepubescent, pubescent, and postpubescent males. *The Physician and Sports Medicine* 14(9):134–43.

Pipes, T. V., and J. H. Wilmore. 1975. Isokinetic vs isotonic strength training in adult men. *Medicine and Science in Sports* 7(4):262–74.

Pollock, M. L. 1973. The quantification of endurance training programs. In *Exercise and sports science reviews*, ed. J. Wilmore. Vol. 1. New York: Academic Press.

Pollock, M. L., J. H. Wilmore, and S. M. Fox. 1978. *Health and fitness through physical activity*. New York: John Wiley & Sons, Inc.

Pollock, M. L., J. H. Wilmore, and S. M. Fox. 1984. *Exercise in health and disease*. Philadelphia: W. B. Saunders Company.

Pope, H. G., and D. L. Katz. 1988. Affective and psychotic symptoms associated with anabolic steroid use. *American Journal of Psychiatry* 145(4):487–90.

President's Council on Physical Fitness and Sports. 1983. Aerobic dance and weight training rate as fastest-growing physical fitness activities. *President's Council on Physical Fitness and Sports Newsletter* September, 9.

Puffer, J. C., ed. 1985. Androgenic steroids and the risk of cancer. *Sports Medicine Digest* 7(2):5.

Radcliffe, J. C., and R. C. Farentinos. 1985. *Plyometrics: Explosive power training*. 2d ed. Champaign, IL: Human Kinetics Publishers.

Rasch, P. J., and R. K. Burke. 1978. *Kinesiology and applied anatomy: The science of human movement*. 6th ed. Philadelphia: Lea & Febiger.

Reid, C. M., R. A. Yeater, and H. Ullrich. 1987. Weight training and strength, cardiorespiratory functioning and body composition of men. *British Journal of Sports Medicine* 21(1):40–44.

Rians, C. B., A. Weltman, B. R. Cahill, C. A. Janney, S. R. Tippett, and F. I. Katch. 1987. Strength training for prepubescent males: Is it safe? *The American Journal of Sports Medicine* 15(5):483–89.

Rogers, C. C. 1985. On the rebound: A fitness love affair. *The Physician and Sports Medicine* 13(9):141–50.

Rowe, P. H. 1979. Case report: Colles fracture due to weight lifting. *British Journal of Sports Medicine* 13:130–31.

Ryan, J. R., and G. G. Salciccioli. 1976. Fractures of the distal radial epiphysis in adolescent weight lifters. *The American Journal of Sports Medicine* 4:26–27.

Sale, D., I. Jacobs, D. Moroz, D. MacDougall, and S. Garner. 1988. Comparison of two regimens of combined strength and endurance training (abstract). *Medicine and Science in Sports and Exercise* 20(2): S9.

Saltin, B., and P. Astrand. 1967. Maximal oxygen uptake in athletes. *Journal of Applied Physiology* 23:353–58.

Saudek, C. E., and K. A. Palmer. 1987. Back pain revisited. *The Journal of Orthopaedic and Sports Physical Therapy* 8(12):556–66.

Sawhill, J. A. 1981. Biomechanical characteristics of rotational velocity and movement complexity in isokinetic performance. Doctoral diss., University of Oregon, Eugene.

Selye, H. 1976. *The stress of life.* New York: McGraw-Hill, Inc.

Serono Laboratories, Inc. 1984. *Asellacrin (somatotropin) for intramuscular injection.* Randolph, MA: Serono Laboratories, Inc.

Servedio, F. J., R. L. Bartels, R. L. Hamlin, D. Teske, T. Shaffer, and A. Servedio. 1985. The effects of weight training, using olympic style lifts, on various physiological variables in pre-pubescent boys (abstract). *Medicine and Science in Sports and Exercise* 17(2):288.

Sewall, L., and L. J. Micheli. 1986. Strength training for children. *Journal of Pediatric Orthopedics* 6(2):143–46.

Shankman, G. A. 1985. Special considerations in conditioning the young athlete. *National Strength and Conditioning Association Journal* 7(3):52–53.

Shapiro, C. M., P. M. Warren, J. Trinder, S. J. Paxton, I. Oswald, D. C. Flenley, and J. R. Catterall. 1984. Fitness facilitates sleep. *European Journal of Applied Physiology and Occupational Physiology* 53:1–4.

Sharkey, B. J. 1966. A physiological comparison of static and phasic exercise. *The Research Quarterly* 37:520–31.

Shellock, F. G. 1983. Physiological benefits of warm-up. *The Physician and Sports Medicine* 11(10):134–39.

Shephard, R. J., D. Killinger, and T. Fried. 1977. Responses to sustained use of anabolic steroid. *British Journal of Sports Medicine* 11:170–73.

Staron, R. S., F. C. Hagerman, and R. S. Hikida. 1981. The effects of detraining on an elite power lifter. *Journal of the Neurological Sciences* 51:247–57.

Stillman, R. J., T. G. Lohman, M. H. Slaughter, and B. H. Massey. 1986. Physical activity and bone mineral content in women aged 30 to 85 years. *Medicine and science in sports and exercise* 18(5):576–80.

Stone, W. J., and W. A. Kroll. 1978. *Sports conditioning and weight training.* Boston: Allyn and Bacon, Inc.

Strauss, R. H., J. E. Wright, G. A. Finerman, and D. H. Catlin. 1983. Side effects of anabolic steroids in weight-trained men. *The Physician and Sports Medicine* 11(12):87–96.

Stryer, L. 1981. *Biochemistry.* San Francisco: W. H. Freeman and Company.

Tahmindjis, A. J. 1976. The use of anabolic steroids by athletes to increase body weight and strength. *Medical Journal of Australia* 1:991–93.

Thorstensson, A. 1976. Muscle strength, fibre types and enzyme activities in man. *Acta Physiologica Scandinavica* supplementum 443:1–45.

Todd, T. 1985. Historical perspective: The myth of the muscle-bound lifter. *National Strength and Conditioning Association Journal* 7(3):37–41.

Tomassoni, T. L., M. S. Blanchard, and A. H. Goldfarb. 1985. Effects of a rebound exercise training program on aerobic capacity and body composition. *The Physician and Sports Medicine* 13(11):110–15.

U. S. Consumer Product Safety Commission. 1980. *National electronic surveillance system: Report for January 1 through December 31, 1979.* Washington, D.C.: US CPSC.

Vanhelder, W. P., M. W. Radomski, and R. C. Goode. 1984. Growth hormone responses during intermittent weight lifting exercise in men. *European Journal of Applied Physiology and Occupational Physiology* 53:31–34.

Verkhoshanski, Y. 1969. Perspectives in the improvement of speed-strength preparation of jumpers. *Yessis Review of Soviet Physical Education and Sports* 4(2):28–29.

Verkhoshansky, U. 1979a. How to set up a training program in speed-strength events (part I). *Legkaya Atletika* 8:8–10. Translated in *Soviet Sports Review* 1981, 16, 53–57.

Verkhoshansky, U. 1979b. How to set up a training program in speed-strength events (part II). *Legkaya Atletika* 8:8–10. Translated in *Soviet Sports Review* 1981, 16, 123–26.

Volpe, S., K. Webb, J. Walberg, and D. Hinkle. 1988. Influence of aerobic exercise on strength training (abstract). *Medicine and Science in Sports and Exercise* 20(2):S86.

Wade, N. 1972. Anabolic steroids: Doctors denounce them, but athletes aren't listening. *Science* 176:1399–1403.

Wells, J. B., E. Jokl, and J. Bohanen. 1963. The effect of intensive physical training upon body composition of adolescent girls. *Journal of the Association for Physical and Mental Rehabilitation* 17:68–72, 81.

Wells, K. F., and Luttgens, K. 1976. *Kinesiology: Scientific basis of human motion.* 6th ed. Philadelphia: W. B. Saunders Company.

Whitney, E. N., and E. M. N. Hamilton. 1987. *Understanding nutrition.* 4th ed. St. Paul, MN: West Publishing Company.

Wilkins, K. E. 1980. The uniqueness of the young athlete: Musculoskeletal injuries. *The American Journal of Sports Medicine* 8(5):377–82.

Williams, M. H., ed. 1983. *Ergogenic aids in sports.* Champaign, IL: Human Kinetics Publishers.

Williams, M. H. 1983b. *Nutrition for Fitness and Sport.* Dubuque: Wm. C. Brown Company Publishers.

Wilmore, J. H. 1974. Alterations in strength, body composition and anthropometric measurements consequent to a 10-week weight training program. *Medicine and Science in Sports* 6:133–38.

Wilmore, J. H., R. B. Parr, P. Ward, P. A. Vodak, T. J. Barstow, T. V. Pipes, G. Grimditch, and P. Leslie. 1978a. Energy cost of circuit weight training. *Medicine and Science in Sports* 10:75–78.

Wilmore, J. H., R. B. Parr, R. N. Girandola, P. Ward, P. A. Vodak, T. J. Barstow, T. V. Pipes, G. T. Romero, and P. Leslie. 1978b. Physiological alterations consequent to circuit weight training. *Medicine and Science in Sports* 10:79–84.

Wynn, V. 1975. Metabolic effects of anabolic steroids. *British Journal of Sports Medicine* 9:60–64.

Yen, S. S. C., R. Rebar, G. VandenBerg, F. Naaftolin, Y. Ehara, S. Engblom, K. J. Ryan, and K. Benirschke. 1972. Synthetic luteinizing hormone-releasing factor: A potent stimulator of gonadotropin release in man. *Journal of Clinical Endocrinology and Metabolism* 34:1108–11.

Yoshimura, H. 1961. Adult protein requirements. *Federation Proceedings* 20:103–10.

Young, D. C. 1984. *The Olympic myth of Greek amateur athletics.* Chicago: Aires Publishing Company.

Ziegenfuss, J., and R. Carabasi. 1973. Androgens and hepatocellular carcinoma (letter). *Lancet* I:262.

Index